Praise for *The Illusio*

'Riveting. Truly revelatory. Jaw-dropping. Stranger than any fiction, you simply could not make these stories up. At last, Dudley Clarke and his extraordinary war as it deserves to be told . . . Great fun and wonderfully written'   Damien Lewis

'[An] enthralling true-life thriller . . . Hutton uses valuable new material and witty insight to restore the reputation of the louche but brilliant Clarke'   Alexander Larman, *Observer*

'A cracking tale. With admiration and pacy prose, Robert Hutton tracks one of the great British characters of World War Two . . . Expect ingenuity and eccentricity by the barrow-load'
                                                          Sonia Purnell

'Brilliant . . . Clarke not only emerges as a genius of deception but also as a colourful and highly attractive maverick who deserves far greater recognition. Hopefully, this utterly compelling book will do just that. Superb'   James Holland

'Superbly entertaining'   *Mail on Sunday*

'A full and satisfying biography . . . Thanks to his extensive research and skill as a writer, Hutton tells Clarke's story in detail without losing the reader's attention'   *Wall Street Journal*

'Warfare has been partly about deception since the days of the Trojan Horse, but by the time of the Second World War it appeared to have reached a peak of sophistication. And, according to Robert Hutton in this well-researched and often entertaining book, the ultimate sophisticate was Dudley Clarke'   Simon Heffer, *Telegraph*

ROBERT HUTTON spent sixteen years covering the British government for Bloomberg and is now sketchwriter for The Critic. He lives in London.

Also by Robert Hutton

Romps, Tots and Boffins: The Strange Language of News
Would They Lie To You? How to Spin Friends and Manipulate People
Agent Jack: The True Story of MI5's Secret Nazi Hunter

THE
ILLUSIONIST

The True Story of the Man Who Fooled Hitler

ROBERT HUTTON

WEIDENFELD & NICOLSON

First published in Great Britain in 2024 by Weidenfeld & Nicolson
This paperback edition first published in 2025 by Weidenfeld & Nicolson,
an imprint of The Orion Publishing Group Ltd
Carmelite House, 50 Victoria Embankment
London EC4Y 0DZ

An Hachette UK Company

The authorised representative in the EEA is Hachette Ireland,
8 Castlecourt Centre, Dublin 15, D15 XTP3,
Republic of Ireland (email: info@hbgi.ie)

1 3 5 7 9 10 8 6 4 2

A CIP catalogue record for this book is
available from the British Library.

ISBN (Mass Market Paperback) 978 1 4746 2604 0
ISBN (Ebook) 978 1 4746 2605 7
ISBN (Audio) 978 1 4746 2606 4

Typeset by Input Data Services Ltd, Bridgwater, Somerset

Maps by John Gilkes

Printed in Great Britain by Clays Ltd, Elcograf S.p.A.

www.weidenfeldandnicolson.co.uk
www.orionbooks.co.uk

For my father, with love

Contents

The Costume Trunk: July–October 1941

The Assistant's Revenge: October 1941–February 1942

The Miser's Dream: February–June 1942

The Cut and Restored Rope: June–July 1942

The Shell Game: July–October 1942

Maps and Illustrations

Dudley Clarke's Theatre of War

FRANCE

ITALY

Y

SPAIN
• Madrid

PORTUGAL

Lisbon •

Atlantic
Ocean

Gibraltar •

Sicily

Tunis •

Malta

TUNISIA

MOROCCO

Tripoli •

ALGERIA

LIB

0   200   400   600 Miles
0   200   400   600   800 Km

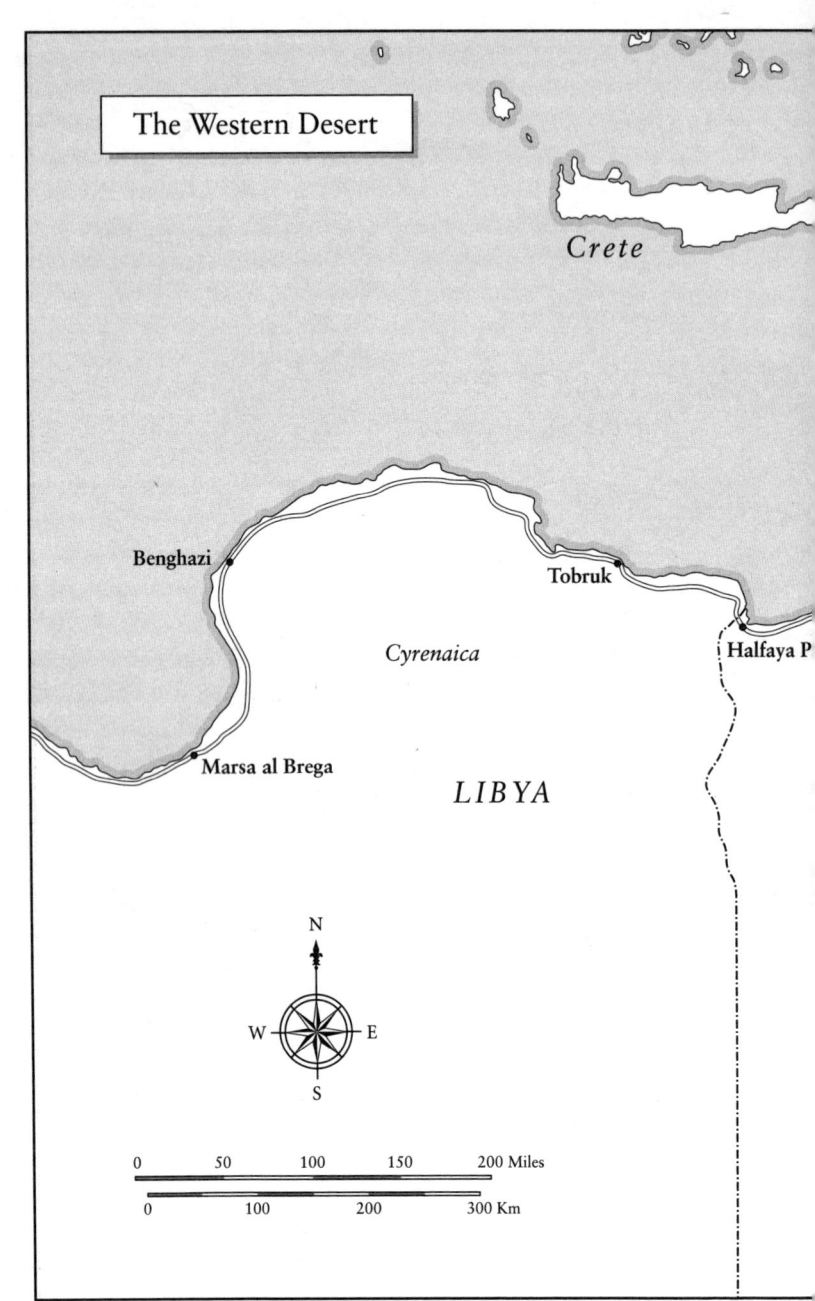

The Western Desert

Crete

Benghazi

Tobruk

Cyrenaica

Halfaya P

Marsa al Brega

LIBYA

N

W ⊕ E

S

| 0 | 50 | 100 | 150 | 200 Miles |

| 0 | 100 | 200 | 300 Km |

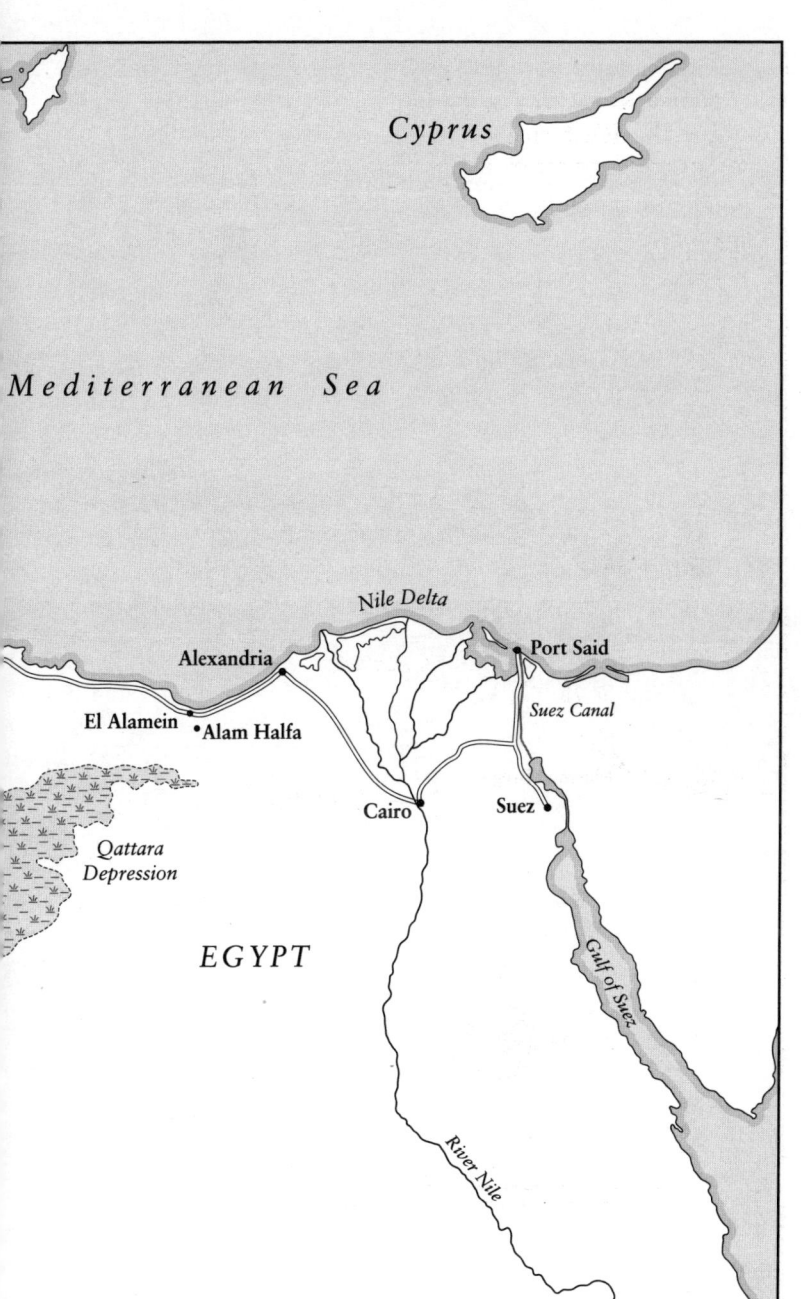

Cyprus

Mediterranean   Sea

Nile Delta

Alexandria   ● Port Said

El Alamein   ●Alam Halfa   *Suez Canal*

Cairo   Suez

*Qattara
Depression*

EGYPT   *Gulf of Suez*

River Nile

Prologue

The smell of burning paper was everywhere. Smoke hung in low clouds over the Nile, drifting there from the chic quarter of the city where the British government and military had made their home. In the grounds of the embassy and General Headquarters, diplomats and soldiers shovelled files onto bonfires, while gardeners poked the pyres with rakes to feed the flames. Now and then a document would get caught in a draught and fly up, intact, with the smoke, out over the walls and into the streets beyond, still clearly displaying whatever secrets its owners had hoped to destroy.

From the buildings moved a steady stream of men and women carrying trays and bags of papers to be burned, the smoke stinging their eyes and getting into their hair and clothes, which already stank of sweat from the heat of an Egyptian afternoon in high summer. They made the occasional joke, affecting unconcern, but there was no disguising the seriousness of their purpose, for there was much to do and no one knew how much time they had to do it.

In the streets beyond, there were queues outside banks and crowds inside, as people fought to get their money out. It was the same at the railway station, where they were trying to get themselves or their families out. Some wanted to get their affairs in order first, hoping to sell their businesses or their homes for whatever cash they could raise. Others, including those who had arrived recently in the city as refugees, knew that the most important thing about escaping an advancing army is to flee while you can. People piled into cars, tying mattresses onto the roofs in the desperate hope they would provide some protection from falling debris.

This was panic. Rommel was coming.

For two years the Allied and Axis armies had been chasing each other back and forth across the deserts of North Africa. At times, each side had seemed on the point of victory, only to have it snatched away. Now, though, the result seemed certain. The maverick German commander had swept past the forces that were supposed to stop him, seized the port of Tobruk and rolled over the Egyptian border.

By now, Rommel had become an almost mythic figure to the troops of both sides: fearless, a master tactician, unstoppable, unbeatable, everywhere at once and apparently better informed about his opponents than their own commanders. The Allies had no one to match him, and they knew it.

And he was only hours away. Between him and the city exhausted soldiers gathered from across the British Empire were dug into the sand, preparing to make a final desperate stand in the desert, far from their homes. But what chance did they have of holding him back when their better-prepared and better-equipped comrades had already failed?

Back in Cairo, in a courtyard behind a block of flats a little way away from the embassy, a small team of men and women were holding their own bonfire of paperwork. Overseeing them, telling them which files to keep and which to burn, was a small man in his early forties with a smooth oval face, a high forehead, and a pipe clamped between his teeth.

While others were falling apart, this chap – the shoulders on his uniform revealed him to be a colonel – was calm. They were preparing to flee, but he was getting ready to stay. Destruction of records was only one of the things on his mind. In his office inside, there were maps spread on his desk, and as a motley collection of figures made their way in and out, he took reports, gave orders and made offers. He was blinking incessantly, but not from the smoke or nerves, that was just his way. He was currently conducting simultaneous negotiations with both the police and the local crime syndicates. He had people out in the city organising disguises and hideouts. If the Germans were going to occupy Egypt, he was going to make their lives hell.

There are people who only become their full selves in war, when the normal rules of civilised life are suspended. Some simply relish the chance to kill. But for others war offers the opportunity to become a sort of respectable scoundrel, doing things no gentleman would usually consider, but with official approval. A pirate, if you like, in the service of your country. Dudley Clarke was one of those men.

All around him was chaos, and he was having the time of his life.

If you had asked a British officer in Cairo in 1942 to point Colonel Clarke out to you in the bar of Shepheard's, the hotel that was one of the hubs of life for Cairo's military smart set, they would have been able to. He was a well-known figure in the city's wartime society, always ready with a cocktail and a story. But if you'd asked what it was that he did, you would have had less success. Those who knew didn't tell, and almost no one really did know. It was something hush-hush, working for the commander-in-chief.

The mystery persisted for the rest of his life. When Clarke died in 1974, *The Times* carried a two-paragraph obituary, describing him as 'a soldier of originality and independence', but not explaining how these qualities had manifested themselves, or what part he had played in the world war in which he rose to the rank of brigadier.

Neither does Clarke appear much in histories of the war, even those dealing with campaigns and operations with which he was intimately involved. When he does, it is generally a passing reference. He sometimes pops up in memoirs, in the background in some scene of great moment, but even then the authors often seem faintly baffled about his presence.

He enjoyed a brief moment of celebrity in 2013, when files were released dealing with his 1941 arrest in Madrid – an episode that might have cost him his career – but those reports too were vague about what his job had actually been. He had another sudden moment of prominence at the end of 2022, when he was portrayed by Dominic West as a louche spy in a Chanel dress in the BBC drama *SAS: Rogue Heroes*. Though the series is based in fact, it largely fictionalised Clarke. That's fair enough: he was a man to whom stories attached themselves.

But if Clarke was obscure, his commanders had a keen sense of his value. 'He is irreplaceable,' wrote General Harold Alexander, then commanding Allied forces in North Africa, in 1943. 'His mental ingenuity, balance, foresight, tact, character and remarkable personality have achieved results which have contributed more to the successful operations in the Middle East than probably any other officer of his rank.'

Others agreed. 'By his outstanding intelligence, professional skill, energy and grasp of the many complex problems he has dealt with he has contributed in an unusual degree to the success of Allied campaigns,' read a citation for the US Legion of Merit signed by President Franklin D. Roosevelt.

What was that work? The short answer is 'deception'. But that is a little like saying that Robert Oppenheimer worked on bombing. Throughout history, military commanders have sought to mislead their opponents. Dudley Clarke set out to do it on a scale no one had imagined before. Even afterwards, almost no one understood the scale of his achievement.

Clarke thought of himself as developing a new kind of weapon. It was a weapon that helped to deliver victory but it also saved lives, hundreds of thousands of them.

Most unusually for a weapon, it saved the lives of enemy soldiers as well. There are many Germans alive today whose grandfathers owed their survival of the war to this eccentric English soldier.

The success of this weapon depended on secrecy. Very few people knew what Clarke was up to. Even the commanders who were cleared to know about his work struggled to understand it. After the war, he was forbidden from talking about it. Others took credit instead, with stories that were at best exaggerated, and often fictitious.

In recent decades, the opening up of secret wartime files has revealed the scale of the Allied deception operations ahead of D-Day, and the use of double agents to plant false information in Berlin. What has generally been missed is that there was nothing done in London in 1944 that hadn't been done first in Cairo by 1942. The men who worked on the Normandy landings were Clarke's disciples, trained by him and using techniques he had invented, tested and refined.

This is the story of how Clarke conceived and built his weapon. Its sources include Clarke's private papers and those of some of his colleagues, but the main one is the files of his team, now open at Britain's National Archives in Kew.

There is no shortage of documentation around Clarke. His own writings include two volumes of personal memoirs, a history and a novel. His papers contain letters and diaries. All these words reveal him to be an entertaining writer who knew how to tell a tale, but also one practised at deflecting unwanted attention and directing the audience's eyes elsewhere. Of one of the most critical moments of his own war, he wrote not a word that I can find. He is an easy man to like but, at the deepest level, a difficult man to know.

And so there are parts of Clarke's story that remain mysterious, hidden even from those closest to him. But it is a good story. Clarke loved good stories.

The Players

ALLIES

Deceivers and allied trades

Dudley Clarke – Head of A Force
David Niven – Movie star, Commando
R. J. Maunsell – Head of Security Intelligence Middle East (SIME)
Tony Simonds – A Force, MI9 coordinator
Eric 'John' Shearer – Director of Military Intelligence, Cairo
Vladimir Wolfson – Naval Intelligence, SIME and A Force officer,
    Istanbul
Kenyon Jones – SIME officer
Warrant Officer Ellis – First wireless operator for Nicosoff
Sergeant Shears – Second wireless operator for Nicosoff
Evan John Simpson – SIME officer
'Professor' Eric 'Titters the Taster' Titterington – Forger
Geoffrey Barkas – Head of Camouflage
John Hutton – Camouflage officer
Peter Proud – Camouflage officer
Tony Ayrton – Camouflage officer
Brian Robb – Camouflage officer
Jasper Maskelyne – Camouflage officer and then MI9 lecturer
Ralph Bagnold – Founder of the Long Range Desert Group,
    Middle East Chief Deception Officer, 1941–42
Dominic Macadam-Sherwen, alias Dominique, Vicomte de la
    Motte – SIME officer
Noel Wild – A Force officer
Michael Crichton – A Force officer
Evangeline Palidou – SIME employee, Blonde Gun Moll
Oliver Stanley – Head of London Controlling Section 1941–42
Johnny Bevan – Head of London Controlling Section 1942–45

Dennis Wheatley – Novelist, London Controlling Section officer
Peter Fleming – Deception officer, Far East
Carl Goldbranson – US liaison to A Force
Harold Burris-Meyer – Sound technician extraordinaire
Douglas Fairbanks, Jr – Movie star, US naval officer
David Strangeways – A Force officer
Daphne Llewellyn – Secretary and organiser of illicit dances,
    Algiers
Harry Gummer – A Force representative, Gibraltar

Soldiers

John Dill – Chief of the Imperial General Staff, 1940–41
Alan Brooke – Chief of the Imperial General Staff, 1941–46
Dwight Eisenhower – Supreme Allied Commander, Europe
    1943–45
Archibald Wavell – Commander-in-Chief, Middle East, 1939–41
Claude Auchinleck – Commander-in-Chief, Middle East, 1941–42
Harold Alexander – Commander-in-Chief, Middle East, 1942–43
Neil Ritchie – Commander, Eighth Army, 1941–42
Bernard Montgomery – Commander, Eighth Army, 1942–43, Allied
    Ground Forces (Normandy), 1944
Bonner Fellers – US military attaché, Egypt
Freddie de Guingand – Chief of staff, Eighth Army, under
    Montgomery
Charles Richardson – Planning officer, Eighth Army
M. E. Clifton James – Lieutenant, Pay Corps 1940–46;
    Commander, Allied Ground Forces (Normandy), 27–30 May,
    1944 (sort of).

Spies

Guy Liddell – Deputy Director MI5
Stewart Menzies – Head of MI6
Thomas Argyll 'TAR' Robertson – MI5, in charge of double agents
Charles Cholmondeley – MI5 officer, secretary to the Twenty
    Committee
Ewen Montagu – Naval Intelligence
Ivor Montagu – Soviet Intelligence

Renato Levi – Double agent, notionally working for German intelligence, actually working for British intelligence
Leonard Hamilton Stokes – MI6 Head of Station, Madrid
Paul Nicosoff – Entirely fictional spy, supposedly working for the Germans in Cairo
Marie – Nicosoff's equally fictional girlfriend
Gilbert Lennox – MI5 officer

Civilians

Sidney Clarke – Uncle, lawyer, magician
Thomas 'Tibby' Clarke – Brother, screenwriter
Hermione Ranfurly – Secretary and diarist, Cairo
Alice Sims, Betty-to-You, later Betty Crichton – Dancer, Cairo
Cedric Salter – Journalist, Istanbul
Alexander Clifford – Journalist, Cairo

Diplomats

Miles Lampson – British ambassador to Egypt
Samuel Hoare – British ambassador to Spain
Arthur Yencken – Counsellor, British Embassy in Madrid
William Torr – Military attaché, British Embassy in Madrid
Francis Haselden – British consul in Huelva, Spain

His Majesty's Government

Alexander Cadogan – Permanent Secretary, Foreign Office
Philip Whitefoord – Deputy Director, Military Intelligence, War Office
Anthony Eden – Foreign Secretary
David Margesson – War Secretary
Lord Gort – Governor of Gibraltar, 1941–42

THE AXIS

Spies

Admiral Canaris – Head of Abwehr
Hans Travaglio – Abwehr officer in Italy
Laszlo Almasy – Desert explorer

Diplomats

Michizo Ohno – Japanese diplomat in Egypt

Soldiers

Erwin Rommel – Commander, Afrika Corps 1941–43,
   Army Group B 1943–44
Georg Stumme – Rommel's Afrika Corps deputy
Gerhard von Schwerin – German army officer
Hans-Otto Behrendt – Intelligence officer, Afrika Corps
Ulrich Liss – Head of Army Intelligence

NEUTRALS

Anwar Al-Sadat – Egyptian army officer
Ignacio Molina – Spanish intelligence officer

Setting the Stage

1500 BC–December 1940

All warfare is based on deception. When able to attack, we must seem unable; when using our forces, we must seem inactive; when we are near, we must make the enemy believe we are far away; when far away, we must make him believe we are near.

Sun Tzu

Chapter 1

A year and a half before the panic of 1942, a 31-year-old captain named Tony Simonds was sitting at his desk in General Headquarters in Cairo, bored out of his mind.

It was December 1940, the end of a year that had seen the map of Europe transformed. Poland, Denmark, Norway, Holland, Belgium and half of France were now occupied by the Nazis. The rest of France was a satellite state, run from Vichy. The Royal Air Force and Royal Navy had stopped the Germans at the Channel, but Britain's army had retreated in disarray first from Norway and then from the continent.

All that had happened thousands of miles away from where Simonds sat. As far as he was concerned, the war was offering depressingly little excitement.

It wasn't that he disliked his job. He'd seen enough of the army over the past nine years to know that military intelligence was a lot more his line than parade grounds and kit inspections. And he enjoyed being stationed in Egypt. There was none of the rationing or blackouts or bombing that were making life in Britain so miserable. Here there was still the feeling of colonial life in the great days of the empire: watching polo matches, lounging by swimming pools, drinking sundowners at the Continental Hotel, lusting after the belly dancers in Madame Badia's Cabaret, and after that, well, Cairo was a city ready to cater for every appetite. You had to put up with heat and dust and stink and flies and disease, but it was also a place of adventure with a sense that anything was possible.

That sense was suspended when Simonds sat down at his desk each day. He was supposed to be in charge of compiling reports into the Italian military's technical capabilities, but the work didn't thrill him. So when his colonel announced he had an errand for him, he was grateful for the chance to escape the office.

He was even happier when he heard what the job was. He was to go and collect Dudley Clarke from the airport. If that made it sound routine, the next sentence hinted that it wouldn't be. He was to wear civilian clothes and, whatever Clarke looked like, he was to maintain his composure and make no comment. Simonds smiled to himself. That sounded about right.

Even in 1940, Clarke was a sort of secret legend. He wasn't famous, but those who knew him swapped tales of his adventures. Simonds had worked alongside him in Palestine before the war, and was in awe of the unconventional way in which he approached military life. If Clarke was coming to Egypt, then adventures would not be far behind.

Nor would surprises. As he watched the passengers step from the flying boat, Simonds understood why he'd been warned to stay unruffled. There was his friend's trim figure. Clarke could often pass unnoticed – he seemed, one fan said, to have a gift for appearing in rooms without anyone seeing him come in – but no one was going to miss him today. He was dressed as an Englishman's idea of the worst kind of American: loud check plus-fours with matching stockings, a bright cloth cap and sunglasses. He marched up to Simonds and introduced himself, in an atrocious American accent, as 'Wrangel Clarke, journalist'. It was all that the younger man could do to keep a straight face.

Clarke never explained what all this had been in aid of. When Simonds told the story later, he would say that the cover of a neutral journalist – America had yet to enter the war – had enabled Clarke to travel through occupied Europe as a spy, but it's not clear whether his friend had actually told him that. Clarke certainly hadn't come by that route.

In reality, it was probably a joke. Clarke enjoyed jokes. He enjoyed play-acting and dressing up, too. It was, ultimately, a bit of an odd thing to do. But then, Dudley Wrangel Clarke was a bit of an odd chap.

He had been born in Johannesburg in 1899, in the run-up to another conflict, the Boer War. He was the eldest son of a Yorkshireman, Ernest, who had moved to South Africa in search of adventure, taken part in a failed coup, got into gold-mining, and married. After the war ended, he took his young family back to Britain and settled in the Home Counties.

Ernest had done well in business: he had a shrewd eye for an opportunity, claiming that he paid for his first house with money he won on the journey back to England when he learned the ship had stopped during the night, allowing him to place a large bet in the daily passengers' contest to guess how far the boat had travelled. He was an affectionate, generous father, who had got into scrapes as a young man and tended to see the funny side when his children did the same. And having succeeded himself, he set his sons up to do even better, sending them to Charterhouse, one of England's great public schools, where young gentlemen were prepared for the future that was expected of them. Charterhouse men entered parliament, ran colonies, became bishops or generals.

Dudley was never likely to become a bishop, and he had already been thinking about the Army when the course of his life was set in the summer of 1914. Fifteen years old, he was on a summer camp with his school's Officer Training Corps. The professional soldiers looking after them rapidly began to disappear, and on the day that the Great War was declared, the boys were ordered to break camp and head home.

War was, to schoolboys raised on tales of empire and conquest, an exciting adventure. Older boys joined up. As for the rest of them, Clarke recalled, 'all we could do was wait to grow old enough to join the Army.' Dudley had never been a great academic, and now books held no interest for him at all.

In time, he would come to see the tragedy of the teenage thirst for military glory. Of the five boys he shared a tent with on that 1914 camp, two were dead within a year. Clarke estimated that a quarter of the 550 boys who had been at Charterhouse when he arrived in 1912 were killed by the end of the decade.

But in 1915, he was desperate to get into the fight. He tried to join the navy as a midshipman, but was refused. Finally, at the end of the year, he turned sixteen and a half, old enough to sit the entrance exam for army officers. He passed, but his score was too low to get him into the Royal Military Academy at Woolwich. He greeted it as a welcome miracle when, a week later, he was told there would be room for him after all. Only later would he realise that the War Ministry's decision to expand its recruitment of young officers reflected the weight of losses at the front.

The Woolwich academy had its share of eccentricities: four-course formal dinners each evening, and dancing lessons for which cadets with 'roughly the right physique' were expected to don skirts. Clarke enjoyed it. But at the end of his six months training, Clarke's hopes of getting into combat were thwarted once again. There was a strict rule against sending anyone under the age of nineteen into action. Instead, he was commissioned as a second lieutenant, and posted to Brighton.

For Clarke, 1917 and 1918 were spent trying, and failing, to enter the war. He begged his father, who was running ambulances for the British Red Cross, to use his contacts to get him a place at the front. But Ernest, who must have had a good sense of what was happening in France, would have been forgiven for not trying very hard. Though Dudley didn't know it, his father had been behind his rejection from the navy.

Determined to make it by hook or crook, Dudley even found his way onto a troop ship to France, and tried to bluff his way to the front, before being sent, gently, back home to England. Hearing that the Royal Flying Corps wanted artillery officers, he applied to become a pilot. He was accepted, but ended up being sent to Egypt to learn to fly. There, in 1918, standing at the edge of a desert airfield, he realised that the fighting was going to end before he had a chance to join in, and wept. He spent Armistice Day in Cairo, struggling to celebrate the end of a war that, for him, had never really begun.

His father, though, urged him not to quit the army. There weren't enough jobs for the men who were being demobilised, and it was a chance for a young man to travel the world. Over the next twenty years, Dudley would see much of the empire, visiting India and serving in Mesopotamia, Palestine and Aden. He would combine the conventional life of a rising officer – staff exams, home and foreign postings – with a quest for adventure. He spent one leave as a war correspondent in Morocco, and visited Germany repeatedly as Adolf Hitler rose to power and then tightened his grip on the country.

To everything he added a dash of glamour. In Palestine, where as a senior officer fighting the Arab uprising his name was near the top of a death list, he drove round the country with a pistol clipped to the steering column of his customised sports car. Interrupted by an insurgent attack on his way to a dance, he'd found himself directing mortar fire in his dinner suit.

All Dudley's fellow officers seemed to have tales about him, some true, many exaggerated or apocryphal. There was the time that, short of funds for a weekend leave in London, he had supposedly pawned a fellow officer's suit, used the money to pay the deposit on a grandfather clock, pawned that, and retrieved the clothes with cash to spare. 'My dear chap,' he'd explained to a friend puzzled about the details of this. 'A grandfather clock is so respectable.' Then there was the whisper about his time in Morocco, that journalism had only been a cover, and in fact he'd been fighting alongside the rebel tribesmen against the French. If either of these was true, Clarke left it out of his own memoirs.

Simonds, a decade younger, had worked for Clarke in Palestine, and enjoyed telling stories about his gentle mocking of authority. Ordered by a new commander to start arriving at his desk at 8 a.m., the late-rising Clarke complied, but then had his breakfast brought to him at his desk by servants an hour later. He waged a long tongue-in-cheek campaign to get himself a Boer War campaign medal, because he'd discovered that anyone who had been on the military ration strength was entitled to one and he had, as an infant, been fed on garrison food during the siege of Ladysmith. For well over a decade he'd been ignoring repeated orders to remove his now-outdated Royal Flying Corps wings from his uniform. 'Dudley never went out of his way to flout, disagree or to insult authority,' Simonds said. 'He merely smiled sweetly, got his own way, or went in another direction.'

But if this seemed to border on insubordination, it was the behaviour of someone with a lively mind, rather than a malcontent. Commanders found Clarke efficient, likeable and quick-thinking. A few saw something more.

General Archibald Wavell, one of Clarke's commanders in Palestine, was among those who had been impressed by the way he would 'tackle any emergency with calmness, almost with unconcern'. But it wasn't simply Clarke's coolness that recommended him. Wavell saw in Clarke a 'somewhat impish sense of humour' combined with real ingenuity. 'I recognised an original, unorthodox outlook on soldiering,' he said. These were qualities he was sure could be useful. Wavell had made a mental note that this officer was someone he'd like to have at hand in a war.

In 1939 that war had come, and Clarke had swiftly been given a series of sensitive missions. It was on one of these, carrying cash and secret orders to the troops that were sailing for Norway in April 1940, that he got his first taste of how badly the British were outmatched by their enemy. The expeditionary force, supposed to help the country fight back against a surprise German invasion, was poorly organised and equipped, too small to make a difference, and utterly unprepared for what it was to face. Almost as soon as he had arrived, Clarke found himself discussing how the army might leave. Entrusted by the Norwegian commander-in-chief with a letter to London begging for more help, Clarke experienced the chaos of war as he was arrested by Norwegians who suspected him of being a German agent, and then dive-bombed by the Germans as he continued his journey, everywhere passing wounded and retreating soldiers, the defenders hopelessly overwhelmed.

He carried his message to London and was promptly sent back to Norway with a reply that there would be no more British soldiers coming, and that those who were there should evacuate at once. This was to prove an even more desperate journey than his last one, as Clarke, his messages delivered, once again escaped the country, this time sheltering from bombers in a drain on the way. He felt a failure. 'Here was a professional soldier at the first clash of the greatest war of all, the ultimate test of the Army in which I had spent over half my life,' he wrote. 'And what was my present contribution to these world-shattering events? To hide.'

But Clarke would be very far from the last British soldier to find himself fleeing the Germans that summer. The following month, Hitler's armies rolled across Western Europe, showing once again that they understood modern warfare better than their opponents. As German forces had closed in on the French coast, it was Clarke, now back in London, who dictated the grim order to the British garrison at Calais that they would not be rescued, and were to stand fast at all costs.

If these were moments of military significance, Clarke's most politically sensitive mission came in the midst of that British retreat, as he was sent to Dublin, in conditions of absolute secrecy, to liaise with the Irish government on how it might respond to a German invasion, and the conditions under which it might ask for British military aid. Such discussions were a matter of huge delicacy in a country that had only recently won its independence from Britain. Clarke's selection showed how highly his commanders rated not just his military judgement and his discretion but also his diplomatic skills. He seems to have got on well with people who two decades earlier would have regarded him as an enemy. His advice that any request should come early if there was to be a chance of holding back the Nazis was met with the dry reply that the Irish had some experience dealing with occupying armies.

Meanwhile, Clarke had been giving thought to avoiding 'the mass slaughter of 1914–18'. In the early months, he pondered whether Hitler's alliance with the Soviet Union would open the door to splitting the Fuhrer off from his generals, who had supported the Nazis because of their opposition to communism. Was there a different way to fight the war? 'I feel more and more convinced each day that it *can* be won by subterranean methods,' he wrote in his diary. He put up proposals for 'underground work against the German Army', but without success.

This was Clarke: a trusted man with a rebellious streak, a team player who could work on his own, a joker who noted everything and could keep a secret, a career soldier with a creative vision. And as he was about to demonstrate, he was a man who could imagine a new way of fighting, and a new kind of warrior.

Chapter 2

If Clarke had done nothing else in the war, his final job in London in 1940 would have secured him a place in history. On his return from Ireland he'd been appointed as military assistant to Sir John Dill, the new Chief of the Imperial General Staff. Dill and Clarke were old comrades. In Palestine a couple of years earlier, they'd been flying in a plane together and Clarke had leaned out to point to something, only to be thrown from his seat in the open cockpit by a moment of turbulence. In the version of the story that Clarke liked to tell, Dill had caught him 'by the ankles' and hauled him back into the plane.

Now Dill had been put in charge of the country's military just as it was at its lowest ebb. The army had been defeated first in Norway and then in France and Belgium. The evacuation of troops from Dunkirk might have been more successful than anyone had dared hope, but it had still involved the soldiers fleeing, their guns left behind them on the beach. There was no escaping the reality that the German army was winning battles and the British army was losing them.

Two days after the retreat from Dunkirk, Dill went to meet some of the soldiers who had escaped. He returned to the War Office troubled. Clarke followed him into his large corner office, with its view towards Trafalgar Square. For a minute or two the general stood at the window, deep in thought. It had been a pleasant summer afternoon, and in the distance behind Nelson's Column, the barrage balloons that were supposed to deter low-flying planes glittered silver in the evening sunlight.

Eventually Dill returned to his desk, and told his aide what was on his mind. The defence of Britain lay now in the hands of the air force and the navy. Unless the Germans attempted an invasion, there was little for the army to do. But his soldiers needed to recover their 'offensive spirit' – to get fighting again.

As it happened, Clarke had been approaching this problem from a different direction, thinking about how other armies had dealt with defeat. He reminded Dill how in South Africa the Boers had retreated and then formed small bands of mounted warriors to terrorise the force that had beaten them. It was the same tactic that people around the world had adopted to make life difficult for the British.

When Clarke and Dill had been in Palestine, they'd spent months dealing with bands of Arabs who struck fast and then disappeared before the better-armed British could chase them. Now they discussed how they could use the same approach against the Nazis, to launch 'a war of continual mosquito tactics which, at small cost to the marauders, would wear down and sicken the ponderous bulk of the more powerful side'.

This wasn't how British soldiers usually fought. It was, as Clarke knew from experience, how lesser forces fought against the British. But then the British army didn't have much experience of being the smaller force in a war. To get regular soldiers to operate as insurgents would require them to unlearn as much as they would learn. They would have to be able to act independently and without support.

At Dill's request, that night Clarke drafted a paper on the subject, proposing the formation of a small aggressive troop of soldiers who could launch swift raids into occupied Europe and then disappear into the night. He even had a name for them, taken from the South Africans he so admired: 'The Commandos'.

It was an unorthodox, eye-catching idea, exactly the sort of thing to appeal to the prime minister, Winston Churchill, who had encountered the Boers himself decades earlier. Clarke was ordered to raise a Commando force and send it on a raid as fast as possible.

Clarke found no shortage of soldiers and sailors eager to strike back at the all-conquering Nazis. His idea wasn't quite as original as he had thought: a few months earlier, a few 'independent companies' had been formed with the idea of training men in guerrilla warfare. These were being disbanded, and the men were keen to carry the work into Clarke's new unit.

In his recruits, he looked for 'intelligence, self-reliance and an independent frame of mind' as well as another somewhat nebulous quality: 'dash'. Anyone wondering what he meant by that had only to look at one of the first officers to volunteer for Clarke's new outfit, David Niven.

Before Niven had been a movie star, he had been a bored junior army officer, the kind of man for whom peacetime soldiering had no attraction. He'd quit and gone to Hollywood, but on the coming of war, he'd immediately returned to Britain to join up. Clarke saw in him a fellow unconventional thinker, someone who could set the perfect tone for the crew of gentlemen pirates and gangsters that he wanted to assemble. But he wanted Niven on his team for another reason, too.

Clarke was a snob. He liked the finer things of life, and he liked to think of himself as someone who mingled with top people. He had a flat in Mayfair that he couldn't have afforded without his father's help. He had a weakness for dropping names even in official reports. To have a Hollywood celebrity on his staff was an obvious thrill. When Clarke wrote later about his time setting up the Commandos, every other man was referred to by his surname. Niven was 'David'.

Stardust aside, the work of setting up the new unit was serious. If some senior officers liked the sound of giving the enemy a bloody nose, others were much less enthusiastic when it came to handing over men or equipment. In particular, there was a desperate short-age of weapons, and army units weren't going to hand back what little they had. Clarke wanted Thompson submachine guns for his soldiers, ideal for close-quarter surprise attacks, but there were only forty in the country – the military hadn't imagined such a weapon would be necessary a year earlier. He was given them, so long as he promised that only twenty would be taken on operations at a time, with the rest to stay in London in case they were needed to fight off a German invasion. It was a mark of how desperate the shortage of weapons was after Dunkirk that anyone thought twenty guns might make a difference to the defence of England.

On 24 June, less than three weeks after Clarke was given the go-ahead, the Commandos launched a cross-Channel assault. As raids go, it wasn't a great one, memorable only for being the unit's first. Just over a hundred men landed on French beaches, a couple of German sentries were killed, and the only British casualty was Clarke himself, his ear nearly shot off by a stray enemy bullet.

But it was a start, and meant that a month after the retreat from Dunkirk, the War Office was able to announce that 'naval and military units yesterday carried out successful reconnaissances of the enemy coastline'. The press release went on to claim that 'much useful information was obtained', which reflected mainly what the Commandos had learned about the logistics of coastal raids, rather than any useful intelligence collected on the ground. But the public were delighted to see that Britain hadn't given up. 'Its tactical significance may be small,' *The Times* wrote of the raid, 'but the tiniest thorn thrust into the heel with which the enemy is grinding down Western Europe has a moral importance which is not to be despised.'

If the first Commando raid was a bit of a damp squib, the second, a few weeks later, was an embarrassment. The target was supposed to be the Channel island of Guernsey, but malfunctioning compasses meant one unit landed on a different island altogether. Others were let down by faulty motorboats. The soldiers that did manage to get ashore failed to find any Germans, though they did knock one islander unconscious. When it came to leaving, their boats were unable to get close enough to the shore to retrieve them. At this stage, three of the soldiers revealed they had lied about being able to swim. Left behind, they were eventually captured.*

It was hardly a surprise that the army should have teething troubles when experimenting with fighting in this new way, but for those in the War Office who had thought the whole idea ridiculous, these failures were all the excuses they needed to begin sabotaging the Commandos. There was a bigger problem, too.

Clarke's vision of the Commandos had been of small independent units carrying out 'little and often' attacks that did damage out of proportion with their size and then fleeing before the German army could bring its weight to bear against them. But Churchill now decided he disliked 'pinprick' raids. A senior admiral was put in charge of what were named 'Combined Operations' – because the navy or air force were used to deliver the soldiers to their targets.

From now on, the Commandos would mount the sort of big attacks with which the top brass were more comfortable. But planning such raids proved cumbersome, and getting approval for them

---

* The following year, Hitler would order the building of vast fortifications on the Channel Islands, only for the islands to be ignored during the Allied invasion of Europe. It's possible this huge waste of resources was partly prompted by the 1940 raid, and it has been argued that this actually makes the visit to Guernsey the most successful Commando operation of the war, perhaps of all time.

impossible. They required more support from other services, which meant they needed to have a great purpose. The vision of a dozen or so men nipping across the Channel to cut throats and make the Germans nervous was dead.

Clarke could feel his project slipping away from him. As summer turned to autumn, he found himself sitting in meetings trying to justify the continued existence of a force that seemingly wasn't allowed to go on any missions. It was at this point, just as he feared his unit might be strangled at birth, that he was ordered to Cairo.

It doesn't seem that anyone was trying to get him out of the way. In other circumstances, this would have been a plum posting: Egypt was the one place where the army was still fighting anyone. But opponents of the Commandos would have been pleased to see Clarke departing. He certainly feared the project might not survive in his absence. There was, however, no point in trying to resist. His presence had been personally requested by the commander-in-chief of forces in the Middle East.

Clarke left London, then, in complicated circumstances, his highest-profile achievement one of unproven value. He was a maverick figure, but was he a useful one, or was he simply another crackpot whose wizard schemes didn't survive contact with reality?

Some soldiers were, like Tony Simonds, in awe of Dudley Clarke. Others found his ideas too strange. Out in Egypt, though, one very senior general thought he was exactly the man he needed.

Chapter 3

A year into the Second World War, things were not, bluntly, going Britain's way. Hitler's Reich stretched from the Arctic Circle down to Biarritz in the South of France.

The one place where the British army was still in the game was Africa, where Britain had both colonies and interests. But there, too, 1940 had seen mainly retreats.

Italy had entered the war in June when Benito Mussolini saw how well things were going for his fellow fascist. Keen for national triumphs, he secured Hitler's agreement that the Mediterranean and Africa would be his theatre.

In Mussolini's mind, a great nation like Italy deserved a great empire. It had for decades had colonies in Libya, in North Africa, and Somaliland, in East Africa. Five years earlier it had advanced into Ethiopia. The borders of its possessions were now, for the most part, British colonies and protectorates: Kenya, Uganda, Sudan, British Somaliland and Egypt. If Italy's empire was to expand, Britain's must shrink.

Mussolini's first attacks of 1940, in East Africa, had gone well, but they should have: he chose to avoid the better-protected Kenya and Sudan, and attack instead British Somaliland, where 24,000 Italian invaders overwhelmed 4,500 defenders.

Meanwhile the target for Italy's forces in Libya was Egypt, and the Suez Canal. The prizes were great: capturing the canal would sever Britain's shortest link to her empire, and help the Italian navy control the Mediterranean. More than that, a British defeat in Egypt would leave nothing between the Italian forces and the oil fields of the Middle East.

Britain's status in Egypt was complicated. The country was neutral, but its young ruler, King Farouk, had signed a treaty in 1936 giving the British the right to defend the country. After the start of the war, the British quickly began treating Egypt as though she were a colonial possession, rather than a sovereign state.

Still, Neville Chamberlain's government had been reluctant to build up strength in Egypt at the start of the year out of a fear of provoking Mussolini. British commanders now estimated their 36,000 troops in Egypt were facing more than 200,000 Italians in Libya.

They had another problem, too. Although a war with Italy had long been anticipated as a possibility, all the planning had assumed that Britain would be allied with France, which held Tunisia, on Libya's western border. Now that France was out of the war, the Italians in Libya no longer had to fight on two fronts.

When it came, the Italian attack on Egypt illustrated the three factors that would dominate the war in North Africa for the next three years: geography, armour and supply.

Although Egypt's border with Libya was hundreds of miles long, most of it was roadless desert that was impassable to an army. In practice, the North African war would be fought on a long narrow strip of land next to the Mediterranean. The flat, featureless terrain rewarded whichever side had the stronger tanks and longer-range guns.

But both sides would struggle to support their own advances. The essentials of life and of combat – water, food, fuel and ammunition, tonnes and tonnes and tonnes of each – had to be brought up along the poorly-maintained road – a road, of course, that hadn't been designed for this level of traffic – behind them. The further an army advanced, the further those supplies had to travel. And travel was arduous. The sand, the heat and the dust sapped men's energy, and were no kinder to machines. The country was poorly mapped. There were no landmarks. Iron ore deposits in the ground and the metal in vehicles interfered with compasses. It was easy to break down or get lost, and in the desert either of those could kill you.

So when the Italian army advanced in September 1940, it was cautiously. Although it had far more men than the British, it was weaker in terms of equipment, in particular tanks. After a small advance, the Italians set up camp and waited for more supplies.

The man commanding British forces in the Middle East was Archibald Wavell, who had been so impressed with Clarke a couple of years earlier when they worked together in Palestine. Solidly built, in his late fifties, greying, moustachioed with a lined face, he was a veteran of the Boer War who had lost an eye in the Great War but gained a Military Cross.

He was famously taciturn. When Clarke had first met him three years earlier, they had driven together from Jerusalem to Haifa. As they set out, Wavell offered what Clarke took to be a conversational opener: 'When did you join?'

'In 1916, sir,' Clarke replied.

Wavell considered this. Clarke, ever the raconteur, claimed it was a full hour before he spoke again: 'I meant: when did you join this headquarters?'

It was hardly surprising that some found him remote. But Wavell's silence – shyness, perhaps – reflected a mind at work. He was considered one of the army's leading thinkers, an advocate of better and more practical training for soldiers and officers. He had been appalled and frustrated by the way he saw infantry thrown against enemy defences in the Great War. To him, good soldiers relied on their wits as well as their weapons, and they deserved to be deployed with thought.

When a friend defined the ideal infantryman as 'athlete, marksman, stalker', Wavell replied that a better combination would be 'cat burglar, gunman, poacher'. The marksman, he said, risked nothing, whereas the criminal put his life on the line.

Wavell loved outdoor pursuits – hunting, shooting and golf – but also poetry. In 1944 he would publish an anthology of more than 200 poems he had at one time or another known by heart. It was an unexpectedly popular collection at the time and has rarely been out of print since. Inevitably there was plenty in there on fighting and death but, he noted, 'war is not only a grim but mainly a dull business and does not tend to inspire poetry in those who practise it.' His choices and the commentaries he wrote on them revealed sensitivity, thoughtfulness, and in the poems that did deal with combat, a keen awareness that a poor choice by a general would cost the lives of his men.

He wrote with a dry humour that was clear even in his official communications, and those who could break through the shell found they enjoyed his company, even when he spoke little. 'I soon learned to respect these silences,' Clarke wrote later, 'and even to understand them, while I somehow came to realise that the general understood me.'

More than understand. Wavell saw in him a fellow creative thinker. Clarke had passed through Cairo in February 1940, under orders to investigate an overland supply route from Kenya to Egypt. Running into him at headquarters, Wavell had asked him then if he would like to join his staff. 'On the spur of the moment – without the least idea of what the job would be – I said "Yes",' Clarke wrote in his diary. 'In his usual silent way that ended the conversation.'

It had taken nine months for anything to come of this, but by November 1940 Wavell had sent a personal note to Dill. 'Wish to form special section,' it began. 'Require uncommon type of officer and can think of no one better suited than Dudley Clarke. Could he possibly be spared?'

There were plenty of reasons Wavell might have wanted Clarke: he was an efficient staff officer who understood the army and the theory of war, and had experience of secret work. He got on well with his fellow officers and was confident briefing generals. Having trained as a pilot and worked in Egypt, Palestine, Aden and North Africa, he knew the region from both the ground and the air. But it was another quality that recommended Clarke to Wavell: he had imagination.

Early the day after his arrival in Cairo, Clarke, now in uniform, made his way down the steps of Shepheard's Hotel. It was his third visit to the city in just over a year. The previous times he had been passing through, but this was a permanent assignment.

He had known Cairo more than twenty years, and liked it. Not everyone did. Some couldn't stand the mix of extreme squalor and luxury – the expensive American cars fighting for road space with overloaded donkey carts. They could never get used to the temperature, the flies, the grime, the beggars on every corner, the hawkers trying to sell you things you didn't want, talking at speed in a language you didn't understand, the stench of sewage that was always in the air. But to Clarke it was a city where in the evenings 'they sold daisy-chains of jasmine on the pavements and every girl who passed carried the sweet smell of the white flowers down the street.' A superstitious man, he was sure that his destiny lay in the Middle East.

In the months since Clarke's last visit, the army's General Headquarters had outgrown their previous building, and moved into Grey

Pillars, an apartment block in the Garden City, Cairo's smartest district.

The area had been built on the banks of the Nile in the European style, with tree-lined winding boulevards that were intended to make the visitor feel as though they had escaped the din and rush of the rest of the city. This relaxing air was a little undermined by the barbed wire that had been put up to protect the approaches to Grey Pillars, with sentries checking passes and keeping out undesirables.

Inside the building there was plenty of din and rush. There were signposts everywhere marked with the initials of different sections and offices. This was the bureaucracy of an army at war, keeping track of men, equipment and supplies, trying to ensure that they went where they were supposed to, when they were needed, and survived the journey.

The building itself bore the scars of battle, not from enemy fire, but from the effort to turn it into office space. Corridors had been boarded up to create rooms, and rooms had been knocked together to make corridors. In the heat of the day it was a crowded, noisy, sweaty place. One visitor was left with the impression of a busy department store trying to cope during structural alterations.

Clarke made his way to Wavell's office, at the end of an upstairs corridor. The wall behind the general was covered in maps, ten feet high, showing the many parts of Africa and the Middle East that he had to worry about. But Wavell kept his desk clear of paperwork, which had the effect of making visitors feel that they were his sole concern, and would roll pencils back and forth across it as he listened to them.

There was a calmness to the general, one acquaintance said, 'as if he knew trouble well and had often stared it in the face and now was not afraid of it any more'. Clarke knew what to expect from the briefing: the 'slow, quiet manner, almost as though he were speaking his thoughts to himself,' in which he set out his thinking.

Wavell welcomed Clarke back, and explained that he was now 'Personal Intelligence Officer (Special Duties) to the Commander-in-Chief'. It was a title that conveyed importance but revealed little. He would, Wavell informed him, have no staff, but they had managed to find him an office, in a converted bathroom. It was an unusual situation, but then the job the general wanted Clarke to do was not one that existed in the British military or anywhere else.

Ten days earlier, on 8 December 1940, Wavell had launched his assault against the Italian forces camped at the border. Operation Compass, as it was called, opened with a bold manoeuvre, where British tanks and infantry passed between two enemy strongholds and then began attacking from the rear. It had achieved complete success, partly because it had been a total surprise. Few even in the British staff had known it was coming. As Wavell put it a couple of years later, 'I have always believed in doing everything possible in war to mystify and mislead one's opponent.'

Wavell described to Clarke how he had ordered intelligence officers to spread rumours in Cairo that more troops were to be sent to Greece. As his forces assembled, they were told it was for another training exercise. Information was planted with 'a Japanese source', probably the consul, whom the British were confident would pass intelligence to his masters, who in turn would pass it to their friends in Italy. To appear stronger than he was, Wavell had ordered the construction of a battalion of fake tanks, apparently covering the British rear. To Clarke, all this was immediately appealing: war by tricks, outwitting a stronger opponent.

The Italians had quickly been forced out of Egypt, and the British had taken 38,000 prisoners at a cost of little more than 600 casualties. For the army, it was also the first victory after a year of defeats. For people at home it was welcome news as Christmas approached.

Compass had exploited surprise but also the Italians' mistakes in the way they had set up their defensive position, leaving a gap that they couldn't defend. That error had been a piece of good fortune for Wavell. Now he wanted to persuade his enemy to make more mistakes. That, he explained, was where Clarke came in. His mission was simple: to persuade the enemy not simply to defend his positions badly, but to put his forces in the wrong place entirely.

There was a word for this job: deception.

Chapter 4

One of the earliest recorded examples of military deception comes in the story of the Siege of Joppa, in the fifteenth century BC. Egyptian forces are said to have got inside the city walls by hiding in sacks that were supposed to contain gifts. This tale has a far more famous echo in a story from a couple of centuries later, elsewhere on the Mediterranean: the Trojan Horse.

In that tale, the Greek besiegers of Troy are supposed to have put their enemies at their ease by sailing away. According to the Bible, the Israelites adopted a similar trick to capture the city of Ai. Their leader, Joshua, hid a small assault force, while displaying most of his troops outside the city. When its defenders came out to meet them, the Israelites fled, and the forces of Ai set off in pursuit. This was the moment for Joshua to unleash his hidden force and set fire to the city. 'The men of Ai looked back and saw the smoke of the city rising up into the sky, but they had no chance to escape in any direction; the Israelites who had been fleeing towards the wilderness had turned back against their pursuers.'

Around a thousand years later on the other side of the world, the Chinese strategist Sun Pin also had his forces feign cowardice, pretending to flee before the army of his rival P'ang Chüan. He told his men to set fewer cooking fires each night, giving the impression to their pursuers that troops were deserting. Aware that P'ang was overconfident, Sun showed him what he expected to see. P'ang, determined not to let his enemy escape, rushed forward with cavalry, arriving as night fell at a valley, where Sun's waiting crossbowmen wiped them out. In Chinese tradition, the ambushers knew where to aim because P'ang had ordered a torch lit to read a message that Sun had left carved into a trunk: 'P'ang Chüan dies beneath this tree'.

Two thousand years after that, in the winter of 1776, George Washington faced the opposite problem as he commanded an undermanned and under-supplied Continental Army in New Jersey. Desperate to deter the much stronger British force from attacking, he made his own side look stronger than it was. He stretched his troops out, billeting them in as many places as possible, so that there seemed to be soldiers everywhere. That made it easier to persuade the enemy to believe the inflated troop numbers Washington's agents were trying to feed them. The British held off, and at the end of the year Washington, having regrouped his forces, crossed the Delaware River and inflicted a swift series of defeats on them.

But for all the millennia that deception had been practised by commanders, there had been a question mark over it. The Greek poet Quintus Smyrnaeus, writing around AD 350, imagined Neoptolemus, the 'battle-eager' son of Achilles, rebuking his fellow Greeks for considering Odysseus's plan to deceive the Trojans. 'Strong men fight their enemies face to face,' he says. 'Let us not now, therefore, think up any trick or any other contrivance. It is proper for princes to show themselves men in battle.'

The spread of Christianity across Europe, with its teaching that personal behaviour mattered more than outcomes, combined with the rise of the chivalric tradition to push warriors away from guile. Although that didn't mean they rejected it altogether. At the Battle of Hastings, William the Conqueror's Normans feigned flight in an effort to lure Harold's Saxons to break their impenetrable shield wall and pursue them. In the late fifteenth century, defenders at Alhama de Granada put up cloth painted like stone to cover gaps that had been made in their walls.

As the centuries went on, commanders sought victory through surprise. The Duke of Marlborough won the Battle of Blenheim by moving his troops further and faster than his enemy had believed possible. James Wolfe captured Quebec by sending his men up a cliff that the French defenders considered inaccessible.

Deception was even celebrated, in certain contexts. Robert Baden-Powell became a national hero in Britain after the Siege of Mafeking of 1899 and 1900, where he used a huge range of ingenious tricks to persuade the Boer attackers that his defending force was far stronger than it was.

But there was a tension between this and the idea that victory should come from honourable and straightforward behaviour. It was summed up in the 1869 *Soldier's Pocket-Book for Field Service*:

'As a nation we are bred up to feel it a disgrace even to succeed by falsehood; the word spy conveys something as repulsive as slave; we will keep hammering along with the conviction that "honesty is the best policy", and that truth always wins in the long run.' This, the author argued, was silly. 'These pretty little sentences do well for a child's copy book, but the man who acts upon them in war had better sheathe his sword for ever.'

The First World War had brought innovations, some in response to technology. Rifles allowed soldiers to hit targets at a much greater distance. British troops who had fought in South Africa two decades earlier in bright red jackets designed to impress the enemy now wore khaki uniforms that were intended to make them hard to spot.

At sea, ships were given 'dazzle paint', jagged stripes that made it difficult for U-boats to correctly judge their course and distance. Some ships were given fake 'Quaker' guns to make them look more dangerous than they really were – a trick that had been working in one form or another since at least the American War of Independence. Others concealed real guns, making themselves look like harmless cargo ships in the hope that submarines would try to save torpedoes and surface to attack them with a gun, at which point the crew would reveal their own weapons and fire back.

But there were distinct limits to the military's innovations, as the deadlock of trench warfare showed. Despite years of stalemate, the military struggled to imagine alternatives to the costly frontal assaults. In early 1917, a British commander on the Western Front proposed catching the Germans off guard by launching an attack after only two days' artillery barrage, instead of the usual seven. The idea was rejected. The commander was Edmund Allenby, a cavalryman by training who was deeply frustrated at the unimaginative tactics he saw in the trenches, and which claimed the life of his only son.

That summer, he was assigned to command the British army in the Middle East, with orders to break the German-Turkish lines and capture Palestine. Determined to do things differently, he quickly agreed a plan for a feint attack at the western end of the line while the bulk of his force advanced in the east. That this was regarded as innovative says a lot about the state of military thinking at the time.

The following year, Allenby went further. Planning a push on to Damascus, he decided to reverse the previous year's approach: he would feint in the west and strike in the east. To assist the enemy in thinking that the attack was coming in the wrong place, he went to elaborate lengths, building a huge camp where the enemy could see it, complete with dummy horses, and marching troops up to it each day, before spiriting them back to their real camps at night, only to have them march up again the next day. When his forces rolled forward, they took 75,000 prisoners at a cost of 5,000 British casualties.

What was surprising, given how successful deception had been for Allenby, was how little effort the British made to learn from this. T. E. Lawrence, who had worked for Allenby, remarked that deceptions 'for the ordinary general were just witty hors d'oeuvres before battle'.

This wasn't simply pig-headedness. There was an assumption that what had worked once wouldn't work again, and that advances in technology would make it harder to deceive future enemies. Both sides, after all, now had fast planes and advanced cameras, allowing them to see far further than the Duke of Wellington could when he remarked a century earlier that 'all the business of war' was 'guessing what was at the other side of the hill'.

Serious military thinkers also offered practical objections to deception. The nineteenth-century Prussian general Carl von Clausewitz, whose theories about warfare remain influential even today, argued that any convincing deceptive move would require so much effort that it would take troops away from fighting that they could more usefully be doing. The only people, he said, who should be thinking about such things were commanders so weak and desperate that they had no other options. This was hardly how a typical British general was trained to think of himself.

At least one person, however, had been paying attention to Allenby's deceptions. One of his staff officers in Palestine was Wavell. He was no ordinary general, and two decades later, and now in command in the Middle East himself, he was determined to apply what he had learned.

In appointing Clarke he was making deceiving the enemy a full-time occupation, rather than an occasional indulgence. Short of men and equipment, with both having to travel by sea from Britain – either on a long route round the whole of Africa or a dangerous one through the Mediterranean – he was looking for anything that would give him the edge.

In effect, Wavell was asking Clarke to put on a show for the enemy. He was the ideal man for the job.

Among the many unusual jobs Clarke had taken on in his career in the army, perhaps the most surprising was 'theatrical impresario'. He'd begun on a modest scale, putting on a play with fellow officers in 1923 in which he took the lead role. But his work escalated to a quite different level when he was asked to organise the Artillery's contribution to the 1925 Royal Tournament, with the instruction that it should be 'the greatest show ever seen in Olympia'. In the ensuing months, Clarke would locate and train oxen, camels, and even elephants, as well as actors to play their African and Indian handlers. By the time of the show, he had 680 men, 300 animals and 37 guns under his command. He'd gone on to write the end-of-term panto for his Staff College class. Then, posted to Aden, he organised the celebrations for King George V's silver jubilee, which culminated in a simulated amphibious assault that he claimed later was so convincing some of his audience fled, believing that the Italians had invaded.

Wavell may not have appreciated it, but the performance he wanted now would be of a particular kind. If deception was an idea the military treated with suspicion, on the stage it was one with a very long pedigree. All theatre relies on the suspension of disbelief – we know the man on the stage isn't really a thousand-year-old Scottish king, and that the dagger before him won't hurt anyone – but there was one group of people who had, for centuries, been leading audiences to look the wrong way and draw the wrong conclusions. They understood the importance of what you display and what you conceal, of misdirection, of lines of sight. The trouble was, no one took them very seriously.

In the 1970s, two American academics, J. Bowyer Bell and Barton Whaley, discovered a mutual fascination with deception, and a frustrating lack of work on the subject. They began to look into it themselves, and eventually concluded that the only people who really understood the field were magicians.

Apart from anything else, they got far more practice. Allenby had spent months working on a single deception. A jobbing stage illusionist performs a couple of dozen every evening. The only people who came close in terms of activity were card sharps and con artists, and their trick rate was still far below that of the average children's entertainer.

As it happened, Clarke had a magician in the family. His uncle Sidney, a barrister by day, was in his spare time an obsessive conjurer, who had been captivated by magic since childhood. He served as chairman of the Magic Circle, the society for magicians, and spent three decades compiling the first exhaustive history of the art.

Sidney, his waistcoat always grey with tobacco ash, was a bachelor uncle in the best traditions of the Edwardian era, doting on his nephews and nieces, putting them up in school holidays, collecting cigarette cards for them, and of course performing tricks. He could be relied upon to greet them with the astonished discovery of half-crowns behind their ears or up their noses. Once, to the delight of Dudley's brother, there was a ten-shilling note in a boiled egg.

He never explained that trick, but there were other secrets he was happy to reveal to the children, as he showed them the ways that people's credulity could be exploited. He'd served as a writer on *Old Moore's Almanack*, the astonishingly long-running book of astrological forecasts, but told them his own successful contributions owed nothing to the movements of the heavens: 'Purely a matter of statistics, my boy. Find out most big fires occur in August and you predict an August conflagration in one of our major cities.'

Dudley, Sidney's godson, inherited his uncle's enthusiasm. His first recorded effort at using illusion to distract the attention of targets – in this case his two younger siblings – was as a twelve-year-old. 'Raining,' he wrote in his diary. 'Gave conjuring show in my bedroom. Sister born.'

Sidney had introduced Dudley to deception and showmanship, and the teenager had got a taste for them on a grander scale as a cadet in Woolwich. Living in London for the first time, he'd fallen in love with the theatre. It wasn't the tragedies of Shakespeare or the comedies of Oscar Wilde that drew him, but the then-popular melodramas, which won audiences by promising thrilling on-stage stunts – simulated car chases and actual horse races, all apparently live before your eyes. He was such a devoted fan of one show that he was invited to watch from the wings as the heroine rode a real motorbike across a rickety plank to escape her pursuers.

By 1940, the music halls that had enthralled Clarke in his youth had been eclipsed by cinema. He'd transferred his affections, or at least widened them to include this new medium. In 1936 he bought a 16mm movie camera, an expensive toy at the time, and he delighted in shooting film. His younger brother Thomas shared that passion and would become one of Britain's great screenwriters, the brains behind the Ealing comedies *Passport to Pimlico* and *The Lavender Hill Mob*. Having spent his teens and twenties sitting in theatres, Dudley would spend his forties in cinemas.

Movies, like theatre and illusion, deceive. In Hollywood, film-makers had quickly learned that clever camera placement could make it look as though someone was dangling from a building, keeping the mattress beneath them out of shot. Meanwhile their Russian counterparts, their thoughts on higher things than mere entertainment, had formed a theory about what made cinema distinctive from other art forms: the ability to cut between different images to tell a story. We see a woman smile, but we don't know what's making her happy until we get the next shot. Is it a child running through the door or a bank clerk filling a bag at gunpoint? The juxtaposition of images is what allows cinema to tell stories.

Generals and their intelligence officers don't simply try to locate enemy armies on a map. They try to understand why those troops are there and where they're going next. In effect, they tell themselves a story about what their opponent is doing. Wavell's hope was that he could persuade the Italians to make the wrong deductions.

There was a great deal that Clarke and Wavell didn't understand about deception at the end of 1940, but one thing they grasped right from the beginning was that they weren't trying to simply persuade the enemy to believe a series of false facts. They were trying to get him to assemble those facts into a false story.

The Multiplying Flags

January–April 1941

The Magician takes three small pieces of coloured tissue paper, squeezes them in their hands, transforming them into hundreds of tiny red, white and blue flags.

Chapter 5

The first story that Wavell wanted Clarke to tell the Italians was about East Africa. While one part of his army pressed westward, attempting to cut off the retreating Italians and capture the ports along Libya's north coast, the general's mind was turning to the next place he planned to fight. Italy's capture of British Somaliland meant it controlled the entire Horn of Africa, posing a threat to ships from the Far East whether they were travelling through the Red Sea to the Suez Canal, or following the coast towards South Africa and around the Cape of Good Hope.

Wavell's plan was to drive the Italians out of East Africa altogether, striking from Kenya to the southwest, and Sudan to the northwest. It would therefore be helpful if the Italians were expecting the attack to come from the northeast, beginning with the recapturing of British Somaliland, by an amphibious assault launched across the Gulf of Aden. When he met Clarke, the general had already sketched out a plan, codenamed 'Camilla', for how he hoped to persuade them that this was exactly his idea.

'The following is a picture of my plans and intentions that I should like to put across to the other side,' he began, before setting out across two pages what he wanted his enemy to believe. The plan opened with a personal point that Wavell believed 'might appeal to the Italian', that this campaign for him was a matter of personal honour. 'The loss of British Somaliland has always rankled bitterly both with my government and myself,' he wrote, portraying himself as a vainer man than he was, working for a capricious leader. 'I got a rocket from the government and nearly lost my job at the time. I have orders to recapture it as soon as resources are available, and am most anxious to remove this blot on my reputation.'

In the false story Wavell was writing, he planned to send a small force into British Somaliland, relying entirely on surprise. The build-up of troops in Kenya and Sudan was, in this tale, a cover for the real attack: 'As part of this plan of deception I am sending two brigades of Indians to the Sudan, hoping that their presence will become known to the enemy and will make them think an offensive in the Sudan is intended.'

Having drawn the picture he wished the Italians to see, he turned to the question he wanted Clarke to work on. 'Now, what means can we take to get this picture across?' he asked. 'The advantage of it seems to me to be that the greater part of it is true, the enemy will see for himself that the greater part of it is actually being done, what we want is for him to place the wrong interpretation on what he sees.'

To help the Italians reach the conclusions he wanted, Wavell planned to rely heavily on his officers' inability to keep a secret. 'We could be a little bit indiscreet in discussing it, and it will be odd if some sort of chat does not run round the bars, etc., in Aden,' he wrote. 'We might issue, again most confidentially, maps of Somaliland to the battalions of the 11th Indian Brigade.'

Would it, he wondered, be possible to put the story over directly? 'We have probably bust the channel we used before,' he wrote, in what seems to be a reference to the Japanese source used ahead of 'Compass'. 'But it should not be impossible to find others and there are many ingenious methods of carelessness with important documents. There are also the usual matters of movement of shipping, wireless traffic, preparation of camps, enquiries about supplies, etc. etc.'

Working on Camilla with Wavell at that point were Eric Shearer, known as 'John', his director of military intelligence, and Raymund J. Maunsell, known as 'RJ', who ran a secretive body called Security Intelligence Middle East. SIME was the combined outpost of both MI5 – Britain's domestic security agency – and MI6 – its foreign intelligence body – in Cairo. Now in his late thirties, Maunsell had originally been commissioned in the Royal Tank Corps, but since 1932 he'd been working in 'security' – what would later be called counter-intelligence – in the Middle East. In practice, that meant in Egypt, the centre of British concerns and the place where, in Maunsell's view, any problem was likely to begin.

Maunsell was a cheery, gregarious man, fond, in his own words, of 'liquorous family bridge and poker parties', who seemed to know everyone and aimed to know everything. His job was made easier by the large number of British ex-pats in the senior ranks of the Egyptian police, who, whatever the attitude of the Egyptian government, were fundamentally on the side of the empire. 'Every schoolboy knows that you build your spy ring slowly and carefully in time of peace,' he said, and he took the same approach to counter-espionage. Having expected war since at least the Munich crisis of 1938, he was well prepared. His team had 'deeply penetrated' the Spanish embassy. He had an agent on the switchboard of the Cairo branch of Dresdner, the German bank, who linked SIME in to telephone calls they wanted to monitor. He had already identified the Germans and Italians he would want to intern.

The Cairo police had a Special Section to deal with 'subversives'. Maunsell ensured that its officers received 'subsidies' to cover 'their official expenditure on the British government's behalf'. This, he observed, 'helped considerably to oil the wheels'. The police in turn paid every doorkeeper in the city 'a small monthly sum' to report comings and goings.

Was any of this legal? In Britain, the security services operated, at least in theory, under the supervision of the government. But Cairo had long been a city where visiting Europeans followed a looser code. That went for sex, and apparently it also went for security work. Maunsell did whatever he deemed necessary, seeming to feel accountable only to himself. Wavell, nominally his commander, was happy to let him get on with it. 'A secure Egypt behind my back is worth two divisions to me,' he told Maunsell. London tried to take an interest in SIME's work, but London was a long way away.

Maunsell seemed to have sources everywhere, but then, he was a useful man to know: someone who could pay a bribe, do a favour or fix a problem. Equally, with the weight of the military and the police behind him, he was in a position to make life difficult for anyone who crossed him. It was hardly surprising that, when a British general dropped a decoded telegram containing details of an important forthcoming operation on the balcony at Shepheard's, the manager sought out Maunsell and handed the message to him.

It helped, too, that he took a relaxed view of human frailty and was unlikely to pass judgement on some of Cairo's shadier businesses. Indeed, his approach when warned about possible security threats was to try to take the heat out of the situation. 'The apparently suspicious behaviour of individuals may often be due to the secret pursuit of homo- or heterosexual relationships,' he said.

A lot of people were a long way from home, and some of them faced imminent death. 'Lonely men and women misconducted themselves all over the place,' he said. That was only his business if it caused a wider problem, as when a rear admiral and his son, also a naval officer, discovered to their mutual fury that they shared a mistress.

Though he took his work seriously, his approach revealed his strong sense of humour. In 1939, a Japanese military attaché – a job that was often an official cover for a spy – had driven a car through Syria and Palestine with a movie camera fixed to the dashboard, filming details of the roads and strategic locations. It was an excellent reconnaissance effort, and Maunsell took great delight in thwarting it as the diplomat passed through Egypt. The camera was briefly impounded and 'with the professional help of the Port Said Police, we were able to substitute for the road report a rather horrible, locally made "blue" film.' All in all, he was a man after Clarke's own heart. They hit it off from the start.

Installed in his bathroom-office, Clarke set to work at once. If he was daunted by the task he had been set, he showed little sign of it. On his first day in the job, he came up with modifications to Operation Camilla, proposing a plan to use wireless traffic to make it look as though the British base at Aden was becoming the focus of military activity.

After the war Clarke would write a novel whose hero was clearly based on his idea of himself. The character 'had the air of a man for whom things run easily,' he wrote, explaining that this was misleading. 'Few ever guessed at the capacity for taking infinite pains which lay well-hidden behind an easy-going exterior.'

Wavell had probably perceived this quality of Clarke's. It would have been one of the reasons he liked having him on his staff. And that willingness to take 'infinite pains' was evident from the beginning of this deception. Clarke drew up a plan in a table with three columns: first a series of dates over the next two months; then what was actually planned for that date; and finally the 'effects' – a bit of stage magic jargon for what he wanted his audience, Italian intelligence, to see and hear.

The first stage was a series of misleading rumours Clarke wanted spread in Egypt, Sudan and Kenya. Troops in Aden and Kenya were given briefings on amphibious landings. Post intended for the 4th Indian Division, a unit already on its way to Sudan, was diverted to Aden. The RAF in Aden were ordered to carry out reconnaissance flights on Somaliland and to bomb coastal defences. Back in Britain, government sources suggested to newspapers that Wavell 'ought now to clear his reputation by recapturing British Somaliland'.

In Egypt there was no way of concealing the fact that the 11th Infantry Brigade was being loaded onto ships that were heading south down the canal, but Clarke ensured that the ships carried enough food to take their passengers all the way to Aden, rather than their actual destination, Port Sudan, half the distance. His hope was that this information would find its way from the docks to the enemy. Despite Wavell's concern that the Japanese consul in Port Said would no longer be deemed reliable after the Compass deception, Clarke decided it was worth making sure he was informed that the ships were bound for Aden.

Maunsell was able to help with this. He explained that the diplomat in question, 'the not inappropriately named Mr Ohno', was his favourite spy. Enthusiastic but hapless, Michizo Ohno had before the war attempted to recruit two inspectors in the Egyptian police to his cause. He'd believed that this would work because they had Irish names, and would therefore be likely to hate the British. Whatever their ancestral views of the empire, the policemen had a very good idea of who was best-placed to look after their interests, and reported the approach to Maunsell, who had told them to accept the offer, so that he could control the information being passed to the Japanese. Ohno's people on the canal were in fact Maunsell's people.

Clarke produced a careful mix of fact and fiction to be fed to the Japanese, including confirmable details about sailing times and specific units along with hard-to-disprove nuggets that pointed towards an invasion of Somaliland.

Finally, Clarke worked out a schedule under which different military outposts were to send signals to each other, with the intensity of messages to and from Aden increasing through January. The enciphered messages were garbage, but that didn't matter. As Clarke knew, intelligence agencies practise 'traffic analysis', watching how the volume and length of messages changes, in the hope of detecting patterns. He hoped the Italians would deduce that the increase in volume of messages between Aden and Cairo was a sign of a forth-coming operation out of Aden.

There were some specific false messages, too. In early January 1941, as the 11th Infantry approached Port Sudan, Aden wired Cairo warning that they weren't ready to accommodate large numbers of extra troops, and suggesting the incoming forces might have to wait at Port Sudan. That gave an excuse for why the troop carriers weren't carrying on down the Red Sea.

Although Clarke was a one-man band, he could draw on other people to help. It was typical that he found the most glamorous assistants he could. Prince Aly Khan, the playboy son of the Aga Khan, had found his way into military intelligence via the French Foreign Legion. He was dispatched to Alexandria as the troops were embarking with a bag of messages for Aden, which he handed to one of the ships' officers.

Others were deployed without their knowledge, including, in a sign of Clarke's ruthlessness, one of his friends.

Tony Simonds was finally getting some excitement. He was off to Ethiopia, on a secret mission to help raise a rebellion against the Italian occupiers. Before his friend left, Clarke took him aside and, in strict confidence, told him that Wavell was planning to attack British Somaliland from Aden. To Clarke's mind, Simonds was going behind enemy lines, where he might accidentally leak information, or be captured and interrogated. Either way, it couldn't hurt to load him up with the false story.

Later, Clarke would describe Camilla as his 'first fumbling steps' in the world of military deception, but they were, if anything, re-markably assured. Not everything worked. On the fake radio signals in particular, he ran into both practical objections and the inability of wireless operators to send more messages.

There was, however, a clear impact on the Italians defending British Somaliland: they packed up and left. Having deduced that an overwhelming attack was imminent, they decided there was no point in trying to hold their positions, and pulled back to Ethiopia.

This was, of course, the precise opposite of Wavell's intention: he'd hoped the Italians would shift troops into British Somaliland, not out of it. He still achieved his military aim, and between February and May 1941, his troops overwhelmed the Italians in Ethiopia and Eritrea. As an exercise in deception, though, Camilla had been at once a total success and a complete failure: he'd fooled the enemy, but they'd gone and done the wrong thing. There was a lesson here, but it would take Clarke a while to understand what it was.

Chapter 6

A couple of weeks after he began working in Cairo, Clarke was passed an extract from the 1940 diary of a captured Italian officer:

> 3 July. Late in the night, the group is informed that enemy parachutists landed near our area.

It must have made Clarke smile. He knew better than most people how far the British had been from dropping parachutists behind enemy lines the previous July. The idea of arriving from the sky had, naturally, occurred to the Commandos that summer, but they had been hampered by a lack of equipment, of trained men, and of suitable planes to drop from. Clarke had gone on a day's parachute training himself, before being told he was too old to jump. Six months later, the first parachute unit had only just been formed.

But parachutists had been an effective psychological weapon for the Nazis: their existence meant a defending force was never sure that its ground was secure. Soldiers had to spend their time chasing rumours and false sightings. Now it was time to play that fear back against the enemy. If the Italians believed there were already parachutists ready to strike in the Middle East, it was a fear Clarke could play on. Wavell was keen to exaggerate the strength of his forces, and the prospect of Commandos dropping behind their lines might encourage the Italians to divert men to protect supplies and airfields far from the action.

Plan Abeam, the first deception operation that Clarke conceived and ran himself, could be dismissed as little more than a practical joke, or low-level mischief-making. It had no goal beyond persuading the Italians that Wavell had a brigade of airborne troops at his disposal. But Clarke approached it with complete thoroughness.

By the middle of January 1941 he had drawn up a five-page 'scenario', detailing every aspect of his imaginary brigade's existence. It had a total strength of around 2,000 men, made up of one parachute battalion and two glider battalions. They had arrived at Suez at the end of December, on board two troop ships, and then travelled by train to a desert camp in Transjordan – modern-day Jordan – close enough to threaten North Africa, but far enough away to be hard to check.

Clarke described the brigade's formation in June 1940, its training near Manchester and then on Salisbury Plain. The parachutists, in his description, carried automatic carbines – lightweight fast-firing rifles suitable for assaults – and were trained in demolition work. The glider troops resembled an ordinary light infantry battalion, but every third man had a Thompson submachine gun. That was, as Clarke was painfully aware, rather more Tommy guns than were currently in England, but the fantasy unit he was building might as well have fantasy kit. He went further: back in London, an inventor had tried to sell the Commandos his design for a new kind of helicopter, and Clarke briefly planned for his imaginary brigade to have 20, carrying senior officers and reconnaissance troops. He was forced to reject this as implausible – the technology wasn't available – but it's an example of his vision as a soldier that he foresaw how troops would be arriving in battle two decades later.

The document he produced was one that only a veteran officer, who understood the army's structures and ways of working, could have written. And if it was supposed to describe a nightmare for the Italians, it sounded an awful lot like the kind of unit he'd dreamed the Commandos would become.

Clarke lifted his fake brigade's story above the ordinary with details such as the parachutists' dislike of dropping from Whitley aircraft, which used a hole in the floor, and their relief at discovering the aircraft in the Middle East and North Africa would all allow them to jump from doors. The glider battalions, he wrote, had only had a month's intense training, and were reluctant to admit that they could have used more preparation.

Having worked out his story, Clarke set about trying to tell it to the enemy. He arranged for additional military patrols in the places where the unit was supposed to be training. Tony Simonds had got to know a young political officer at the Jewish Agency, which represented the interests of Jews in Palestine and beyond. Clarke asked him to see to the spreading of rumours in Syria, Palestine and Iraq of a glider crash that had killed twenty soldiers, and of the Bedouin being forbidden from entering part of the desert.

Then Clarke indulged in a little undercover work of his own. Notified that a known Japanese spy was travelling to Palestine a couple of days later, he booked himself onto the same sleeper train, wearing a red 'Airborne Division' armband, and with a parachutist's wings sewn onto his uniform. He discarded an envelope addressed to 'Colonel Clarke' at 'HQ Airborne Division' in Salisbury. On arrival in Palestine, he visited the local commander,* who promised Clarke he would ask the Arab Legion to close the part of the desert where the parachutists were supposed to be training.

With Operation Camilla still ongoing, Clarke decided his airborne troops might as well play a part. He had a rubber stamp made up for the unit's headquarters, and used it on a receipt for maps of British Somaliland and Harar, just over the border in Ethiopia. While in Palestine, he left the receipt in a hotel, in the hope that it would be picked up and passed to enemy intelligence. Maunsell planted another receipt in Cairo.

The press was an obvious way of getting information to the enemy. Clarke released pictures that purported to show an Ethiopian parachutist training alongside British troops. The suggested caption, used in the forces paper, was: 'Ready to descend on Italy!' The Ethiopian was, in reality, a Cairo laundryman, but the choice of nationality was an interesting one, suggesting that the British were training up vengeful soldiers from the country the Italians had brutally occupied. The notion of Africans being sent on raids against Italy would be particularly provocative to fascists.

But the sly part of this deception was an easily overlooked detail in the picture. Behind the subject, three airmen could be seen chatting to a fourth man, his back to the camera. He had one stand-out feature: a distinctive spiked helmet, as worn by the Arab Legion which policed the Transjordan desert where the troops were supposed to

---

* Lieutenant General Philip Neame, who had the distinction, held to this day, of being the only person to have won both a Victoria Cross (for throwing bombs, Neuve Chapelle, 1914) and an Olympic gold medal (for shooting rifles, Paris, 1924).

be training. It was intended to be the kind of clue that a military censor might miss, but that a sharp-eyed enemy intelligence officer would congratulate himself on spotting.

The airborne unit needed a name, and Clarke took it from a new outfit in England. The 11th Special Air Service Battalion had been formed out of troops that had parachute and glider training. Later in 1941 it would be renamed the 1st Parachute Battalion, becoming the basis of the modern Parachute Regiment. Over in Cairo, Clarke decided his paratroopers would be the 1st Special Air Service Battalion. It was a more significant decision than he appreciated at the time.

Helpfully to Clarke, the 11th Special Air Service Battalion was about to go into action – and, indeed, to descend on Italy. In early February, Operation Colossus saw them dropped into the south of the country to attack an aqueduct. Like other early Commando raids, the mission itself had what might politely be called mixed results: the aqueduct was hit but the paratroopers were captured. But it had effects on morale on both sides: the British now had forces who could, in theory, strike anywhere.

The final touch came in April, when Clarke borrowed two trustworthy soldiers from the Staffordshire Yeomanry, who were based in Palestine. Having been requested for 'special escort duty', Lance Corporal Smith and Trooper Michael Gurmin were met at Cairo station and taken to a secure barracks, where they were given their real mission. They were to remove their existing unit badges from their uniforms, and sew on new ones, including parachutists' wings. 'From tomorrow onwards you are to take the part of Lance Bombardier Smith and Gunner Gurmin,' they were told, 'of the First Special Air Service Battalion (Parachutists) and you must keep this up throughout your stay in Cairo.'

Smith and Gurmin were issued with a briefing on the roles they were to play: how they had come to join the Special Air Service, and their training and travels since then. They were supposed to be in Egypt accompanying their commanding officer and awaiting further orders. At the end of their briefing came a special note: 'The following is, of course, information that you would normally keep very secret. It may, however, be useful for you to note it so that you can let a word or two out if you get the opportunity.' The details they were supposed to leak included the strength of their supposed unit and its armaments.

With that, the pair were sent out to enjoy themselves for four days, first in Cairo and then in Port Said, in the hope that they would be spotted by an Axis informant known to travel on the train – probably another Japanese agent. They had quite a time of it, visiting the pyramids, a football match, a cabaret, and going dancing. They 'attracted an enormous amount of attention', chiefly from fellow Allied soldiers but also from civilians and Egyptian officers. Under orders to be judiciously indiscreet, Smith and Gurmin chatted freely. 'We answered a lot of questions,' they reported back, 'particularly going to Port Said, where an infantry company sergeant major and staff sergeant were very interested, so we told them a fair amount.'

Plan Abeam was an experiment, really. It had no great aim. But it showed Clarke's approach. When Dominic West portrayed Clarke on TV, he described putting all the Abeam material together into a folder and leaving it in his briefcase where a Spanish attaché could find it. That was exactly the sort of blunt approach the real Clarke rejected.

Having worked out the story he wanted to tell in detail, he fed it piecemeal to the enemy by multiple routes. There were scraps of paper to collect, uniform badges to spot, an unusual helmet to pick out in a photograph. He left clues for enemy intelligence agencies to find and let them draw their own conclusion. By making them work for the story, he hoped to make them sell it to themselves. Anyone smart enough to notice a distinctive helmet in the background of a photograph would surely be so pleased with themselves that they'd be keen to believe the tale that it supported.

The problem with the experiment was finding out the results. Had any of these clues, so carefully distributed, made their way back to Italian intelligence? Had they been accepted, and if so, had they been put together as Clarke intended? He had no way of knowing. There were encouraging signs: in June Clarke was delighted to receive a report of gossip going round Cairo that any parachutists spotted dropping near the city would be British. (In fact, they would be British dummies: that week the RAF had dropped several to the south of the city to simulate SAS soldiers in training.) The story that a parachute unit was present in Egypt was now definitely in the public domain.

But it would be months before he was handed captured documents showing the enemy listing a parachute battalion among the British forces in the Middle East.

Abeam's most significant legacy came that July. At the start of the year, 2,000 Commandos had sailed for the Middle East, with ideas that they might be useful to Wavell. But here too, the military hadn't really known what to do with this large raiding party, and the unit had broken up. Among its frustrated members was a lieutenant in the Scots Guards, David Stirling. He, like Clarke, believed that the Commando idea was a good one that had been badly implemented. The key, he felt, was to keep things small and nimble.

Lying in hospital after a trial parachute jump that had gone wrong, Stirling had time to consider how things might be done differently. One of his visitors was Clarke, who had got to know Stirling well since he arrived in Cairo. Clarke liked to hold court in Shepheard's, where he now had a permanent room. Many officers congregated in the Long Bar, where women were banned. Amazingly, they took this to mean that it was a safe place to discuss secrets. The joke was that you could learn whatever you needed to about the British forces in the Middle East simply by standing there for an evening. Clarke liked to position himself somewhere where he had a wall at his back and a view of the door, a habit from his days on a Palestinian death list.

Tall, posh – he came from one of Scotland's great families – and charming, Stirling fitted well into Clarke's gang of chaps who had creative thoughts about warfare. Few, if any of them, knew exactly what it was that Clarke did, only that it was something secret. 'Nobody could poke into what he was doing, because he'd retort by telling funny stories about something quite different,' recalled one. 'He was so pleasant to meet that he could get away with that.' For all his congeniality, there was a separateness about Clarke, a way in which he was closed off from those around him. Much later, one of his friends would describe him as someone who could be alone in a crowd.

As Stirling recovered in hospital, Clarke talked to him about the Commandos. He was still sure there was merit in the original idea. The important thing, in his view, was fostering independent-mindedness in soldiers. Much of military life seemed to aim at achieving just the opposite. 'Nearly every conception of guerrilla

warfare was opposed to all the British soldier had ever been taught.'
Ordinary soldiers, Clarke explained, were stuck with their officers,
whereas a guerrilla chose the band he would join. The only discipline that should be necessary for an elite soldier was the threat of
being returned to their regular unit.

The mistake Clarke had made with the Commandos was trying
to build a large force under the eyes of the War Office in London: so
many senior people had got involved that it became impossible to
do anything. Out here in Cairo, far from the eyes of officials, it was
possible to experiment.

Stirling proposed putting together a much smaller outfit – just fifty
soldiers initially. Clarke, one of the few people he confided in, encouraged him. This unit would be much closer to the original vision
of the Commandos. It would certainly be independent-minded.
Without much support from the hierarchy in Grey Pillars, Stirling's
men would have to 'borrow' supplies from other units.

Clarke was happy to put a word in for his friend, and he had the
ear of the commander-in-chief. He also had a contribution of his
own. It would be helpful, he said, if Stirling's new unit was called the
Special Air Service, as this would put flesh on the bones of Abeam,
rewarding any Axis intelligence officers who had followed the trail of
clues. As an additional touch, he suggested calling the first recruits
'L Detachment', implying the existence of detachments A to K.

The Special Air Service that was made flesh by Stirling bore
almost no resemblance to the unit that Clarke had sketched out in
Abeam. It was far smaller, and after its first attempt to drop behind
the lines by parachute ended in disaster, it stayed out of the air. But it
was completely in the spirit of what he'd imagined the Commandos
would be: little teams of men with 'dash' who thought for themselves, attacked out of nowhere and then disappeared.

In the years since its formation, the SAS, as it is now universally
known, has shown a keen understanding of the advantage of creating a legend about itself. To this day it has a policy of neither
confirming nor denying stories about its actions, allowing it to be,
in people's minds, everywhere and nowhere, a terrifying force that
might strike at any moment. So it is fitting that it took its name from
a fictitious unit created to scare the enemy.

It was also appropriate that among Stirling's early recruits was
one of Clarke's two fake SAS men, Michael Gurmin.

The SAS wasn't the only descendant of the Commandos. In the middle of January 1941, as Clarke was putting together Abeam and implementing Camilla, he was invited to meet William Donovan, President Franklin D. Roosevelt's unofficial envoy to the British, who was on a fact-finding tour of the Mediterranean.

Clarke was the ideal person to charm and impress him: a natural storyteller, he was in his element sipping cocktails on the terrace of the Continental Hotel, revealing some secrets, keeping others. Equally Donovan, a well-connected former soldier whose exploits in the First World War had won him the nickname 'Wild Bill' and been the subject of a James Cagney movie the previous year, was exactly the sort of American that the status-obsessed Clarke was eager to meet. Among the subjects they covered was guerrilla warfare.

Donovan had liked the sound of the Commandos, and believed the US would soon need a similar force. Five days later the men met again to discuss the subject in more detail, and Clarke promised to draft a paper on his experiences. Apologising for knowing nothing about the US Army except for what he'd learned from his hours in the cinema, Clarke set out the approach he'd taken, and offered some proposals for a US force. He emphasised the importance of choosing a name with 'an adventurous sound, with historic associations, and above all an essence of the offensive spirit about it. "Rangers" might be a possibility.'

The US Army Rangers were formed in 1942, becoming America's first modern elite unit. They were consciously modelled on the Commandos, and early recruits trained and fought alongside them. Most American historians do not accept that the unit's name came from Clarke, but he determinedly claimed the credit, saying he'd named two of Britain's elite forces, as well as one of America's.

It was a good boast to make, but Clarke had contributed more than names. His vision of turning regular soldiers into guerrillas who could fight independently and strike far behind the enemy lines lives on in today's special forces units. It's no coincidence that the green beret adopted by Britain's Commandos during the war became the symbol of elite troops around the world. It's not hard, either, to see shades of the Commandos in the guerrilla activities of the US Office of Strategic Services, which Donovan would found months later, and which would grow into the Central Intelligence Agency.

The creation of the Commandos, the SAS and the Rangers was the work of many hands, but those who had been at the heart of things understood Clarke's contribution. 'Very much a pro,' Stirling said, citing Clarke's important influence on his thinking. 'He championed the independent company concept.' The general who led the Commandos for the final years of the war was even clearer in a 1945 letter to Clarke: 'If it had not been for your activities, the Green Beret would never have seen the light of day.'

Chapter 7

While Clarke was finding his feet as a deceiver in Cairo, the most important work in the deception field was being done 500 miles to the city's west, as Wavell's forces continued to pursue the Italians across the Libyan desert. Britain's 10th Royal Tank Regiment had been formed following the army's initial breakthrough in December. It ought to have been of limited fighting value as its tanks were made of wood and canvas. When they wanted to move, they were folded up and packed onto lorries. But sometimes, it turned out, wood and canvas was enough. The 10th joined the troops preparing to attack the town of Mechili, only for the Italians to flee during the night, convinced of the overwhelming strength of the British armour. In reality, the Italians had 300 fighting tanks to Britain's 50.

The advancing British forces were coming to terms with one of the realities that would dominate the next two years: the way the desert wore down machines. Sand and grit got everywhere, sitting inside mechanisms and grinding away the moving parts of engines and guns. The poor roads and worse off-road conditions wore away at suspensions, tyres and tracks. As armies advanced, they stretched their supply lines, up which everything from water and fuel to spare parts and ammunition had to be carried: the one certainty of the desert was that it would yield nothing to help them. The very trucks that carried the supplies suffered the same attritional damage as the advancing tanks.

Even fake tanks weren't immune, it turned out. The wood warped in the heat. The parts were damaged by repeated packing and un-packing. In mid-February, the 10th, its tanks literally falling apart, was disbanded.

But back in Cairo, Clarke had come up with a way to create extra tanks that would never wear out. New machines from Britain were still months away, but perhaps the enemy could be convinced they had already arrived.

When the magician fans out the cards in their hand and flashes them briefly at the audience, the implication is that it's a full deck, but who has time to count them? Who even tries? They say it's a deck of cards, and they're definitely holding cards.

The 3rd Indian Motor Brigade had just arrived in Egypt. It didn't have tanks, or anti-tank guns. In fact it was mainly armed with rifles. But it had trucks, and the word 'motor' in its name. Clarke spread rumours in Cairo that it was part of the 10th Armoured Division. That implied the existence of two other brigades, and a lot of tanks. No one saw the tanks, but the 3rd Indian's trucks might function as proof of their presence.

Clarke would now learn that Egypt was as hard on men as it was on equipment. In early February, he fell sick with jaundice, a common disease among troops in the Middle East, the result of poor sanitation. He was hospitalised for three weeks, a frustration for a man with a mind as active and fertile as Clarke's. Maunsell visited him almost every day to discuss rumours that they could propagate to the enemy, but compared to the frenetic level of activity Clarke had sustained in his first two months in the job, there was little output. Even after his discharge, he was still weak, and he was sent to Cyprus to recuperate.

Having satisfied himself that there was work to be done in deception, Clarke was now arguing that he needed more staff. The fact that everything had ceased while he was sick had shown the danger of leaving it all to one man.

His masters agreed, and Clarke was allowed to begin building a team. The unit would need a name. This would necessarily have to be misleading – he couldn't very well call it the Deception Section – and characteristically, he decided he might as well put some more flesh on the bones of his imaginary SAS unit. Its main headquarters were supposed to be in Transjordan, so he would suggest that his unit was the local branch, the 'Advance Headquarters, "A" Force' – hoping curious minds would guess that A stood for 'Airborne'. It didn't hurt that 'A Force' had a pleasingly glamorous sound to it.

Turning to staff, he had heard there was a secretary in Grey Pillars who had won a gold medal for her skills. This made her, by Clarke's reckoning, the best typist in England. It was typical of him both that he decided he had to have her working for him, and that he managed to get her. It was typical, too, that the rest of his recruits were particular types of chap. You didn't need to have gone to Eton and Oxford to join A Force, but it did seem to help.

Clarke, of course, had attended neither, and as with his recruitment of David Niven back in London, there were signs here of insecurity on his part. The lifestyle he aspired to – flat in Mayfair, cocktails at the Ritz, dinner at the Savoy – was that of an aristocratic officer in one of the army's more socially exclusive regiments, a cavalryman, say. He could afford it because of his father's money, but that wealth had been self-made, rather than inherited with a title and an estate. And though Clarke palled around Cairo with the officers of the Eleventh Hussars – now riding armoured cars, rather than horses – he was himself an artilleryman, even if he still wore his Flying Corps wings. In a subtle way that perhaps only an Englishman of his generation could understand, this consummate insider was also an outsider.

Finally, Clarke wanted a new office. He needed to talk to intelligence sources, and inviting someone into Grey Pillars created the risk that they would take away more information than they had brought in. He was allowed to lease two flats on Sharia Kasr-El-Nil, convenient for two of the city's most fashionable spots, Groppi's coffee shop and the Mohammed Ali social club. The block had been a high-class brothel, and Clarke was happy for the business to continue on the upper floors. The arrangement worked well. Neither set of tenants wanted to advertise what they were up to, and both saw that guests who wanted to avoid questions now had a plausible alibi for visiting. A Force did occasionally, to their general delight, have to deal with confused soldiers who had arrived in search of a good time. There is no record of how the brothel dealt with lost visitors wanting to discuss military deception.

There remained the question of how to explain all this to the curious. It was easy to say that members of A Force should simply not discuss their work, but like a good illusionist, Clarke understood the importance of diversion.

When Wavell had appointed Clarke to his staff, he had given him responsibility for various 'undefined secret activities', including being the local representative of MI9. This covert organisation had been set up at the start of the war, to assist British soldiers behind enemy lines in evading capture and helping those who had been caught to escape.

Although it meant more work, to Clarke's devious mind it had an advantage: if people wanted to know what he was up to, his MI9 work could be offered as a 'useful cloak' to conceal his main work. He was deceiving about his deception, using a secret to cover a bigger secret. It was Clarke all over.

It wasn't simply a cover. There isn't room here to tell the story of the Middle East branch of MI9 under Clarke's command. Some numbers will have to do the job instead. Between 1941 and 1945 it helped in the rescue of 2,807 Allied personnel from behind enemy lines, as well as roughly 9,000 Greeks and 94 Poles. And close to a million service personnel were given escape and evasion training. As with the Commandos, if Clarke had done nothing but oversee MI9, he could have been considered to have had a very good war.

As the war went on, Clarke developed some informal rules: he recruited no male officers below the rank of major, unless they'd proved themselves by being wounded or winning a medal, and he wouldn't let female officers direct clandestine operations – these were often on the MI9 side – fearing they would fall in love with the men they were sending into the field.

Back in 1941, just as Clarke was getting his new unit established in its new headquarters, everything changed.

Wavell had thought that the spring of that year might see further British advances, but Hitler had other ideas. Frustrated by the failure of his Italian allies, the Fuhrer ordered his generals to capture Yugoslavia and then move into Greece. Meanwhile, fearful of a total collapse in North Africa, he had dispatched one of his favourite generals with orders to shore up the Italian defences and stop them being pushed any further back. But the man he'd sent was never going to settle for that. By March, Erwin Rommel was ready to attack.

Chapter 8

On 24 February 1941, the new edition of *Life* magazine hit newsstands across America. Its striking cover image was of a group of soldiers standing at ease in the desert, dust on their boots, shirts open and sleeves rolled up, rifles lightly held, faces turned towards the sun. 'ANZAC CONQUERORS' was the caption. It was based on the mistaken assumption that the New Zealanders their photographer had persuaded to pose in Egypt had been fighting alongside Australian forces in Libya. In fact these young men had yet to see combat, though they would get plenty of it soon enough.

The bigger mistaken assumption was that the war in the desert was won. That day Winston Churchill signalled Wavell his approval for a plan to send the New Zealanders in the picture, along with 57,000 other troops, to reinforce Britain's Greek allies, who had held off an Italian invasion but now faced a German one.

Also that day, a British patrol near Benghazi encountered something new to North Africa: a German tank unit. The patrol stood no chance: two scout cars, a truck and a car were destroyed, and the Germans took three prisoners. For the new German commander in Tripoli, it was an encouraging portent. 'No casualties on our side,' Rommel noted.

Wavell was aware that the Germans had arrived in Africa, but he had gone along with Churchill's request to pull troops out of Libya and send them to Greece. Having seen the way the Italians fought, he was confident their troops could be discounted, and he didn't feel the Germans were yet strong enough to manage a serious counter-attack on their own. It was a point on which the German high command agreed. In the middle of March, Rommel flew to Hitler's headquarters, where he was told to sit tight until the end of May, when he would receive reinforcements, and could try to advance a little way, perhaps as far as Benghazi.

But Rommel wasn't a man to sit around. He was a career soldier who knew how to get the best out of his troops. In the previous war, he had made his name as a daring infantry commander who was willing to attack much stronger forces, using innovative tactics so that his soldiers appeared where they were least expected and pulled off astonishing victories. Given command of a panzer division ahead of the German advance into France, he had pushed forward again and again, sometimes turning off his radio so that he couldn't hear orders telling him to stop and consolidate. To Rommel, attacking was everything: you saw a weakness in the enemy's line, and you threw your full strength at that point. Success came from spotting your opportunity and being bold enough to exploit it.

At the end of March, breaking his orders, and without waiting for reinforcements, he did just that. The Allied defenders were even weaker than he could have realised. It wasn't just that troops had been pulled away to go to Greece. Those who were left had little or no battle experience. They were short of anti-tank guns. Tanks worn out by the drive west had been sent back to Cairo for repair and refitting. Those that remained often needed repair just as badly. The commander in the field who had swept the Italians from Cyrenaica had fallen sick, and his replacement had no experience of desert warfare. More fundamentally, the reason that the British had stopped where they had was that they had reached the limit of their supply lines.

The Germans meanwhile looked stronger than they were. Rommel had ordered his own fleet of dummy tanks built out of wood and canvas and fitted on top of cars – Wavell was no longer the only innovative general in North Africa. But even without this fake show, they were strong enough.

Wavell had known before the attack how vulnerable his forces were, and had given permission for them to fall back, but what followed looked a lot more like headlong flight than a fighting retreat. Rommel was overreaching in his assault, with his tanks forced to stop because they had run out of fuel. Had the Allies had a commander of his mettle, they might have seen this weakness and pushed the Axis forces back. Instead, they ran.

A week after Rommel launched his attack, Clarke was summoned back from his sick leave in Cyprus to see Wavell. Something was needed to stop, or at least slow down, the German advance. What could this new A Force do to give Rommel pause?

Wavell, who had yet to get the measure of his new opposite number, knew what the German ought to be worrying about: his supply lines. Nobody was more familiar than Wavell with the difficulty of supporting an army as it advanced across Cyrenaica. Clarke was ordered to persuade Rommel that an attack on his rear was imminent.

By this time Clarke had been in the deception business for all of three months. So far he'd run operations that had been conducted on his own terms and targeted at the Italian forces who, it was clear, were no match for the British. Now he was being asked to put together a plan on the fly, to deal with a far more dangerous enemy. In a year and a half of fighting, the German army had defeated the British army every time they'd met, and the current encounter was proving no different.

Such was the urgency of the situation that Clarke didn't even bother with a codename for the operation he was sketching out. It became known as simply 'Plan Anti-Rommel' – 'A-R' for short. He tried to put himself in the mind of the German general. 'Enemy probably knows we have a sea-borne expedition ready to launch against his coast somewhere,' he began. 'He will probably be nervous about his flanks and rear in any case. He probably even expects an attack on his communications before the end of April.'

Clarke wrote down all the units that might plausibly be able to threaten Rommel's rear. It was a short list. There were some genuine Australian troops who hadn't gone to Greece, and then there were the two false units he'd created: 10th Armoured Division and the 1st Special Air Service. The genuine SAS force was still in the future, at this point not even a gleam in David Stirling's eye.

How could these be made threatening? Dummy gliders had been built for the SAS brigade. Clarke sent them to Crete, which was closer to western Cyrenaica than Cairo, to support the idea that airborne units were going to launch an attack far behind the lines. Apart from that, he was going to have to rely on rumours. With Wavell he came up with a list of stories that ought to give an advancing commander pause: that the 10th Armoured Division was advancing into the desert with a plan to attack the enemy flank and that Commandos newly arrived in Egypt and the SAS who were supposedly in Crete would both launch strikes deep into Libya to cut off Rommel's supply lines.

He drew up a list of pieces of information he wanted passed to the enemy: 'The 7th Division Guards Brigade went from Egypt to Cyrenaica on 6th April'; '6th Division Headquarters in Cairo were packing up on April 7th'; army officers had been drinking with their naval counterparts in the Continental Hotel and had been heard talking about 'kicking the Boche in the pants'. The list went over several pages. Some of the items were true: 6th Division HQ were indeed packing up. Others weren't.

The problem was getting these whispers over to the enemy. A press photo was released of new American tank equipment that was supposedly being supplied to British troops in Africa. London, Clarke had been told, had some sort of 'special source' for passing information to German intelligence. He sent a couple of items their way. The ever-reliable Japanese intelligence agent, Ohno, still seemed to trust his source on the Suez Canal, so information could be passed to him. The rest Clarke handed to Maunsell, to distribute as best he could.

Behind his desk at A Force HQ, Clarke pinned up a poster produced by the Ministry of Information. 'PRACTICE AND PREACH SECURITY MINDEDNESS!' it urged readers, under a series of cartoons of careless military men and their families making offhand remarks about their movements. Each piece of information was fed into the centre of the poster, where they were assembled into an accurate 'Report From Spy HQ to Germany'. The lesson, for anyone who hadn't already got it, was spelled out at the bottom: 'Mind your own tongue – and check indiscretions in others.'

It was not one of the great wartime posters: cluttered, confusing and with a slogan that was the opposite of memorable. A later US poster would do a better job, showing a Nazi hand piecing together a jigsaw puzzle of words to spell out a message about a convoy. But what this one did very well was show the process that Clarke was trying to reverse-engineer. He started with the final report he wanted German intelligence to produce, then generated a list of facts that could lead to that conclusion, then produced pieces of gossip, things that might have been seen or overheard that would support those facts. 'The actual messages will of course be passed in a much more devious form,' he assured one of Wavell's aides as he sought permission to go ahead with his plan.

The main flaw with the Ministry of Information's poster, although no one knew it at the time, was that it was set in Britain. It featured nine different Nazi informants, all passing information to a spymaster. This was a fair reflection of the fears of British authorities, but it was far from the reality. German intelligence had no functioning spy network in the UK at the time, and the agents it was sending over were being rapidly picked up by MI5.

It was closer to reflecting the security situation in Egypt. Britain was an island, meaning agents had to be landed by boat or plane, both risky routes. A spy who wanted to travel to Egypt from neutral Turkey had only to get on the train.

And that was assuming they weren't already there. Egypt was theoretically an independent country, but the British treated it in much the same way as a colonial possession. To officers such as Clarke, it probably felt like one.

But not everyone was happy about that. Many Egyptians resented the way the British treated them and reckoned that from Egypt's point of view, a British defeat might be a good thing. Some of them were keen to pass secrets to the enemy, if they could find a way.

Then there were the supposed neutrals. Although Britain wasn't yet at war with the Japanese, no one was under any illusions about whose side they were on. But diplomats such as Ohno were allowed to wander the country freely, noting the arrival and departure of ships and troops, listening to gossip in the bazaar.

And beyond those with ideological or patriotic motives for passing information to the enemy, there were plenty of people happy to make good money doing it. Everything else in Cairo was for sale, so why not secrets? Clarke's confidence that gossip spoken too loudly in bars and waste paper carelessly discarded would find its way to enemy intelligence was well founded.

Magicians like Clarke's uncle Sidney think a lot about 'angles': who can see which part of the stage from where. In rehearsals, assistants sit at the extreme corners of the auditorium to check that wires and secret compartments aren't visible – and that the tricks are. Clarke's problem was that he didn't know exactly where the audience for his nuggets of fake intelligence was sitting. Maunsell's team at SIME had a good idea about some enemy sources, but they had no reason to think they'd found all of them. Ultimately, Clarke's audience could be anywhere.

From the perspective of 'security mindedness', Cairo was a nightmare, a mix of soldiers, alcohol, women and spies. But for a deceiver, it was an opportunity. Like a magician, a deceiver finds their work is pointless if no one is paying attention. Clarke was confident there was an audience in Cairo. It was now a question of making sure they were paying attention to the right (or, depending on your point of view, wrong) things.

The question was, were they? It was all very well spreading rumours in bars and hoping that they would make their way back to Berlin. What Clarke really needed was more solid ways of getting information to his audience.

As it turned out, whether or not Axis intelligence was paying attention to Clarke's carefully drafted clues, Rommel wasn't. While Clarke was pulling together his elaborate story and securing agreement for his various leaks, the Afrika Corps was charging across the desert, following much the same paths the British had taken four months earlier.

The kind of puzzle pieces that Clarke was passing over to Axis intelligence would need time to work their way through the system before anyone would assemble them into a picture. But Rommel wasn't interested in waiting for that to happen. The best information he was getting about British forces came from his encounters with them.

A century earlier, the Duke of Wellington had talked about the importance of a commander being able to guess what he couldn't see. This was a gift that Rommel possessed in spades. His experiences in the previous war and in France in 1940 had left him with an uncanny knack for drawing inferences about what he couldn't see based on what he could. This was why his daring attacks so often delivered triumphs.

In the first few days of April he watched how the defenders responded to his advance. His men were taking prisoners by the hundred, and Rommel concluded that the defenders 'intended to avoid, in any circumstances, fighting a decisive action'. He was like a poker player who had bluffed and found that his opponent didn't dare call him. 'It was a chance I could not resist,' he said. He would keep up his pursuit.

On 11 April, three months after it had fallen to Australian troops, the city of Tobruk was once again under siege, this time by the Axis. Tobruk is the easternmost port on the Cyrenaica desert. Wavell feared that if Rommel took it he would be able to use it to bring up supplies almost to the Egyptian border. For Rommel, leaving it in British hands and pressing on to Egypt meant leaving an enemy toehold at his rear. He was determined that the city should be taken.

A Force officers suddenly found that their MI9 duties were urgent. One visited Tobruk to brief the defenders on escape and evasion techniques. It was well-meant, but an unfortunate clue to how commanders in Cairo viewed their likely fate.

And as this nightmare was unfolding on the southern side of the Mediterranean, another one was developing in the Balkans. The troops Churchill had ordered redeployed from Libya were enough to make Wavell weak, but not enough to make the Greeks strong. Over the course of April, the Germans swept through Yugoslavia and Greece. The forces that had arrived to help hold them off instead joined the general retreat, pulling back to Crete at the end of the month.

An A Force team had visited the island in the middle of the month to find a good location to display the dummy 'SAS' gliders when it became clear that there was no point in pretending the island was going to be a base for attacking anywhere else: it was about to be attacked itself. That part of Plan A-R was cancelled, and the gliders that were en route were destroyed when they arrived on Crete, to prevent German invaders discovering their existence.

Soldiers can be sceptical of the work of intelligence agencies, and with good cause. Reports are often based on out-of-date rumours and half-truths passed on by agents who have incentives to make the information they glean sound more important than it is. Even when they are accurate, they can be wrong: British codebreakers would read messages from Germany commanding Rommel not to advance and assume, incorrectly, that he would follow orders. They hadn't understood that Rommel knew Hitler would forgive him disobeying instructions if the result was victories.

Clarke was trying to tell Rommel a story using rumours passed slowly through a variety of sources in Cairo. But Rommel, by now sporting a pair of sand goggles that he'd been given by a captured British officer, could see a different story with his own eyes. And

Rommel was a bad target for the story Clarke was trying to tell him. As his forces reached Tobruk he ordered an assault even before they had scouted the city's defences. This was not the behaviour of a man who would be persuaded to worry about what might go wrong. Neither was he a general inclined to spend time worrying about supply lines.

His subordinates warned him about the state of their vehicles, about shortages of fuel, about the condition of the road ahead, but Rommel was dismissive. 'One cannot permit unique opportunities to slip by for the sake of trifles,' he wrote, offering what might as well have been his motto.

Plan Anti-Rommel was an interesting idea, but a failure at every level. It wasn't clear that the message reached German intelligence. Even if it had, there was no time for it to be processed, and even had the story got to Rommel, it wasn't one he was interested in listening to. This was not a commander who was going to be persuaded to slow down for fear of over-extending himself, or indeed to be concerned with tedious details about supply logistics. For Rommel, destiny lay ahead of him, not behind. He could tell that the British were running away, and that was all the intelligence he needed. As a deceiver, Clarke hadn't yet learned that he needed to know his audience.

It was a mark of how fast the war was changing that in mid-April Wavell suggested a new rumour, that he had laid 'very extensive minefields' inside the Egyptian border, including some that could be detonated remotely. Three weeks earlier he had felt secure. Now he feared Rommel was going to make it all the way to Cairo.

The Turk

The Magician brings onto the stage a large cabinet, at the back of which are a carved head and torso dressed in Ottoman robes and a turban. They open the door in the cabinet to show the mechanism underneath, and then place a chess board in front of the Turk, and invite members of the audience to challenge it to a game.

Chapter 9

At the end of April 1941, Clarke boarded a plane to Cyprus. He was wearing civilian clothes, and though his passport was in his real name, it was inaccurate in a crucial respect. Towards the back, a British official has written a message: 'Holder of this passport is permitted to leave and enter Egypt freely so long as he remains holder of British War Correspondents Licence No 219.' Clarke was pretending to be a journalist again, but this time, it wasn't a joke.

After a night as the guest of the British governor on Cyprus, he boarded a civilian flight to Turkey. Travelling incognito, with only a letter from Wavell to the British ambassador in his pocket to confirm his covert mission, Dudley Clarke was now a secret agent.

In the desert, Rommel was stuck, still trying to take Tobruk. Just as the British had been three months earlier, he was now close to the limit of his supply lines. He was still confident that he could take Cairo, especially if he were given more troops and tanks. Germany had a large and powerful army which was just about to complete its conquest of Greece. Where better to send those men next than the desert, to run the British out of Africa and the Middle East as well?

Clarke was looking for new routes to get his story to the enemy. He and Wavell had agreed that he might be able to spread rumours supporting Plan Anti-Rommel in neutral Turkey. There was also work for him wearing his MI9 hat: British soldiers who hadn't managed to join the main evacuation from Greece would be looking for other ways back to their own side, and Turkey was an obvious place to head.

After seeing the ambassador in Ankara, Clarke took the overnight train to Istanbul. It wasn't his first visit to the city. That had been nearly twenty years earlier, when it had been known as Constantinople. He had been a spy that time as well.

The story Clarke told was that in 1922, on leave from the army, he had followed a whim to travel on the Orient Express, something he couldn't really afford. He arrived in Constantinople with an empty wallet, and an idea of how to fix that problem. The British, who were supposed to be keeping the peace in the city, were facing Turks fighting to create an independent homeland, in a stand-off that threatened to become violent. Clarke, hoping to find an army cashier who could advance him money to pay his passage home, presented himself in civilian clothes at British headquarters on the pretext of offering his services as an officer. He claimed later that his hope was that he would simply be sent on his way with enough cash for a ticket.

Instead his offer was taken up, and he was asked to take a room at a boarding house whose owner was suspected of being a spy. Clarke quickly realised that his landlord was 'living a double life in a state of near terror', and began using him to pass misinformation to the Turkish forces.

This was clandestine work, out of uniform and in a foreign country. He was armed with a small Browning automatic pistol that he had brought with him for protection as he travelled through Eastern Europe. When he told the story decades later, it was with an amused detachment. But at the time, a young man thirsty for excitement and with a vivid imagination must have been conscious that he was following the footsteps of John Buchan's fictional officer-spy, Richard Hannay, the hero of *The Thirty-Nine Steps* and other novels. Too closely at times. In a story that echoed Hannay's adventures in *Greenmantle*, published six years earlier, Clarke said he at one stage found himself surrounded by an angry mob in Constantinople. He only escaped by claiming that he, too, was a Turkish nationalist.

Clarke's account of this Constantinople adventure may have improved in the telling, but it's clear that this had been his first taste of secret work, and he'd enjoyed it. The visit ended with him escorting a fleeing Turkish dignitary onto a Royal Navy ship in the night. The young lieutenant had found himself chatting over drinks with senior naval officers, some of them convinced that he was a far more important covert agent than he really was. It had been dangerous at times, but also fun, and Clarke liked having fun.

Now he had returned, a real intelligence officer on a real mission in a real war. Unlike Egypt, occupied and defended by the British, Turkey really was neutral. The previous war had led to the final collapse of the Ottoman Empire, and the Turkish government had no desire to get involved in another senseless loss of life.

That made the country, like the other neutral nations of southern Europe, an ideal base for intelligence work by the fighting powers. The Abwehr, Germany's foreign intelligence service, set up shop with the goal of building networks in the Middle East to gather information on the British forces there. For the British, meanwhile, it was a good spot from which to try to put feelers into the Balkans. Foreign correspondents, of the sort Clarke was pretending to be, also based themselves there. Just as it had done for the best part of a thousand years, Istanbul was serving as a crossroads and an information exchange between east and west.

Clarke checked himself into the luxurious Park Hotel. In itself, this was a bold act. The hotel was opposite the German consulate. Its restaurant and bars were known to be full of German spies. British agents tended to prefer the gloomier Pera Palace. But it was German spies that Clarke wanted to meet.

That evening, he kept an 'unobtrusive rendezvous' with a man whose name hinted at his unusual background.

Commander Vladimir Wolfson had been born into a Jewish family in Kyiv in 1903. His father, a lawyer, was wealthy enough to employ a Scottish governess, who taught her charges fluent English. In the chaos following the 1917 revolution, young Vladimir found himself invited onto a Royal Navy cruiser that had come to Odessa to rescue White Russians, to act as a translator. Whether he intended to leave with them or not, he was stuck on board when the city fell to the Red Army, and was taken onto the crew as a midshipman. From then on, he was 'more English than any Englishman'. He attended Cambridge, married, and joined the Shell Oil company, which sent him to Palestine and Egypt. When war came, he was called back up and posted to Istanbul as 'assistant naval attaché'. It was meant to sound unimportant. He was the man on the ground for the Naval Intelligence Division.

Wolfson talked Clarke through the situation in Istanbul. The Turkish police kept watch on foreign spies, but allowed them to go about their business so long as they didn't spy on Turkey. The Abwehr had got around this by making spying on Turkey the job of its Bulgarian operation. The Istanbul station was left in peace to get on with spying on the Middle East.

The most straightforward job Clarke had for Wolfson was to run the local outpost of MI9, getting British troops out of Greece and shepherding them back to their own side. The next job was rather more surprising. Clarke wanted to get in touch with some Axis agents.

His goal was twofold: he had specific disinformation to spread as part of Plan A-R, but he also wanted to set up permanent channels for passing information to the enemy. His cover as a journalist was ideal for this. A decade and a half earlier, Clarke had spent a leave as a war correspondent for the *Morning Post*, covering the French fight against rebel tribesmen in Morocco, an episode that sounds less like Buchan and more like Evelyn Waugh's *Scoop*. Camped out in a hotel with 'a dozen or so' reporters from a selection of nations, he'd learned the dirty secret of the press on assignment: the level of cooperation between people who are theoretically rivals: 'We worked closely together, even pooling stories or methods of despatch at times.'

Even when they're not sharing resources, reporters are tremendous gossips, exchanging information and observations as they try to work out what the story is. And though most are secretive when they have a scoop, there are some who just can't stop themselves from sharing juicy stories. Clarke wanted to meet people who would either put his misinformation into the stories that they wrote or mention it to their Axis contacts, who might pass it on in turn.

Guided by Wolfson, it wasn't difficult for Clarke, playing the part of a journalist recently arrived from Cairo, to join the gang of reporters who had, like the spies, settled on Turkey as a good spot from which to watch events in Europe and the Middle East.

There was an informal gathering of foreign correspondents – including Germans – each day at the Cafe Hatay, presided over by the Turkey correspondent of *The Times*. There Clarke met a Hungarian Jew who was writing for papers in Stockholm and Budapest. 'He has been in London a good deal and is pro-British in sentiment, but mixes with Axis and American journalists,' Clarke noted. 'He would probably send to his papers anything which comes under the heading of news and would undoubtedly discuss it in journalistic circles of various nationalities.'

There was 'a young and impetuous American who probably believes almost anything he is told'. He'd been in Berlin until the previous October, and was in the habit of meeting up with German and Japanese journalists. 'He is essentially a news hound and will jump quickly at anything that looks like news.'

And there was a Swedish journalist who'd previously been in Berlin. 'He has contacts in Axis circles and is talkative,' Clarke wrote. 'He is fond of the ladies and a frequenter of the brighter haunts of Istanbul.' At least one person in the embassy believed that 'news given to him would reach the enemy'.

It wasn't just reporters that Clarke met. There was a Hungarian banker who had been educated in England and professed 'strong British sentiments which may not be entirely genuine'. He was deemed 'a useful contact in international circles'.

Clarke's 'channels', as he called them, even included a carpet seller at the Grand Bazaar. 'He is very talkative and inquisitive, asks innumerable questions and is only too happy to discuss any aspect of the war,' Clarke said. 'He is probably quite the best for spreading Bazaar rumours and for getting news to the Turks. He speaks excellent English and is a great football fan. He says that he is a member of the Arsenal and has played for them as a reserve. Anyone going into his shop and talking football can say anything they like.'

He went on, offering an insight into how he'd passed the time in the man's shop: 'If conversation flags he should be encouraged to show some erotic Persian pictures which will give ample time for talking.' The war situation, Clarke said, always came up in these confidential chats.

Then there were those about whom he had no firm evidence, but some suspicions. 'There is a little man belonging to the Iraq consulate, who looks like rather a fat edition of Charlie Chaplin. He haunts Tokatliyan Bar at about noon and 7 p.m., after which he is usually found in the Taxim Casino. He is not inclined to talk, but would probably pick up any documents which were dropped within his reach.'

In his imagined capacity as a reporter, Clarke had asked someone at his hotel to help him find a typist. The Russian woman who arrived was immediately suspect in his mind, simply as a result of being suggested by the staff at a hotel where the Abwehr had so much influence. 'I have no reason to doubt her reliability,' he said, but one of the hotel staff had found her, so it was possible she 'may show papers to him or his associates.' In Istanbul in 1941, it was safest to assume that everyone was working an angle.

Clarke spent three weeks in the city. In his account, no one guessed that he was anything other than what he claimed to be, a fellow scribbler and, to correspondents keen to hear the latest from the front, a man with fresh gossip. It's also possible that some of them suspected he wasn't quite right, but decided to play him along – someone who's trying to mislead you can still be a source of information.

In either case, he gave them lots to work with. He suggested that any German advance into Egypt would be walking into a 'well-prepared trap'. The British were 'keeping back in Egypt a large reserve, including recently arrived armoured units'. He described the remote-controlled minefields that Wavell had suggested, too.

He speculated in a knowledgeable tone of voice that the recent flight to Scotland by Hitler's deputy, Rudolf Hess, had followed a failed attempt to assassinate the Fuhrer. He even wrote 'stories' for his newspaper, presumably in the hope that someone would take a look at them, either his Russian typist, or another reporter, or one of the hotel staff.

Clarke and Wolfson didn't stop at general rumours. They hatched a plan to put someone masquerading as a British traitor into direct contact with a German agent. It was still in the early stages when Clarke left. And they discussed a way to send fake stories in the name of journalists in Istanbul to their newspapers. Such subterfuge would of course be discovered when the false story appeared, so it was a high-risk approach. 'This scheme will only be used for messages where speed of transmission is all important,' Clarke wrote. 'No one journalist should be used more than once but each Axis journalist can if necessary be used in turn.'

Before he left Istanbul, Clarke agreed a code he would use to signal the stories he wanted passed round in Turkey. Messages were already encrypted, but ciphers could be broken, and decrypted messages could be left lying around. So since the start of his deception work, Clarke had added another very simple layer of concealment. 'The word "COUNTER" should be read as "ENCOURAGE",' he explained in a briefing note. 'For instance, a message saying "PLEASE COUNTER LEAKAGES REGARDING" means "PLEASE ENCOURAGE LEAKAGES".'

He agreed codewords he'd use if he wanted a particular channel to be deployed. 'Chaplin' was the man from the Iraqi consulate; 'Hatay' meant simply dropping a word in at one of the daily cafe chats.

Was any of this going to work? Clarke was putting a lot of faith in the idea that the Abwehr were listening to gossip from reporters, and that words dropped to hotel staff and merchants at the bazaar would find their way to enemy intelligence. If that sounded like the sort of thing that happened in novels or films, the reality was that there were no handbooks for intelligence officers in 1941. More than one read spy fiction hoping to find tips and tricks. Both Clarke and Wolfson were learning as they went along.

As it happened, two days after Clarke arrived in Istanbul to begin setting up his misinformation channels, another man arrived in the city on a parallel mission. He, too, was an adventurer and a performer, though a less respectable one than the English lieutenant colonel. He made his way to the building over the road from Clarke's hotel, the German consulate, where he asked to speak to someone connected to the Abwehr. He was an agent just returned from Egypt, and he wished to make a report.

Chapter 10

Renato Levi was in his late thirties when he was invited to become a spy. Up to that point, his life hadn't amounted to much. He'd been born into a prosperous Italian Jewish family in 1902, been raised between Bombay, where his family operated a shipyard, and Switzerland, where he was educated. He married an Australian and moved there for a decade before returning to Genoa with his wife and son in 1937. His mother owned hotels in the city, and he was supposed to help her run them, but she complained he wasn't much help. Others saw something in him.

Just before Christmas 1939, he was approached by a tall, broad man, a little older than he was, named Hans Travaglio. He was, despite his surname, German, a jolly man, good company and generous. Levi liked him. After they had got to know each other a little, Travaglio asked an intriguing question: would Levi be interested in working for German intelligence?

Travaglio was no amateur spy. Weeks earlier, he had been involved in the first intelligence coup of the war, when he had pretended to be an anti-Nazi Luftwaffe officer in order to lure two officers of Britain's foreign intelligence service, MI6, to a meeting in the town of Venlo, on the Dutch-German border, where they were abducted. The incident had thrown British intelligence into chaos, and put lives in danger: one of the MI6 men was, incredibly foolishly, carrying a list of agents' names and addresses. So that Christmas the Abwehr and its man in Genoa were justly feeling pretty pleased with themselves.

What was it about Levi, such a disappointment to his mother, that caught Travaglio's eye? Some of the characteristics that make a poor son might make for a good spy: a relaxed attitude to conventional morality, an aptitude for bluffing one's way through life relying on charm. But it may have been as simple as the fact that, through his marriage and his time in Australia, Levi had picked up a British passport. At that point in the war, with Italy neutral and France unoccupied, this was a man who could travel to Britain easily.

Levi replied that he was indeed interested. However, he had ideas of his own. He sought out the British consul in Genoa and reported the approach. He claimed later he wanted to help the Allies because they were fighting the Germans, and the Germans hated Jews. But he was also a thrill-seeker, and this was an opportunity for excitement. And there seemed the possibility that there might be money to be made from this caper. As for the idea that it might be dangerous, Levi didn't seem to give it much thought.

At the start of 1940, Travaglio dispatched his new recruit to Paris with a list of questions about the French military. There he was met by an MI6 officer, who passed him to France's intelligence agency, the Deuxieme Bureau. It wasn't a profitable relationship. The French didn't seem to know how to use this new asset, and Levi ended up returning to Italy without the information he'd been asked to get. He decided to bluff it out, expressing outrage to his handler at the ridiculousness of his mission, a tactic that, somehow, worked. It probably helped that France had collapsed in the face of the German army, meaning his failure didn't matter.

Besides, if Levi hadn't yet been much of a success as an agent, he was proving his value to Travaglio in other ways. Abwehr officers were given dollars with which to pay their agents. Levi, however, knew black marketeers who would pay almost twice the official exchange rate for US currency. He and his new Abwehr colleagues saw a business opportunity. They would change the dollars into lira, pay the agents with those, and pocket the difference. It wasn't always straightforward: Levi was arrested while trying to change thousands of dollars, and the Germans had to pull strings with the Italian police to get him released. But this spying game was proving just as profitable as Levi had hoped.

The Abwehr was now changing its focus, and Travaglio asked Levi if he would be willing to go to Egypt. Italy had entered the war, and the Abwehr were working with their Italian counterparts, the Servizio de Informazione Militare, known as the SIM. Its head signed off a plan where Levi and a wireless operator would travel to Cairo via Istanbul, and a wireless set would be sent for them in the diplomatic bag of a friendly country that still had an outpost in Cairo, probably Hungary.

Neither the Italians nor the Germans were keeping close tabs on Levi. In the second half of 1940 he was able to make two trips to Yugoslavia, where Britain still had an embassy, to keep MI6 abreast of developments. Over in Cairo, R. J. Maunsell's team was notified it could soon expect a guest.

At the end of 1940, Levi and his radio man set off for Istanbul, and almost at once things went wrong. Five days after they arrived, they were arrested when police swooped on a gang that was circulating counterfeit English currency. The details of how they had become mixed up in this racket aren't explained in Levi's files, but they're not hard to guess. Probably Levi had seen another chance to make a bit of money on the side. He may have believed he'd be able to pass the cash off as genuine in Cairo, where there were plenty of British soldiers. And he may well have believed that his relationship with MI6 would afford him some protection. He was certainly carrying £200 in forged £5 notes when he was arrested, and his explanation to the police was that he was working for the British.

He'd had the good sense to check in at the British consulate in Istanbul before his arrest, and so the diplomats had at least some idea of who he was. They can't have been impressed, but after three weeks they secured the release of the two spies. The wireless man had by this stage had enough. He may have lost his nerve for the spying lark altogether, or he may have felt that Levi was not the sort of person that he wanted at his side in dangerous moments. In any case, he turned back.

Levi though was undeterred by these setbacks and carried on to Cairo, where he arrived in February 1941 and was met by Maunsell's deputy, Captain Kenyon Jones.

Security and Intelligence Middle East operated out of a block of flats close to Grey Pillars, but outside the barbed wire. The building, modelled after a European fashion, reminded Maunsell of Kensington. It was guarded by an Egyptian who had lost his legs in an accident – or been born without them, Maunsell never established which – who spoke multiple languages and had an ear for when the rhythms of the city were turning dangerous. He moved around on a trolley, or his hands, and quickly impressed Maunsell, who gave him a pistol. SIME officers became used, on late visits to the office, to being challenged from ground-level in the deep Cockney accent that the guard had picked up from British squaddies. Maunsell's reply to

'Who goes there?' was the positively Kipling-esque: 'Your father and your friend.'

The team occupied three rooms. In one – the one with a huge air conditioning unit – sat Maunsell, with a large safe containing SIME's deepest secrets. In a second were typists, tapping out and filing and cross-checking the details of all Cairo's suspicious characters. In the third and smallest room were the other SIME officers, overseen by Jones.

Approaching thirty, Jones was a burly farmer's son who had played rugby for Oxford and Wales as a Number Eight, a position at the back of the scrum that requires not only impressive physical power but also speed of foot and mind. Despite the discomforts of heat or disease, he was irrepressibly cheerful. His colleagues whispered that he could be seen going for dawn runs around the city each morning before breakfast. Even after two years in Egypt, one of them noted, 'he still disseminated a faint atmosphere of barns and hayfields'.

Maunsell took the view that he had smart people working for him who should be allowed to get on with their jobs. He tried to maintain a friendly atmosphere: 'I didn't give a damn how they wore their uniforms, or indeed what they wore.'

Jones liked it. He enjoyed the 'interesting and unusual' jobs that came his way, and Levi seemed a particularly promising one. 'Since he was vouched for, he was treated in a friendly fashion,' he later recalled. Jones gave him a false name and found him somewhere to live. Levi told him he hoped that if he helped the Allies he might be helped to get back to Australia 'where he had much enjoyed living'.

For Jones, it was an exciting moment. Here was an actual enemy agent who had set himself up as a 'double', working for the British against his imagined employer. Better, he'd already spent more than a year inside the Abwehr. What stories might he be able to tell? What hidden enemy networks inside Egypt might he reveal?

He was in for a disappointment. Levi had been told there would be a message waiting for him at the Carlton Hotel about his wireless. There wasn't. He'd been given the names of two people in the city who would be able to help him in his work. Neither was any use.

As for Levi himself, Jones soon realised he was unreliable, especially where money was concerned. He was, according to the SIME file on him, 'a natural liar, capable of inventing any story on the spur of the moment to get himself out of a fix.' This was not necessarily a disadvantage in a secret agent, but it represented a bit of a problem for his handler.

His local leads exhausted, Levi showed no interest in developing new ones. 'It was quite obvious that his main concern in life was women,' said Jones, 'and he was not making any contacts among the large Italian colony.' The two men would meet twice a week. The Welshman found the Italian 'an intelligent, easy-going, lazy fellow, one who had lived by his wits and was quite confident of his ability to go on doing so.'

Jones had concluded that the Germans weren't going to be able to send a wireless set. Tighter procedures around diplomatic packages had ruled out the original plan. It seemed baffling that, having gone to the trouble of recruiting an agent and inserting him into enemy territory, they would do nothing to enable him to send messages home, but over the course of 1941, British counter-espionage officers would conclude that the Abwehr was far less formidable than they had previously thought. Agents were often sent out poorly equipped and with little training. Both capturing them and persuading them to switch sides proved less of a struggle than it should have been. One of Dudley Clarke's close friends, who had been in Berlin before the war and now headed the German section of military intelligence, expressed bafflement that the efficient people he had got to know could be so stupid.

Levi wasn't bothered. 'Renato amused himself with his lady friends and lounging around the bars and cafes of Cairo,' reported Jones. But his SIME handlers had had enough. Jones, 'somewhat tired of his company', suggested to Levi that the British find him a transmitter, a plan he agreed to enthusiastically. Jones approached the army's Signals Section, explaining that he wanted to help a German agent send messages to Italy. They were, understandably, 'somewhat sceptical'. The idea of playing back agents was a new one, and the harassed officers, busy with the fall-out of Rommel's advance, replied that their job was to hinder, not help, enemy spies.

Eventually, though, they pointed him towards a Warrant Officer Ellis, who liked to build radios, and who was willing to make what was needed: a small set that would have the range to reach Italy, but would sound at the other end like a home-made one that Levi might have been able to obtain illicitly.

The next challenge was to develop a code – Levi hadn't been given one by the Abwehr, of course. One of Jones's colleagues suggested the Playfair cipher, nearly a hundred years old, but still tricky to crack.

Finally there was the question of how to tell Levi's controllers about the new wireless. Levi wanted to return to Italy himself and do it. This was a huge risk. The Abwehr would be bound to question him on his time in Cairo. If they detected inconsistencies in his story, they might realise he was playing them false. The danger then was that he would be persuaded – or forced – to turn again, and become a triple agent. But Levi was confident it would work. 'He seemed to have no idea that he might be risking his life,' Jones said. 'As a result of his successful activities in France, Italy, Turkey and then in Egypt, he had acquired an amazing self-confidence and complete belief in his own ability to travel anywhere and deceive anybody.'

In the end, Jones and Maunsell agreed it was the only course. What Levi needed now was an explanation of how he had come by the radio set, and indeed who was operating it while he was back in Italy. Jones suggested he say that, 'after great difficulty', he'd paid an Italian £200 for an amateur wireless set, that he'd installed it in a flat and found an operator, 'Paul', who would begin twice-weekly transmissions at the end of May. 'Paul' had been left with about £150, all that remained of the £500 the Abwehr had given Levi.

Jones wrote the story out 'and drilled him thoroughly in it – at least as far as it was possible to drill him in anything, since he was one of these happy-go-lucky improvisers who depended on his wits to get him out of any jam.'

Frustrating though it was for Jones, Levi's confidence in his own improvisational activities wasn't entirely misplaced. He began to flesh out the character of 'Paul' for himself. He gave him a surname, 'Nicosoff', and a back story with just the right amount of vagueness to be plausible: 'I believe he is a Syrian, but he told me he was born in Egypt.'

And so Jones bade his agent farewell and sent him off to Istanbul, hoping for the best. When Levi had first come into contact with British intelligence, he'd been given the codename 'Lambert' – probably a historical joke, after Lambert Simnel, a fake fifteenth-century claimant to the English throne known as 'the first pretender'. By now, however, another name had stuck. He was to be known, for reasons that were never recorded, as 'Cheese'.

At first, things seemed to be going well in Istanbul. Levi presented himself at the German consulate and lived to tell the tale to a British intelligence officer afterwards. Over the course of May, as Dudley Clarke was planting stories with journalists in one part of Istanbul, Levi was holding a series of meetings with both German and British intelligence in other parts of the city. The Abwehr officer who was handling him 'seemed very pleased with the work done in Egypt'. Indeed he thought he ought to head back there.

Levi, however, was determined to get back to Italy, saying he wanted to see his family. Finally, at the end of the month, Berlin agreed. Cheese said farewell to his British contact, set off for Italy, and went silent. In the months that were to follow, that silence would be the source of increasing anxiety to British intelligence in Cairo.

While Levi was being debriefed in Istanbul, Jones and Ellis were trying to get the wireless connection working. On the date set for their first transmission, the pair of them sat together in a hut, Ellis tapping out the Morse code as Jones read the signal to him. 'To our great disappointment we could make no contact whatsoever,' Jones said. They tried again without success, and then Ellis realised the problem. The wavelengths he'd given to Levi had been settled on some months before, but different atmospheric conditions meant signals on them would no longer reach Italy.

Fortunately, Jones had agreed a backup channel to send messages to Levi, a simple code they could use in telegrams to Istanbul to pass on brief messages. He sent off new arrangements, and on a Monday in the middle of July, he and Ellis tried again. This time, they got through. Jones was thrilled as Ellis began to scrawl down the message back from the wireless station in Italy that was handling communications for the Abwehr. He went back to his room 'as though floating on air'.

When he reported the news to Maunsell the next morning, he was a little deflated when his chief asked an obvious question that he couldn't answer: now that they had a channel to German intelligence, what were they supposed to do with it?

Chapter 11

In mid-May 1941 Clarke travelled to Ankara, from where he intended to fly back to Cairo. Here he was met by the defence attaché, who had news for him. His mission had changed.

Just before Clarke had set off for Turkey the previous month, Wavell had explained he was considering invading Syria and Lebanon. The countries were controlled by the French, which meant they were now in the hands of the Vichy government, which was collaborating with the Nazis. Wavell feared the Germans would use them as an air base from which to attack his forces. In the intervening weeks, tensions had risen. Now the British attack was imminent. Clarke decided to take advantage of his civilian cover and take a trip behind the Vichy lines.

He spent the day bringing the attaché up to speed on the deception channels in Istanbul, and the other man suggested he might have his own means of dropping stories to journalists in Ankara. Satisfied that A Force's interests in Turkey were in safe hands, Clarke boarded a train.

Before the war the Taurus Express had been one of the world's great railway journeys, linking up with the Orient Express to offer the possibility, with a couple of changes, of a three-continent trip from London to Cairo or Baghdad. The international traveller in Clarke, who had used his leaves from the Army to explore the world, was a little thrilled to be taking a sleeping compartment on this famous route – four years later, in an official report on the journey, he would name the train he'd taken twice, in successive paragraphs.

At noon the following day, the train reached Adana, the last stop in Turkey. The British consul was waiting, with instructions to stop all British subjects from entering Syria. Men of military age were in particular danger of being interned. On the platform, passengers digested this news. 'The wildest rumours flew around,' Clarke reported. 'Britain was at war with France! Wavell had marched into

Syria! The RAF had bombed Beirut!' For a man who was making misinformation his trade, it was an interesting experience of being on the receiving end. 'It was impossible to sift the false from the true, and a harassed Consul was no better informed than anyone else.'

Most importantly for Clarke, he avoided being taken off the train, and with the few others who wanted to go to a place that might soon be at war, he travelled on, through Syria and on to the Lebanese port of Tripoli. Clarke tried to put about a story that a recent anti-British coup in Iraq didn't enjoy the support of the whole Iraqi army. It was a tale that had gone over well with foreign correspondents in Turkey. Here, closer to Iraq, they laughed, and informed Clarke he had fallen for British propaganda. There was a lesson for the apprentice deceiver there, too.

That was as far as the train would take him, but Clarke persuaded a Jewish refugee family he'd met to give him a lift in their car. They may have concluded that this smooth-talking Englishman, who knew Palestine so well, would be handy if they had any trouble getting through the British lines. They would certainly have been more sympathetic to the British than to the Vichy French. From Clarke's point of view, travelling with them gave him an ideal cover for reconnaissance work.

As their car approached the bridge over the Litani River in southern Lebanon, one of the first objectives an invading army would need to seize, he persuaded the family to pull over so that he could get a closer look. Three weeks later, the bridge would be the site of fierce fighting. 'The road followed the coast the whole way,' Clarke recorded, 'and it was possible to observe the troop movements and defence preparations all along the route.' His willingness to put the family at risk for his own ends revealed again his ruthlessness. 'More than once the car was stopped by troops or police,' he said, 'and there were some anxious moments.'

The atmosphere in Beirut was 'very tense indeed, and troop movements were evident in all directions,' he wrote. 'It was not the time to linger longer than was absolutely necessary to get the information required.'

Clarke was an ideal choice for this sort of work. A few years earlier, he'd been fighting the Arab uprising in Palestine, so he understood how the terrain could be used for ambushes, working for and against the regular soldier. He didn't need to take notes. 'I happen to be blessed with a photographic memory,' he said. It was 'quite useless for acquiring knowledge, since the photograph fades after a few days', but that wasn't a problem in this case: by the evening he was in Jerusalem, making a report to the general who was planning the coming attack on Lebanon and Syria. The next day he flew on to Cairo, for a 'long interview' with Wavell, describing all he had seen and done.

There was a word for what Clarke had been doing, scouting enemy defences dressed as a civilian. It was in a different category from pretending there were parachutists in the Transjordan desert, and even from pretending to be a journalist in a neutral country. It was called spying. And if he had been caught, he would have enjoyed no protection as a prisoner of war.

When the young Dudley Clarke had volunteered for the army twenty-five years earlier, this wasn't the sort of soldiering he'd had in mind. Then he had dreamed of getting to the trenches, or flying above them, of being a leader of men. But this war had put him in a quite different niche, as an unconventional soldier fighting in unconventional ways.

At the beginning of John Buchan's *Greenmantle*, Richard Hannay is asked to go on a mission that 'does not come by any conceivable stretch within the scope of a soldier's duties.' He is warned that 'in this job you would not be fighting with an army around you, but alone.'

Hannay always takes these jobs with a noble distaste, telling the reader how much he would prefer to be back in the trenches. But after two decades of thrillers written by not just Buchan but also Eric Ambler, Somerset Maugham and Leslie Charteris, spying was glamorous, a fantasy for many men. Clarke, operating with the huge amount of leeway he was given by Wavell, was getting the chance to live it out. He was having fun. A little too much fun, as it would turn out.

The Sands of the Desert

May–July 1941

The Magician stands with a large transparent bowl filled with water, and three bowls of coloured sand. The sands are poured into the bowls and stirred, turning the water inky black, but when the magician reaches into the bowl, he is able to pull out fistfuls of dry sand of each colour.

Chapter 12

While Wavell was preparing to advance into Lebanon and Syria, his forces were in full retreat elsewhere. At the end of May, after just over a week of fighting, British forces began to leave Crete. The German victory in Greece was now complete. It had taken two months – another British defeat to add to France and Norway.

Wavell's fear was that Cyprus would be next. He sent a message to Clarke, who was back in Jerusalem, asking if A Force could delay an attack by two weeks, to give him time to reinforce the island. Clarke had one immediate thought. There had recently been a scare in Palestine after plague rats had been spotted coming off a ship at the port of Haifa. An army doctor was summoned. What effect might fears of plague have on an invading force? Clarke asked the doctor. When he got his reply, he sent a message back to Wavell suggesting that a rumour of a bubonic plague outbreak on Cyprus could cause the Germans to inoculate their troops, which would add a week or two to their schedule. 'A slender hope,' wrote Clarke, 'but at least it seemed worth trying.'

Wavell, however, rejected the idea, replying that the same rumours would make it very difficult to move civilians from Cyprus to Egypt. Even Clarke's enquiries to medical officers in Palestine had inadvertently started a rumour of an outbreak. Instead the general urged Clarke to find some way to exaggerate the strength of the British forces on the island. There were about 4,000 men on Cyprus. How could German intelligence be persuaded that there were several times that number?

The first part of the solution was to spread rumours that reinforcements were imminent. Maunsell's network of leakers were put to work in Cairo. Clarke asked an intelligence officer in Jerusalem to put it about that several regiments had been sent to the island. The week after Wavell's message to Clarke, a story appeared in the *New York Post* that Cyprus was being reinforced.

Over in Cairo, headquarters sent signals to Cyprus using a cipher that the Germans were thought to have broken, announcing the imminent arrival of troops and anti-aircraft units. To explain why this wouldn't lead to any increase in anti-aircraft fire against Luftwaffe planes, the signals included an instruction for the new batteries to 'remain silent against ordinary raids, reserving their fire for main attack if and when it comes'.

An immediate issue was how to explain to forces on Cyprus the meaning of these messages. Brigadier Reginald Rodwell, the commander on the island, received a separate message from Cairo instructing him to ignore the signals. Clarke then dispatched an officer to coordinate deception activity on the island, carrying a letter for Rodwell from Clarke. 'This was started very hurriedly before we had a chance to coordinate it with you,' he wrote, by way of apology, before going on to set out the breadth of his plan.

It was easy enough to spread rumours, but his assumption was that Axis intelligence knew better than to believe everything they read in newspapers, or even everything they read in a deciphered signal. On their own, these individual stunts were like small pieces of sleight-of-hand: possibly impressive, but not convincing. Clarke was trying to persuade a sophisticated audience, and to do that, he needed to put on a complete show.

The 4,000 soldiers on Cyprus represented the strength of one brigade. They were commanded by a brigadier. Clarke wanted to suggest there was a whole division on the island, which would typically be three brigades and supporting troops – around 16,000 men in total. A division would be commanded by a major-general. So along with his instructions, Clarke had sent Rodwell some new insignia to pin onto his shoulders: a crossed baton and sabre. He was now a major-general. The hope was that Axis intelligence, seeing his promotion, would conclude that the presence of a major-general implied the presence of a division.

For Rodwell, the sad news was that this was not a real promotion. He bore this manfully, offering to pay for the insignia even though they were temporary. 'I might want them again if the war goes on long enough!'

How had this gone down in London? It had been agreed within the day that the troops on Cyprus would now be known as 7th Division. At another moment, it might have been more difficult to get the request through, but it had come in Wavell's name, and Clarke's unconventional ways were understood and appreciated in London. More than all of that, to an army desperate to avoid another defeat after months of them, any measure that might stave off an attack that the troops on Cyprus were in no position to defend against was surely worth trying.

If Rodwell was a touch disappointed that his promotion wasn't genuine, he greeted Clarke's deception plan with enthusiasm, and agreed to draw up a plan for the island's defence as if he were a real major-general with a real 7th Division at his disposal. Clarke's man on the ground, meanwhile, launched into a frenzy of activity aimed at simulating what would be happening if thousands of reinforcements were genuinely arriving. Buildings were hastily requisitioned to act as headquarters for the additional units that were supposedly en route, and everywhere signposts appeared giving directions to the troops who were supposed to be there. Facts about the supposed reinforcements were slipped into conversations with civilians.

But to the small number of officers who were in on the truth, the mission was less welcome. 'Officers to whom I have spoken were depressed by the self-evident fact that no defence of the island was possible with our present resource and by the fact that plans seemed made for nothing but an evacuation,' Clarke's man reported. 'They seemed to have no prospects except those of being killed, taken prisoner or ignominiously evacuated.'

British soldiers had good reason to feel depressed that summer. Churchill had been putting pressure on Wavell to attack Rommel and relieve Tobruk. On 15 June, with deep misgivings, Wavell ordered the start of Operation Battleaxe, which was supposed to push Rommel back across the Libyan desert. It was a disaster.

Nearly two years into the war, the British still hadn't got to grips with armoured warfare, and in Rommel they had an opponent who was a master of the art. As the British tanks advanced, the German guns picked them off with devastating effect. The battle saw Wavell's forces lose 91 tanks, while Rommel lost 12. 'By the 18th June all was over,' Clarke recorded, 'and we were back where we had started, on the Egyptian side of the frontier.'

Wherever, it seemed, the British fought the Germans, the Germans won. And now, as well as having an apparently superior army, the enemy had a superior leader. During his charge across France, German war correspondents had christened Rommel's force 'the Ghost Division' for its ability to materialise behind Allied lines. Now they came up with a nickname for the commander: 'Der Wüstenfuchs' – 'the Desert Fox'. It was adopted by both sides: here was a cunning general who was able to thrive and win in a place hostile to both man and machine.

There was barely any deception attempted ahead of Operation Battleaxe. The best reason for the Germans to think an attack was unlikely was that it was a bad idea to launch an assault in Libya while also fighting in Syria – 'how can we undertake offensive operations on two fronts in the Middle East when we have not got sufficient for one?' asked a general in London when he heard Churchill talking about the proposed attack.

But it's unlikely deception would have worked anyway. Rommel had little need to rely on intelligence from Berlin. He had his own sources on the battlefield. Apart from anything else, he could see the British tanks drawing up in the days before the attack.

If the evidence of his eyes wasn't enough, Rommel had ears, too, in the form of an outstanding wireless monitoring unit. It analysed the patterns of encrypted messages and listened to the large amount of Allied voice radio chatter that carried on with only the most basic attempts to conceal what was being said (at one point some-one attempted to conceal a reference to 'London' with the impene-trable phrase 'capital of England').

The German listeners became experts at making sense of this information. They got to know the different transmission style of each headquarters unit's wireless operator, meaning they could tell who was talking to who and, by triangulating their signals, where they were and when they'd moved.

So Rommel's team noted that the Allied wireless patterns in early June were similar to what they'd seen before an attack the previous month. They knew that leave had been cancelled. They noted that reconnaissance flights had increased. Their own planes saw track marks in the sand from transport vehicles, and an expansion of one of the British camps. The radio listeners concluded that armoured forces were advancing. Finally, on 14 June, they heard the codeword 'Peter' being passed down from headquarters. From that evening, Rommel's forces were waiting for an attack.

Clarke didn't know how lax his own side's radio security was, but he was aware of the difficulty of concealing your intentions when there is no natural cover. 'The enemy's air reconnaissance could scarcely fail to observe' the tank build-up, he noted sadly. But how could you conceal an army in a desert?

In the meantime, he decided to call on some old tricks. In a workshop on the outskirts of Cairo, the Royal Engineers had for months been working on an improved design of dummy tank. Transported folded up in the back of a truck, they could be put up and taken down in less than five minutes. Close up, they weren't going to fool anyone, but from a distance they worked.

A unit of fifty soldiers, made up of infantrymen under the command of a tank captain, were redesignated the 38th Battalion of the Royal Tank Regiment. As the surviving tanks of Battleaxe fell back, the 38th were sent out to make up their numbers and dissuade Rommel from following up his victory with an attack into Egypt. It was strange work: trying to be seen, but aware that if attacked they would be utterly defenceless. They would stay in the area for three months until, in mid-September, a German armoured probe into the British lines got too close to them, and they were ordered to burn their dummies and flee.

Two more dummy battalions were quickly assembled, one headed to Cyprus and the other to Palestine. Clarke decided the Palestine battalion should travel by train, in the hope that the dummies, covered by tarpaulins, would be spotted and reported by Axis spies. It was a good idea that got off to a bad start when the Palestinian train driver, under the impression that he was carrying dozens of tanks, was audibly astonished by the light weight of his load as he pulled out. When one of the 'tanks' was blown off its truck, Clarke admitted to a 'distressing struggle for Sense of Security over Sense of Humour'.

Not everyone was impressed by Clarke's efforts. As he was trying to arrange dummy equipment for Cyprus, RAF Intelligence told him they wouldn't be bothering with dummy planes 'as they do not consider they deceive any German photographic recces'. Clarke noted dryly that a few days earlier the Luftwaffe had lost two planes in an operation to bomb the dummy aircraft he'd set up west of Cairo.

Rodwell sent back from Cyprus the defence plan for the island he'd drawn up, using the extra forces he was supposed to have. Clarke and Maunsell had a special use for that. In the middle of July, after what Clarke described as 'a great deal of care and trouble', it was passed to a woman 'who was known to be in touch with Japanese intelligence circles and friendly with a German female agent in the town.'

Sadly the A Force files give no more details of this transaction or what happened next, but they do include a note in German signed 'K' that suggests selling the plan to Maunsell's favourite Japanese diplomat: 'Don't ask for less than one hundred Egyptian pounds for this. It's worth at least twice that to Ohno.'

Rodwell had questioned whether the deception about the troops on the island could last more than a few weeks, and Clarke had originally reassured him that it didn't need to: real forces would begin arriving soon. By mid-July, 50th Division was being sent. But then, instead of letting the deception fall away, Clarke decided to keep it going. There were now supposed to be two divisions on Cyprus, and so the island was given a 'Corps HQ' – a military necessity for so many soldiers.

In August, he sent a note to SIME suggesting a line that one of their double agents might offer his Japanese contacts: 'The garrison of Cyprus appears to be larger than is necessary for the defence of the island. It is believed that these additional troops are in Cyprus so as to be available for any sea-borne expedition which the British may contemplate. Although nothing definite is known, there is talk of a landing on one of the Dodecanese islands, although some people think that a landing on the coast of Cyrenaica may be an objective.'

Having sold the lie that there were enough troops to defend Cyprus, he was now going one better, suggesting there were so many there that they were in a position to threaten other places. This was in part a function of necessity: for it to be plausible that there were so many soldiers on the island, there had to be a reason for keeping them there. But an idea was forming in Clarke's mind of a further way he could use the machine he was building.

Chapter 13

A Force weren't the only people who were giving thought to deceiving the enemy in the desert. Major Geoffrey Barkas had arrived in Cairo a few weeks after Clarke, under instructions to teach soldiers about camouflage. He was forty-four, only three years older than Clarke, but those years had made the crucial difference in the Great War. While the teenage Clarke had been trying to find a way to the front, Barkas had been commanding a platoon at Gallipoli, before picking up a Military Cross at the Somme.

In the 1920s he'd gone into the movie business, writing and then directing films. One of them, a documentary about the first flight over Everest, had won an Academy Award. When war came again, he hoped he might be able to put his skills to use making documentaries or propaganda. Instead, after some false starts, he was assigned to a new camouflage unit, alongside a motley crew of artists learning the business of concealment. Barkas spent the second half of 1940 trying to teach the basics to troops, assisted by a poem he wrote about the sad death of 'Driver George Nathaniel Glover', who 'scorned the use of natural cover, and never, never could be made, to park his lorry in the shade'. Then, at the end of the year, he was posted to Cairo, to take the secrets of concealment to the desert.

It seemed, initially, an unpromising location: there was precious little of either natural cover or shade in which even the most enthusiastic driver could hope to park his lorry. But Barkas had developed a theory of camouflage: 'Whatever Nature (or man) has placed upon the surface of the earth forms some kind of pattern to the eye,' he wrote. 'Whatever additions man makes to the objects or marks on any patch of ground will inherently tend to be conspicuous if they run counter to the existing pattern, and inconspicuous if they continue the pattern.' The camoufleurs set about identifying the patterns of both desert and military.

One of the things Barkas had studied back in England was the way that armies left their marks on the landscape. Different types of unit had developed different ways of operating, and their individual marks were distinctive to the analysts hunched over reconnaissance photographs: 'It scrawls its signature upon the ground.' Here was a new pipeline. There was a minefield, or an artillery unit. His question followed naturally: could those marks be concealed, or disguised? Or could other things be made to look like them?

This brought him into A Force's orbit. For the movie-mad amateur cinematographer Clarke, nothing could have been better than the arrival of a real filmmaker – an Oscar-winner to boot. 'A very good man,' he wrote, urging that Barkas be consulted on the construction of dummy tanks. 'Quite the best of the photographic experts in British films.'

Barkas brought a new rigour to the construction of the dummy tanks. His team had the understanding of light and shade that comes from artistic training, and new ideas about how the eye could be fooled. They painted shadows onto the dummies to make them more convincing, and photographed them at different distances and angles to assess their authenticity. Real tanks left track marks behind them, so track-makers were built to make the dummies more convincing.

John Hutton, a New Zealand-born painter and mural-maker, had an idea for what he called 'shadow houses': complicated patterns painted on the ground and the roofs of airfield hangers that, from above, gave the impression of built-up areas. They would never fool photo-interpreters – for one thing the 'shadows' were only in the right place for half an hour a day – but they aimed to puzzle enemy pilots tasked with attacking the airfields, forcing them to make multiple approaches to identify their target, thereby giving defenders more time to fight back. When he tried them out at Beirut, the RAF congratulated him on their effectiveness, but added that sadly they were making it much harder for their own pilots to find the runway. The scheme was dropped by mutual consent.

Next to men already known for their skill with brush and pencil, Barkas was dismissive of his own artistic abilities, but he was, like Clarke, uniquely equipped for the role in which he found himself. His time behind the camera had given him a grasp of how things were supposed to look and how to manage creative temperaments.

Meanwhile his time in the trenches meant he also understood the way the army worked.

The camouflage team scoured Egypt for soldiers with useful peacetime skills: carpenters, painters and model-makers. And there were arrivals from the training school in England: prop-makers, set designers, and a magician.

Not just any magician, either. Jasper Maskelyne was the third generation of a family whose name was synonymous with British magic. His grandfather had established a permanent show at the Egyptian Hall in London, and was renowned as the inventor of a number of tricks including the levitation illusion. By the late 1930s, magic wasn't the money-spinner it had once been, but Jasper was a skilled performer. He also understood how to construct props that concealed and revealed. Barkas asked him to set up a 'Camouflage Experimental Unit', to come up with new ideas.

However, for one member of Barkas's team, camouflage suddenly became a matter of personal survival. Peter Proud, another cinema man, had been a set designer before the war. Now he found himself among the roughly 15,000 troops in besieged Tobruk.

The grim struggle for this ancient port dominated the summer of 1941. For Rommel, capturing it would have given him a way to bring food, water and fuel up to within 80 miles of the Egyptian border by sea. And even a general as careless of supply lines as the German commander wasn't going to risk much more of an advance while his enemy had a stronghold like this to his rear.

The town was held in the early months of the siege by the 9th Australian Division. Even for soldiers who prided themselves on toughness, it was a brutal business. Much of the North African fighting of the Second World War involved motion, great advances and retreats by the two sides' armoured units. But at Tobruk, both sides dug in. For the defenders, there were all the privations of desert life – unbearable heat in the day, freezing cold at night, sand and flies everywhere – with the added dangers of continual shelling and bombing. Their diet consisted of bully beef, biscuits and vitamin pills and everything – even much of the water the defenders needed – had to be brought in by ship on moonless nights.

In the midst of this, Proud set about doing what he could to conceal truth and project falsehood. He recruited a team from the stragglers who had got separated from their units and were stuck in

Tobruk, and sent them out on scrounging missions. A consignment of spoiled flour was mixed into a paste he used to paint onto vehicles, helmets, tents and anything else that needed disguising, using sand to darken it where necessary. In the harbour, the barges used to ferry in supplies were hidden under netted covers stretched between half-sunk wrecks. Tobruk's three remaining Hurricane fighters were also hidden, and a fake airfield built to draw fire. To provide further targets for the enemy, Proud set up dummy gun pits and vehicle parks.

It was in his protection of the town's water-distilling plant that Proud put his cinematic skills to best use. There was no point trying to hide the distillery. The Italians, who had occupied Tobruk until a few months previously, knew very well both its location and its importance. So Proud took a more subtle approach. He assembled a team who hid in trenches near the plant and waited for the next attack. The moment a bomb fell close enough, they went to work. They dug fake bomb-holes, and darkened them with coal dust and waste oil so that they'd appear deeper. They scattered cement dust and rubble, and rolled broken-down vehicles on their sides. They blew up an unused cooling tower, and on the roof of the distillery, working to plans Proud had drawn up beforehand, they painted a huge patch of tar to simulate a gaping hole.

Peter Proud knew an awful lot about how to make things convincing for the camera, and from the air, this looked just like a destroyed building. The bombers, sure they had done their job, left it alone.

Back in Cairo, change was afoot. Churchill, anxious for victories and unsympathetic to explanations of the difficulties of modern desert warfare, had lost patience with Wavell before Battleaxe, but the operation's failure settled the question. At the end of June, the prime minister sent the commander a cable, telling him that 'after the long strain you have borne, a new eye and a new hand are required in this most seriously menaced theatre.'

He was to be sent to India, and the commander there, Claude Auchinleck, was to come to Cairo. Auchinleck had moved swiftly to put down the coup in Iraq that summer, and Churchill had persuaded himself that this showed he was a more dynamic general.

For Wavell, there was no disguising the fact that it was a demotion. The news can hardly have come as a surprise to him, and he bore it with equanimity. Men under his command had suffered worse fates than dismissal, and he knew it. One of the many poems he could quote from memory was Siegfried Sassoon's 'The General', which describes a First World War commander cheerfully greeting soldiers who are about to be slaughtered because his plans are flawed.

'We have had some setbacks, some successes,' Wavell told the gathered war correspondents at Grey Pillars. One of them wrote afterwards: 'I saw suddenly how sincere he was, how hard he had tried – tried, fought, organised, argued and held on. There went out of Cairo and the Middle East that afternoon one of the great men of the war.'

At some point in his long army career, one of Auchinleck's soldiers had christened him 'the Auk', and the name had stuck. He didn't have Wavell's reputation for brilliance, or his erudition. But he was not a complete stick in the mud. 'Handsome and charming' was the conclusion of one of Cairo's young Englishwomen. Before the war he'd argued that the Indian army could have Indian, rather than British, officers. In military circles, this qualified him as a progressive.

Still, for Clarke, running what amounted to a private army in A Force, the change of commander was a perilous moment. Would the new man have the same enthusiasm for its unorthodox methods as his predecessor?

Auchinleck had seen his first action in Egypt during the previous war, so understood the challenges involved in fighting in the region. He had been warned that Churchill would want early results, but he refused to budge. Operation Battleaxe had shown that the British were outmatched in terms of equipment, training and tactics. There was no point wasting more lives and machinery simply to prove the point again.

This, of course, infuriated the impatient prime minister, but Churchill had outmanoeuvred himself. Having installed a new commander, he could hardly remove him. The Auk wanted time, and even if Churchill resented him for it, he would have to give it to him.

Churchill was only one of the people from whom Auchinleck wanted time and space. The other was Rommel. No one in Cairo was now under any illusions about the German commander's abilities or his character. After the failure of Battleaxe, a counter-attack to take advantage of the Allied forces' weakness was surely a possibility.

Wavell had spent five days handing over to Auchinleck, and may have helped to persuade his successor of the value of a deception operation, because the new commander summoned Clarke to ask what he could do to persuade the Germans to stay on the defensive. 'He needed just four months of steady preparation, without serious enemy interference, to build up strength,' Clarke wrote.

Auchinleck's view was that the best way to achieve this would be to persuade Rommel that another British attempt to relieve Tobruk was imminent. Clarke set to work coming up with a story for a deception operation he codenamed 'Collect'.

After his successful defence against Battleaxe, Rommel was indeed sure that with reinforcements, Egypt could be his. This was an astonishing position for a man who had landed in Africa less than five months earlier with orders to do nothing more than shore up his ally's defences. But if Hitler was delighted by his general's triumphs, he had his own reasons for not wanting to commit resources to the desert war. A week after the battle, Rommel found out why he wouldn't be getting the extra troops he wanted.

The Costume Trunk

July–October 1941

The Magician opens a large trunk to remove three trays, each with a different costume, and shows that the trunk is now empty. The audience selects one costume, which is placed back into the trunk. When the trunk is reopened, a lady steps out in the costume.

Chapter 14

At 4 a.m. on 22 June 1941, Germany declared war on the Soviet Union. Operation Barbarossa, involving millions of troops and thousands of tanks and planes, had begun.

The Germans had worked hard at their own deception operation ahead of this attack, spreading rumours that the troops massing in Eastern Europe were only there to prevent Britain from realising it was about to be invaded. The Luftwaffe had launched a 500-bomber raid against London in May, to give the impression that Berlin was still looking westward. But in the end the complete surprise the Germans achieved was down to one man: Josef Stalin. The Soviet leader had been warned that an invasion was imminent by his generals, by his spies, by his border guards and by the British. He refused to listen to any of them.

His soldiers, unprepared, ill-equipped and badly led, collapsed. Brigades, divisions, whole armies fell apart in front of the Wehrmacht advance. Though Churchill very much wanted the Soviets to stay in the fight, he held out little hope it would actually happen. For nearly two years, the Nazis had beaten every army they'd fought. There was no reason to think that Soviet soldiers, poorly trained, badly armed, under a commander who rejected realities he didn't like, would do any better.

The impact on the war elsewhere wasn't simply that Hitler had no tanks to spare. If, as both London and Berlin expected, Germany was swiftly victorious, Britain's position in the Middle East would face a new threat. That summer, Hitler was looking at plans to send in troops through Turkey or, once he had advanced far enough into the Soviet Union, across the Caucasus.

From Cairo, watching the Germans advance apparently unopposed along the northern coast of the Black Sea, this looked very plausible. To Auchinleck it seemed almost a bigger threat than the much closer forces of Rommel. Wavell's campaign in Lebanon and

Syria had just come to a successful conclusion with the British in control of both countries. But now Auchinleck had to protect his northern flank, a thousand miles away from where his forces were currently facing the enemy. How was he supposed to do this when he didn't have the strength to beat the Germans on one front? The immediate priority was to make these borders look better defended than they were. Clarke settled on a story that Canadian tank units were in the desert in Syria, heading north to protect this front. Canadian currency and armoured car badges appeared in towns along the route that they were supposed to have taken. The French police in Lebanon were suspected of still being loyal to Vichy, which made them a possible route of information to Axis intelligence. They were told that a French-Canadian soldier from a tank unit had deserted.

The only problem with this plan came when the police replied that they'd captured the man. Trying to conceal his surprise, Clarke sent an escort to collect him, and discovered that he was a Belgian-born trooper from a British tank unit who had been left behind in Greece and had managed to make his way through Turkey by pretending to be a French reservist. 'Poor man,' Clarke said. 'We did the best we could for him, but were quite unable to explain the reasons for his inhospitable reception at the end of a truly gallant escape.'

Back with the story of 'Collect', the invasion of the Soviet Union gave Clarke a plausible narrative. Churchill was under strong domestic pressure to do something to help his new ally. Clarke wove that truth into the tale he wanted to tell Rommel. 'The War Cabinet are anxious to hit Germany as hard as possible while she is heavily involved in Russia,' he wrote, adding that they'd asked the Auk 'to start offensive action at the earliest possible date'.

The date Clarke set for his fake assault was 9 August. 'Please take all possible steps to have it rumoured by Service personnel,' Clarke told Maunsell. A series of specific clues were dropped: two senior officers booked hotel rooms in Palestine for early August and then sent unencrypted telegrams cancelling them; three trusted officers were told that if they wanted to get out of any social engagements in the coming weeks, they should explain that they were expecting to be sent 'up the line' to the front; officers on leave from the Western Desert were asked to say that they expected to be recalled. To encourage some anxiety about the German rear, Clarke sent a cable to the British consul in Tangier requesting he locate a British sailor who was supposed to be in hospital there and 'urgently' ask him specific questions about the defences of Tripoli's harbour.

Then, a week before the supposed date of the attack, it was 'stood down' and the word put about that it had been delayed by three weeks. This was at least partially successful. At the end of the month Rommel wrote to his wife that there was 'a lot of blather about an imminent attack by the British'. Although he personally was unconvinced. 'It's probably pure gossip. They're scraping together troops for Iran.'

That comment showed both Clarke's growing success as a deceiver – he'd got his story in front of the enemy commander – but also the limits of what was possible. Rommel wasn't going to believe the Allies were going to do something if he didn't think that they had the troops to do it.

The second August attack was also 'delayed', with rumours now pointing to 15 September. 'We hoped to keep him on the defensive all through the Autumn,' Clarke wrote. 'What was more, we hoped also that by crying wolf several times in succession, we might lull him into a sense of apathy and false security.'

Once again, there was a parallel from the world of stage magic. For an illusionist, misdirection isn't just about *where* the audience is looking. It's also about *when*. By tensing their muscles and adding an edge to their voice, an illusionist conveys the idea that something important is happening, and then when they relax or tell a joke, they send a signal to the audience that they too can let their attention slip a little. A spoon-bender might make several 'failed' attempts before, as the audience looks elsewhere, they do the trick by simply bending the spoon with their hands.

On a Saturday night in the middle of August, Clarke was summoned before the Auk to discuss Operation Collect. The general had orders for its next phase. The timing was tight, as Clarke was leaving town early the following morning, but he had always functioned best after dark, getting 'a new lease of life after midnight'. In Palestine before the war, a colleague had noted that he and Clarke got on 'splendidly', because 'I work all day, and he works all night.' He liked to sit in late showings at cinemas, turning over problems in his mind or with a colleague. His staff in A Force didn't record their feelings about being summoned to late meetings at whichever nightspot their commander happened to be occupying while doing his thinking.

The following day, having worked out the next stage of 'Collect' and issued his midnight orders, Clarke boarded an Imperial Airways flying boat to Khartoum. After spending five days flying across Africa and then up its west coast, his plane landed on the mouth of the River Tagus at Lisbon. He was travelling, as he had been in Istanbul, incognito, claiming to be a journalist. His plan was to repeat his Turkish success in another neutral country, Portugal.

Lisbon was an obvious spot for Clarke to ply his trade. The city had become a transit hub, and that made it the ideal base for spies – 'more prolific even than Istanbul', Clarke observed. As an overnight stop on the route between the Middle East and Britain, it was, he said, a 'valuable centre for the collection of information from careless or venal travellers.' It was also one of the places from which Germany tried to infiltrate spies into the UK. By 1943, Germans made up a seventh of the city's entire diplomatic corps. The only country with a larger delegation was Britain, responsible for nearly a quarter of the diplomats in Portugal.

One focus for German intelligence-gathering was transatlantic ships bringing supplies destined for Britain. Combining two of the world's oldest professions, the Germans had developed a network of informers in the waterfront brothels who passed on details gathered from drunken sailors on shore leave.

Masquerading as a journalist, Clarke haunted bars and hotels, noting who went where, and to whom they spoke. He had been briefed on which Germans were believed to be spies, and which Portuguese were seen as Nazi sympathisers. For his part, he played the gossipy hack, revealing that the British expected to renew their assault on Rommel in mid-September, and signalling that he might be willing to pass on more information in the right circumstances. 'They were a colourful set,' he said of the people he'd met. 'Germans, Portuguese, Spaniards, international Americans, French and Swiss, of both sexes and mostly of doubtful occupation.'

Clarke was clearly having fun. One of his maxims was that 'no new experience or pleasure should be lightly passed by while they were still there to be enjoyed.' Lisbon, he was appreciating, was a very nice place to pass the war, or just to take a break from it.

For all the skill with which A Force was beginning to supply puzzle pieces for enemy intelligence to assemble, there were huge advantages sometimes to just telling your target the picture that they ought to be looking for. In the three months since Clarke left Turkey, his 'channels' in Istanbul had become his 'main instrument for getting false information quickly to the enemy'. The possibility that Germany might invade Turkey meant he was keen to open up an alternative route.

After a month in Lisbon, Clarke felt he had done well, establishing no fewer than sixteen routes for passing information to the enemy. He had also set up a communication plan with MI6 there. As ever, a message would contain a codename – in this case it was 'for Jack from Mayhew' – and then the request to 'counter' – meaning 'encourage' – a particular line.

Clarke divided the information he wanted to pass over between 'rumours' and the more serious 'leakages'. A rumour would 'give away nothing vital' – for instance that armoured troops in the Middle East were rearming. A leakage, on the other hand was 'intended to deceive the enemy's General Staff'. This would generally be more specific intelligence, apparently more useful – that a shipment of medium tanks was due to arrive at Suez the following week. With a leakage, Clarke said, 'it is more important to conceal its source of origin than to ensure its transmission'. If a leakage was recognised as being planted by the British, he warned, it risked revealing the real plan.

For leakages, Clarke proposed that A Force would prepare fake documents that would be sent by air to Lisbon, where they could be dropped in spots including the toilet of the Atlantico Hotel, a favourite haunt of Germans in the city, or the Deck Bar in the seaside resort of Estoril.

For rumours, he drew up a list of people he believed to be in contact with the man identified by the British as the chief German agent. How good the list was is debatable. High up on it was a leading Portuguese banker and a man that many in British intelligence believed to be in league with the Axis.

It wasn't hard to see why the spies thought this. The man dined regularly with the German ambassador, and his bank did a lot of business with the Axis powers. But another view was that he was simply a networker. He knew everyone, not just Germans. And his wife was Jewish, making him an unlikely Nazi. His abiding interest, not unusually in his line of work, seems to have been making money. That may have left him morally compromised, but it is a long way from being an Axis source.

Other people on Clarke's list included a man who haunted the Deck Bar at lunchtime and in the evenings, earwigging conversations; the Lisbon correspondent of the *Daily Express* – 'he is always short of copy, and is certain to give any juicy rumour a fair wind'; and a woman whom Clarke ungallantly described as the 'parrot-nosed one in Parque Hotel', who was 'in constant touch with Germans'.

But the most amazing channel that Clarke proposed using to pass leakages to the Germans was at the top of his list, headlined 'Letter Box 563'. A Force, Clarke said, would draft messages for this channel, which the MI6 station in Lisbon was to copy out in block capitals, sign 'BOX 563' and put in a letter. It should then be sent to none other than the military attaché at the German embassy.

Clarke's records are frustratingly vague on his Lisbon trip, and offer no further details on this channel. He was clearly confident anything he sent would be believed: he planned to use this link for 'leakages' – the type of false story that, if it were detected as such, risked compromising all his work.

Which leaves a fascinating – and unanswered – question: who did the German military attaché believe the trustworthy source 'Box 563' to be?

The most straightforward explanation is that Clarke, masquerading as a sympathetic journalist, had got himself recruited as a German spy, and agreed a means of communication. This would have been a very high-risk approach. If the Abwehr found out his real identity, then they would know that everything he was sending them was intended to mislead them. That would make Clarke a very useful source indeed, but not in the way he imagined.

There is, though, another possibility. In the years leading up to the war, Clarke had visited Germany several times, observing the country's increased militarisation, but also making contacts. In April 1939 he had gone to Berlin on a working holiday and, through a friend who was a diplomat, met several officers in German military intelligence. 'This was not without some profit,' he wrote after the war, 'for two at least were to cross my path again before very long on the other side of the fence.'

Clarke gave no further explanation for this cryptic remark, but we do know the identity of one of these Germans. Gerhard von Schwerin was a Prussian with whom Clarke had found a sort of kinship: they were almost the same age, and their careers had followed similar trajectories from teenage Great War volunteer to respected peacetime staff officer. In June 1939, Schwerin visited London. Ostensibly, he was there to take a look at Britain's military. Keen to show Germany that war wasn't a one-way bet, the War Office cooperated.

But Schwerin had a secret mission: he was there to urge the British government to abandon its policy of appeasement and confront Hitler. He hoped that a show of British strength might persuade his government to back down. Officials heard him out but he left unconvinced that anything would change. The German spent several evenings in Clarke's flat that summer, talking late into the night about military life and politics. He was far from certain that his country would win any war, but told Clarke that whatever the outcome, 'the aftermath will still be Communism'.*

By early 1941 Schwerin was very much on the other side of the fence, as one of Rommel's commanders heading across the desert towards Cairo. By the end of the year he was on the Russian front. With the outbreak of war, Schwerin had left military intelligence behind him and, whatever his personal antipathy towards Hitler, there's little evidence that he was involved in any active resistance to Naziism.

But Clarke was close to one German officer who had flirted with betraying the Fuhrer. Might he have known others? Is it plausible that the recipient of letters from Box 563 knew exactly who was sending them, and was happy to pass them on in an effort to deceive his own leadership?

Some members of A Force certainly believed that their chief had contacts with Abwehr officers who were working to undermine Hitler. It may well be that this simply reflects the awe in which those who worked for Clarke held him: a man of mystery who simply knew everyone. But it's hard to know which is more improbable:

---

* Clarke later claimed that on the eve of war, he had found Schwerin's visiting card on his doormat with the words '*Auf wiedersehen*' written on the back. However he didn't mention it in his diary at the time, which feels like an extraordinary omission.

that an undercover British officer persuaded German intelligence that he was their man, or that he had someone in German intelligence working for him.

Clarke's Lisbon channels would be less successful than the ones he set up in Turkey. The local MI6 station had no one willing or able to take on Vladimir Wolfson's role as a shepherd of misinformation, and as the war went on A Force tended to rely on Istanbul. It's now impossible to be definitive about whether Box 563 was ever used. Many of A Force's records were destroyed both during the war and afterwards. In the thousands of pages left after the war, I can find no sign of a message being sent.

But to have set up the system at all was a risk that seems uncharacteristic for Clarke, whose approach was usually so meticulous and careful, never trying to pass the whole story by one channel, never drawing attention to what he was doing. Perhaps he was finding his standard route of getting stories over to the enemy was simply too slow. Or perhaps the thrill of a month as a real-life Hannay had gone to his head.

Chapter 15

In Cairo, by September Auchinleck was preparing to attack. That meant A Force moving to a new phase of Operation Collect. So far the idea had been to keep the Germans on the hop by building up false warnings of a coming assault, only to stand them down. But now they wanted the enemy to relax, and think that no attack was imminent. How could they suddenly reverse their message? John Shearer, Auchinleck's head of intelligence – like Clarke, an inheritance from Wavell – had an idea about that.

Shearer wanted to use Cheese. The codename that had been given to Renato Levi was now being applied to the imaginary wireless operator he'd told his handlers he'd installed in Cairo before he left. So far, little had been done with him. After Kenyon Jones's first thrilling moment of contact in July, the signals sent by Cheese had been low level. The responses to his messages from his German handlers in Italy hadn't been enormously encouraging, either: the replies had been poorly encoded, and often repeated questions that had already been answered. There was not much to suggest that the enemy viewed Cheese as an important asset. Still, in Cairo, they took a little encouragement from the slipshod nature of the communication. They'd heard nothing from Levi since his return to Italy. Perhaps, they told themselves, the carelessness was a sign that he was working the other end personally. It would certainly be in his character.

At first, their messages were composed with caution. A Force and SIME didn't know what Levi was telling his handlers about the spy network he'd built up in Cairo, and they didn't want to send anything that contradicted him. Their solution to this problem was to do some invention of their own. Cheese signalled that he'd developed a 'good South African contact'. Because this was an invention at the Cairo end, they could do with him what they liked.

With Auchinleck's attack approaching, this contact was built up. His name was 'Piet', the Germans were told, and he was a non-commissioned officer working in a secure job at Grey Pillars. He had a motive for treachery: he liked women, and was short of cash. The imaginary agent Cheese now had an imaginary sub-agent.

To cover the coming offensive, codenamed 'Crusader', Shearer wanted to put over a sophisticated story, and he didn't see how he could hope that it would be communicated in the piecemeal way that Clarke had been working. It needed to be told directly to the enemy. Cheese offered a route to doing that. Shearer drew up a plan. Such was its secrecy that he didn't commit it to paper, instead telling it to an officer who was on his way to London, and who dictated it on arrival.

What was particularly surprising about the story Shearer wanted to tell was that it involved revealing what A Force had been up to for the last couple of months. 'The British purposely spread rumours that they intended to attack on the above dates because they were themselves apprehensive of being attacked by the Germans,' Shearer wrote in an outline of the tale he aimed to transmit. 'After their abortive offensive in June, they realised that the Germans were considerably superior in tanks, both in respect of numbers and performance.' This all had the benefit of being true, as everyone in Cairo was painfully aware. 'The British therefore put out the rumours that they were about to attack, to cover their own weakness.'

Rommel would be told that the real preparations now underway for 'Crusader' were simply more efforts to dissuade him from attacking. As Clarke had done, Shearer wove things that the enemy would have observed into his narrative. There were the dummy tanks of the 38th Royal Tank Regiment, destroyed that month as the Germans advanced, which showed the British had been playing tricks. Then there was the ongoing removal of exhausted Australian troops from Tobruk and their replacement with Poles. 'The plan is that the Poles should cover the evacuation, and should then be left to their fate,' Shearer said. 'Owing to the well-known reputation of the British for fair play, it is believed that Rommel would not credit such a dastardly plan.'

To Clarke, it felt a little too clever. 'Ingenious,' he concluded, 'but not an easy plan to implement'. He did not, as a rule, approve of magicians revealing their secrets.

Whatever private misgivings Clarke had about Shearer's plan, he was in no position to do anything about them. After a month in

Lisbon, he received orders to go to London. His activities in Cairo had been watched with increasing interest, and now the top brass wanted to hear about them.

When Clarke had left the city ten months earlier, it had been in the midst of the Blitz, so he had some idea of what would greet him. In May he had received a telegram from home: 'Regret your flat completely destroyed'. But knowing about something isn't the same as seeing it. He mournfully approached the street in Mayfair that he'd called home. All that was left of the flat he loved, he wrote, was 'a dusty heap of brickwork'.

Meanwhile his Commandos were still viewed as unproven. They had carried out a successful raid, on Norway's Lofoten Islands, blowing things up and capturing prisoners and codebooks, but Clarke's original vision of constant 'butcher and bolt' raids had not materialised.

But if these were causes of grief and frustration, most of his visit was a pleasure. To soldiers kicking their heels while they waited to get into the war, he was that treasured thing: a visitor back from where the action was. People wanted to hear his impressions of the desert war and of the apparently unbeatable Rommel.

More than that, he was a man with an idea to sell. To the War Office in London, the idea of actively pushing false stories in order to lead your enemy into making mistakes was a new one. Clarke had a gospel to proclaim, and he set about it with enthusiasm.

On a warm, cloudy Monday at the end of September, just over a week after he'd arrived in England, Clarke made his way up St James's Street, round the corner from the Ritz Hotel, to an apparently vacant building. Number 58 had a 'To Let' sign outside, but he went in anyway. This was the London headquarters of MI5, Britain's security service, charged with protecting the country's secrets from Nazi spies.

He was there to see MI5's military liaison, but after that meeting, he was taken to meet Guy Liddell, the deputy director. Clarke's account of his work in the Middle East had a relevance to the spy-catchers of St James that he couldn't have appreciated.

Cheese, Clarke learned, was very far from the only double agent working for British intelligence in 1941. Right from the start of the war, MI5 had been capturing German spies and using them against their controllers. Some, like Renato Levi, had volunteered for this, turning themselves over to British intelligence before they'd even been caught. Others had accepted switching sides as the only sensible course after capture.

Success had bred success, thanks to the Abwehr's unfortunate habit of telling its agents about each other so that they could work together. There was now an entire organisation of MI5 officers running spies that the Abwehr still believed to be loyal, overseen by the 'Twenty Committee', which took its name from a Latin pun – its business was to double-cross: 'XX'.

But although it was building an impressive force of double agents, MI5 had so far only deployed them to catch other spies. People talked about the idea that they could pass false information back, of course, but no one could agree what it should be, or to what end. Now Clarke had turned up on their doorstep, with some very clear thoughts on the subject.

Where Clarke was outgoing, Liddell was softly spoken to the point of shyness. He was a thoughtful spycatcher whose character is captured in the codename given to his Top Secret diaries: 'Wallflower'. These reveal a wry outlook on the world, a man wrestling to balance the need to keep the country safe with the desire to have a country worth saving.

He was impressed with Clarke, though. 'I said that if we had a really good liaison and knew more about his schemes we could probably give him considerable help,' he recorded. He quizzed Clarke about the practical arrangements, both in terms of putting over stories and deciding which tales to tell in the first place. Liddell was impressed, and even a little jealous. To his mind it confirmed what he'd been telling his bosses, 'namely that they had a machine but they did not make proper use of it'.

A couple of days later, Liddell went to lunch with the chief of MI6, Stewart Menzies, famously known as 'C'. His mind was still on what Clarke had told him. 'We discussed in general terms the extent to which we could probably assist Egypt in their schemes of deception,' he wrote afterwards. 'Stewart was quite sure this could and should be done.' Menzies even proposed bringing in MI6's office in New York, which was running covert propaganda efforts to stir up Americans against Germany. One of its techniques was the planting of false news stories in US papers. Clarke's work was very much in this line.

That Thursday Clarke appeared as guest of honour at two separate very secret meetings. In the morning he descended the stairs into the War Cabinet bunker, deep under Whitehall, to brief a meeting of intelligence chiefs – including Menzies – and planners about his work and ideas. Then, after lunch, he made his way across St James's Park and back to MI5, where he had been invited to a meeting of the Twenty Committee.

These had been taking place weekly since the start of the year. Attendance was good thanks partly to the organisers' efforts to ensure that, however bad rationing got, there were always currant buns available. Clarke, fresh from Cairo and Lisbon, may not have appreciated how precious these were.

The committee's job was to coordinate Britain's double agent work. A large part of that was reconciling the need to keep secrets with the requirement that the spies Germany sent to Britain should have something to report.

Anyone running a double agent faces this problem. If the agent is to be valued by the people who think they're in control, then they need to send back good information. But what is it safe for the enemy to know? With many double agents in play, the problem was multiplied: their reports should neither contradict each other nor look coordinated. They should seem valuable without imparting anything of real value.

It didn't help that the instinct of the authorities was often that the enemy should be told as little as possible. But the bigger problem was that no one could agree how these double agents should be used. The military, asked for deceptive ideas that could be passed over, generally had few suggestions beyond putting over the idea that morale was high and troops were well-equipped.

For Clarke, who was used to drawing up and executing plans swiftly on the authority of his commander, this bureaucracy was a jarring change of pace.

The committee was anxious to hear of his experiences with German intelligence. Much of their war felt a little theoretical, a game of chess against a distant enemy. Here was someone whose suntan testified to his practical experience. Clarke, always happy to have an audience, held forth. German intelligence was, he explained, best on things its forces were in direct contact with. The enemy's knowledge of what was going on further away was poor.

They talked about how London could help Cairo, and T. A. 'TAR' Robertson, who ran MI5's double agents section, invited him to come back the next day for a more detailed discussion.

Liddell joined that chat too. He was supportive in principle of the idea of using agents in Britain to pass deception to Germany, but cautioned Clarke that he saw the double-cross network as a long-term operation. Any 'downright lying', he said, risked revealing that agents had been turned. That, of course, was precisely what Shearer was preparing to do in Cairo with Cheese. Liddell, with more double agents under his control, was handling them with more care. The most he would allow was for them to send their German controllers 'tentative half-truths'.

Clarke now turned his attention to a bigger target. Getting the support of spies was all very well, but if deception was going to work, it would need the support of the military. He had set out his thoughts in a 'Most Secret' paper that he had circulated at the highest levels of the War Office.

After nearly a year as a deceiver, having seen both successes and failures, Clarke here wrote down for the first time his vision for the work. What he was talking about, he explained, was far more than mere propaganda – misleading information that might lower enemy morale. It was actually possible to sell false stories to the enemy commanders. What was more, this was a goal worth taking time over. Senior officers, he said, 'must be prepared to go to endless inconvenience and even serious risks' for the prize of 'strategic surprise through deliberate deception'.

MI5's agents weren't being used properly, he said – Liddell, frustrated at the lack of military cooperation with the Twenty Committee, may well have encouraged him to make this point – and the information they were passing was too sparse, and of too low a quality. Only if they gave better material would they be able to win the Abwehr's confidence in the way that they would need to if they were to start spinning lies.

But this wasn't enough. Like a good magician, Clarke knew that he needed to show things to the audience, as well as tell them. '"Oral" sources of information will never sustain a deception unless some "visual" support is produced to confirm it,' he wrote. 'The degree of success of the deception will usually depend upon the scale on which visible evidence is provided to support the whispered story.' That would mean dummy units, at the very least.

All of these pieces need to work together. 'The complete picture must never be presented through any one source: the enemy must be left to build up a jigsaw puzzle himself,' he wrote. 'The pieces, consisting of rumours, leakages and visual evidence, must be supplied to him through varying sources.'

One of Clarke's staff explained this to a colleague a little more colloquially: 'Never give the Boche the thing on a plate – give him the little bits and let him piece them together and think he has been clever.'

That was the means, then, but what was Clarke's goal? It was breathtaking in its ambition. 'All lies, however big, must themselves form pieces in one grand jigsaw puzzle,' he concluded. 'The basis of all future deception should be a completely bogus plan for winning the war.'

Deception was as old as warfare, but what Clarke was describing was something quite new. It was not simply a question of whether an attack was going to come on the left flank or the right, but whether it was going to come in Norway or France, through Italy or the Balkans. This had never been a possibility before because war had never been fought on such a scale before. Clarke had grasped that the global nature of the war made deception a more powerful weapon than ever. Soldiers in the wrong trench can move when an attack comes elsewhere. Armies in the wrong country are useless. And if they can be kept in the wrong place long enough, it might even be possible to defeat them without having to kill them.

It was a message his audience was ready to hear. Hitler's forces were pushing hard into Russia, apparently on course to repeat their triumphs in Western Europe of the previous year. Rommel had shown what the German army was capable of in Africa. Britain felt weak in comparison. As the Joint Intelligence Staff pointed out in their own paper supporting Clarke's arguments, 'we, unlike the Germans, have not the troops, shipping or the interior lines necessary to give threats the backing of reality'. Deception could make them look stronger than they were.

Chapter 16

The following week Clarke was summoned to address the Chiefs of Staff Committee, Britain's highest military decision-making body. The three men in charge of the fighting services met each morning at half past ten in a grand room on the second floor of a vast government building overlooking St James's Park. Clarke made his way through a great pair of bronze doors guarded by armed sentries, past the machine-gun post that protected the route up to the prime minister's private apartment – Downing Street had been deemed insufficiently bomb-proof – and up the wide staircase that was designed to impress upon the visitor that they were in the governing halls of the world's greatest imperial power.

Outside the room where the chiefs met was a hat-stand bearing their caps and a small collection of senior officers, waiting for their turn to be called in. Clarke was second on the agenda.

To a lieutenant colonel less self-confident, this might have been a daunting prospect, but it's unlikely to have troubled Clarke much. Apart from anything else, he counted two of the three chiefs as allies: his old commander, John Dill, and Air Chief Marshal Charles Portal, who'd served alongside Clarke in the Middle East before the war. The only moment in the meeting when he found himself lost for words was when, as the other chiefs asked questions, Dill passed Clarke a note inviting him to his wedding the next day.

Step by step, Clarke took the room through his experiences and his ideas for taking deception to a new level, and added another point: deception-planning should ultimately be in the hands of a single man.

Two days and one wedding later, he returned to the committee to hear its verdict. They were persuaded of his case. Two years into the war, they knew they needed all the good ideas they could get. The only real question was who should take charge of deception in London. The intelligence chiefs had written a description of the ideal candidate: 'must possess considerable ingenuity and imagination, an aptitude for improvisation, plenty of initiative, be something of an actor, in addition to having a sound military background'.

It wasn't a very subtle hint about who they backed for the role, and Dudley Pound, the First Sea Lord, acted on it. He asked Clarke whether he would be willing to take on the job.

It must have been tempting: after leaving London under a bit of a cloud the previous year, he would be returning in triumph, to a job right in the heart of the war-planning operation, on what was surely a fast track to promotion. He would have a global remit, and when the moment came, he would oversee the deception operations for the Allies' return to the continent.

Which is why it was so surprising to the committee that Clarke refused. The reason he gave was that he was working for Auchinleck, 'who alone was conducting active operations at the time, and I felt sure my place was to stay with him'.

Was that the whole truth? There was of course Clarke's love for the Middle East. He would also have been painfully aware of how the bureaucratic wrangling and frustration of the War Office compared to the free hand he enjoyed in Cairo. In London he would find himself wrestling with MI5, MI6 and the military establishment. In Egypt, where he worked well with Maunsell and had the support of his commander, he had only to think of a plan to put it into action.

Two weeks in Britain in the autumn might also have reinforced to Clarke how much better life was in Cairo, where there was no blackout or rationing. He liked fine food and drink and even at the Ritz, one of his favoured London hangouts, both were in short supply. Back in Cairo, he could spend his evenings dining and sipping cocktails in Shepheard's, surrounded by admiring younger men like David Stirling and Tony Simonds, and holding forth on unconventional warfare.

Perhaps, too, he was aware that A Force was as close to a private army as he was likely to get. It was hardly likely that the person who got the London job would be allowed to spend weeks on end playing at spies in neutral capitals. And, as he said, Auchinleck was the only person fighting the enemy at that moment. In October 1941, the war was simply much more fun in Cairo than it was in London.

The chiefs must have looked a little put out at this. To placate them, Clarke tried an analogy aimed at the English upper classes.

'You can't pinch a man's butler when he has only been lent to you for the night,' he said, and at that they laughed, and agreed to let him return to Auchinleck.

The crucial point, as far as he was concerned, was that they'd agreed to his main proposal, the establishment of a 'London Controlling Section' – another deliberately vague name – reporting to them, to plan, implement and coordinate deception operations. Less than a year after setting out for Egypt, Clarke had designed a new weapon of war, and put it at the heart of British operations. He was riding high.

On Monday, 13 October, Clarke boarded a flight at Whitchurch airfield, outside Bristol, bound once again for Lisbon. Shearer's message setting out the next phase of Collect had arrived while he'd been in London. In line with Liddell's injunction that MI5's Double-Cross network would transmit only half-truths, it was agreed that the only thing the Germans would learn from their European agents was that there was good reason to think there could be no Middle East offensive before Christmas.

One such reason was that the troops might be needed elsewhere. Part of the 'Collect' story was that the British were considering sending troops to the Caucasus, to help the defence of Russia. That, went the argument, would leave too few troops in Egypt to attack Rommel.

After three days in Lisbon, Clarke concluded that 'the news of "no desert offensive before Christmas" was successfully percolated into the German embassy'. He didn't record how he achieved that. Had he posted a letter from 'Box 563', or spoken to his 'controller' in person? He must have done more than simply talking loudly in a lot of bars.

There was another neutral country where he could try to get some channels going, and on Thursday, 16 October, Clarke left Lisbon for Madrid, with the goal of passing 'confirmatory evidence' to the German military attaché. And it was there, the following evening, that he was arrested.

This was a disaster. Spain may have been neutral, but its fascist government leaned firmly towards the Nazis. The Abwehr employed between seventy and a hundred people in Germany's Madrid embassy. Clarke was a British officer travelling out of uniform, under a false cover – a spy, in fact. If he were captured on the battlefield, he would expect to be treated as a prisoner of war. But what rights or protections would he have now if the Germans decided they wanted to grab him and interrogate him?

There's no question that bundling Clarke into a car, whisking him to Germany and then torturing him would have been a worthwhile exercise. Few people, if anyone, outside Britain knew as much as Clarke did about his country's intelligence secrets. He had sat in on the committee that controlled MI5's double agents. He hadn't yet been formally informed that Bletchley Park, British intelligence's code-breaking headquarters, had got into Germany's 'unbreakable' Enigma, but as intelligence adviser to successive commanders-in-chief in the Middle East, he may well have been aware that an unusually reliable source was providing incredible levels of information about Rommel's supply lines and Axis shipping in the Mediterranean. He knew from things that had been said at the Twenty Committee that the Allies had 'secret sources' that were telling them things about the Abwehr's thinking.

On a military level he knew the precise detail of British forces in the Middle East, and Auchinleck's plans for them. He was responsible for MI9 escape lines in Greece, the Middle East and Africa. Barely a week earlier, he had been in the War Cabinet bunker. If someone could get Clarke to talk, he had an awful lot to say.

What made all of this far more complicated were the circumstances of his arrest. Lieutenant Colonel Dudley Wrangel Clarke, Royal Artillery, GSO 1 (Intelligence) at GHQ Middle East, Personal Intelligence Officer for Special Duties to the Commander-in-Chief, Officer Commanding A Force, founder of the Commandos, had been, in the words of an urgent cable sent to the Foreign Office in London, 'arrested in a main street dressed, down to a brassiere, as a woman'.

Chapter 17

It hadn't been an easy few months at the British embassy in Madrid. In some ways, things were going well. The diplomats were succeeding in their first, above-all-else goal of keeping Spain from joining the war on Hitler's side. To this end, spies in the embassy were funnelling huge bribes to sympathetic generals. Probably more significant in this cause had been Wavell's defeat of the Italians at the start of the year, a sign that the war wasn't a one-way bet for a fascist leader. Unable to agree terms with Hitler, the dictator Francisco Franco was so far staying on the sidelines.

But behind the embassy walls there were tensions between the ambassador, Sir Samuel Hoare, and the spies there operating under diplomatic cover. Hoare had been an intelligence officer himself in the previous war, working in Russia and then in Rome, where his most famous recruit was a journalist who at the time supported fighting Germany: one Benito Mussolini. Hoare had paid the future dictator £100 a week to produce pro-war propaganda. It is possible that subsequent developments in Italy explained the ambassador's cynicism about the value of intelligence operations. Or perhaps he simply felt MI6 was putting his careful work with the Spanish government at risk.

His suspicions had, to his mind, been confirmed that summer when MI6 discovered that one of their officers in the embassy, a Frenchman, had contacted the Vichy French government and 'divulged many secrets'. The traitor was lured to the embassy, knocked out and sedated as part of a plan to spirit him out of the country. This went wrong when, as the car carrying him was passing through a village in southern Spain, he woke up and began shouting for help. Desperate to subdue him, his captors hit him on the head with a revolver, accidentally killing him. His body was disposed of, and his wife told he'd been drowned when the ship he was travelling on was sunk. German and Vichy diplomats, however, got hold of the truth, and complained to the Spanish Foreign Ministry. Radio France broadcast a report of the incident. 'It could not have been a worse affair,' Hoare sighed in a message back to the Foreign Office.

Clarke's arrest came just as the embassy was putting out these fires. His crime seems to have been his outfit: a knee-length floral dress, high heels, stockings, a necklace, gloves to the elbow, and a tight turban to cover his military haircut. He had accessorised with a small handbag. It wasn't unflattering, but it wasn't especially convincing either. Clarke wasn't a tall man – a shade under five foot eight – or particularly broad, but he was six inches taller than the average Spanish woman at the time, and his Adam's apple was clearly visible. The turban didn't entirely conceal his receding hairline, either.

In a way, it shouldn't have been a diplomatic problem: Clarke was claiming to be a journalist, not a soldier or a government official, so even if he'd done something stupid, it was just another case of a Brit abroad getting themselves into trouble – a routine consular issue. But there was an uneasy sense that there was more to it. Composing a cable to London on the evening after Clarke was arrested, Arthur Yencken, the Counsellor at the embassy, tried to pull the facts together.

'Dudley Clarke, "Times" war correspondent, arrived in Madrid on October 16th on his way to Egypt via Gibraltar,' he began. Clarke had visited the embassy, where he told William Torr, the military attaché, 'that he was also employed by the Joint Intelligence Bureau, Near East, and was under the War Office.' They'd then been joined by Leonard Hamilton Stokes, the local MI6 head of station. Torr and Hamilton Stokes had been 'particularly struck by his intimate knowledge of military secrets and plans of the Naval Intelligence, Middle East.'

After Clarke's arrest, one of the embassy staff had managed to get hold of the interpreter who had helped the police interrogate him. He said the Englishman had claimed to be a novelist who 'wanted to study the reactions of men to women in the street'. The police view apparently was that this was 'a homosexual affair', and their inclination was to fine Clarke and let him go.

Clarke told a different story to the British consul who visited him in custody that morning, that 'he was taking the feminine garments to a lady in Gibraltar and thought that he would try them on for a prank.' However, Yencken observed acidly, 'this hardly squares with the fact that the garments and shoes fitted him.' The diplomat was clearly thinking along similar lines to the police.

The problem was the enemy. 'The Germans apparently think that they have got on to a first class espionage incident and will certainly make the most of it.' The police had searched Clarke's luggage, and found 'another complete set of women's clothes, a war correspondent's uniform and a note book with a number of names of people in London in it. Also papers and a roll of super-fine toilet paper.' The last item had 'particularly excited the police who are submitting each sheet to chemical tests', confirming they were considering the possibility that Clarke was a spy.

If the perplexed Yencken was unaware of Clarke's importance, it was hardly his fault that his clandestine colleagues chose to keep him in the dark. Hamilton Stokes knew exactly who Clarke was and what he was supposed to be doing in Madrid. But as Clarke was sticking to his cover story with the police, the spies followed his lead in the embassy. The most surprising thing was that they told Yencken anything at all. Probably, as Clarke was known to have met them both at the embassy, they judged that a complete denial of knowledge was implausible.

Yencken's Saturday night cable to Sir Alexander Cadogan, the permanent secretary of the Foreign Office, was prompted not by security fears, but concern about an embarrassing scandal involving a correspondent from a leading newspaper. 'I need hardly point out the damage this incident will do to us and the "Times" here,' Yencken wrote. 'Jokes have already begun about "the editor" of the "Times" masquerading as a woman.'

In London they couldn't have cared less about jokes, or indeed the reputation of *The Times*. Hamilton Stokes was having his own cable exchange with his boss, Sir Stewart Menzies. In reply to anxious messages from Menzies about what secrets Clarke might reveal, the station chief replied that the police remained of the view that the unusually-dressed Englishman was a 'homosexualist' but that the Gestapo was pushing the line that he was a spy.

If Cadogan wasn't aware of Clarke's identity, Menzies must then have told him, because that Sunday saw a flurry of activity in Whitehall. Cadogan sent the telegram on to Philip Whitefoord, the

Deputy Director of Military Intelligence at the War Office. And at this point, the military showed that it still knew how to form square around an endangered colleague. Whatever trouble Clarke might have got himself into, he was a well-liked and well-connected officer. Whitefoord and his bosses told the Foreign Office that the most important thing was that, once released, their man should be got over the border either to Gibraltar or Portugal, and then allowed to carry on to Cairo.

'He has verbal information for General Auchinleck which no one else can give at the moment,' Whitefoord said. The Auk would also be able to deal with 'the disciplinary side of the affair,' he said. 'Clarke is on his staff.' The spooks and the diplomats, in other words, could do their job and get Clarke out of jail, and then they could get their mitts off him. In Cairo, Auchinleck weighed in, demanding Clarke be sent back to him 'as soon as possible'.

Cadogan pushed back, insisting that whoever was going to receive Clarke in Lisbon or Gibraltar be told the circumstances of the arrest 'so that they may all know that they may have a lunatic to deal with'. That seemed to persuade the War Office.

'Clarke arrested Madrid disguised as a woman,' Whitefoord's cable to Gibraltar began. 'We hope fact that he is a British officer may be unknown to Spanish authorities and must be kept secret. Please keep him under strict surveillance and despatch to Middle East by next plane. If he shows signs of mental derangement he should however be sent home by first ship.'

Cadogan, meanwhile, cabled Madrid. 'If Clarke is released, you should get him to Gibraltar by quickest means,' he began. 'It would be well that he should be accompanied by someone responsible. You should ascertain from Clarke nature of his papers which Spanish authorities may have examined and whether documents might compromise anything.'

He closed with a warning that should have impressed upon the diplomats the seriousness of the matter: 'In no circumstances should it be revealed that C. is a British officer.'

Amid the flurry that his arrest had caused in both Madrid and London the man himself seemed strangely untroubled. The consul who visited him under arrest found him 'calm and unconcerned'. Clarke's ability to stay cool under pressure was one of the things Wavell liked about him. A Force staff appreciated it too. 'Everything

was always funny,' one of his officers said. 'This extraordinary quality not only made employment in A Force a joy; it had an extremely
practical value since it took the drama out of nail-biting operations.'
But sitting in a Spanish cell must have been a test of even Clarke's
sangfroid. This had the potential to go very badly.

It was not until the Tuesday evening that Yencken cabled back to
Cadogan: 'Mr Clarke was released last night and ordered to leave
Spain within 48 hours. He is leaving tonight for Gibraltar accom-
panied by His Majesty's Consul. Police authorities have returned all
Mr Clarke's papers which, according to him, are without exception
personal, private and entirely uncompromising.'

From Yencken's point of view, it was a happy ending, although
someone did indeed leak the story. MI6 intercepted a report from
Madrid to Berlin about the arrest of 'Wrangal Craker, the Madrid
correspondent of the London "Times"' – the Spanish police don't
seem to have established Clarke's real name. It said that, perhaps as
a result of the 'unusual circumstances of these times' and the 'working methods of British agents', he had been 'dressed as a woman',
although he had 'unusually big feet with a remarkable . . .' at which
point the message was, sadly, marked 'undecipherable'.

After sending his telegram, Yencken slipped a couple of photographs into an envelope and addressed them, 'Personal and Secret'
to Cadogan. 'Dear Alec,' he began. 'I enclose two photographs
which the Spanish police took of Dudley Clarke after his arrest.'

The first showed Clarke wearing the outfit in which he'd been
arrested. The second showed him back in a pinstripe suit, with
bow tie and pocket handkerchief. Intriguingly, both had the air of
slightly awkward studio portraits, rather than shame-faced police
mugshots. More pictures were doing the rounds: Clarke had posed
both sitting and standing. Given the circumstances, he didn't look
all that perturbed.

When they arrived a week later, Cadogan put them back into the
envelope with a note to send them on to Menzies: 'C might like to
see.'

The views of C on this aren't in the public domain, but over at
MI5 Guy Liddell, who a few days earlier had been so impressed by
Clarke, was now revising his opinion, expressing the view of the
professional spy about the amateur. 'I am afraid that after his stay in
Lisbon as a bogus journalist he has got rather over-confident about

his powers,' he wrote in his diary. 'It would be much better if these people confined themselves to their proper job.'

A couple of weeks later, Liddell had heard the full story, including the circumstances of Clarke's arrest. 'At the time he was dressed as a woman complete with brassiere etc,' he said. 'Why he wore this disguise nobody quite knows.'

Having escaped the clutches of the Spanish police and got beyond the reach of German intelligence, Clarke still had to account for himself to his own side. The hopes of Whitefoord and others that he might swiftly be sent on to Cairo, and the whole matter brushed under the carpet, were dashed before he even got out of jail.

On Monday, 20 October, Cadogan had held an emergency meeting on Clarke's arrest. Any doubt about how seriously this was being taken can be dispelled by looking at who was present: Anthony Eden, the Foreign Secretary; David Margesson, the War Secretary; John Dill, the Chief of the Imperial General Staff, and Winston Churchill, the Prime Minister. These were the men who were running the war.

Dill was always going to defend his protégé. But the situation facing Clarke was serious. When Cadogan had suggested Clarke might be a 'lunatic', it could have been interpreted as a charitable interpretation. He wouldn't have been the first soldier to have cracked under the pressure of war, and there were, from a military point of view, worse explanations. In the thinking in 1941, in Britain as much as in Spain, men wearing women's clothing was linked to homosexuality – which was, officially at least, banned from the military.

The reality was a little more complicated. The King's Regulations stated that 'confirmed homosexuals whose rehabilitation is unlikely should be removed from the Army by the most expeditious and appropriate means'. But in fact senior soldiers were often tolerant. They were too short of fighting men to start turning any away. Many had served in India, where attitudes were different from England. In Cairo, Shepheard's Hotel – where Clarke lived – was known to be a meeting place for gay officers, and the Royal Military Police made no effort to interfere.

As for Maunsell, in charge of security in Cairo, he couldn't have cared less. Every so often, someone would approach him awkwardly to inform him, in tones of hushed embarrassment, that a member of SIME staff was having an affair with another man. Maunsell, who reckoned this was true of about four of his officers over the course of the war, found people's concerns about his men ridiculous: 'They all behaved in a perfectly civilised way and I had no reason to believe their proclivities interfered with or threatened their work.'

The attitude of Dill, therefore, would probably not so much have been that Clarke wasn't gay as that it didn't greatly matter if he was. The difficulty was that he had been caught up in a scandal. Worse, whatever the truth about his attire, he had put himself, and everything he knew, at risk. Churchill was firm. If Clarke was released, he must be sent back to Britain.

So it was that on Wednesday, 22 October, nine days after he had departed Britain in triumph, Clarke boarded a merchant ship travelling from Gibraltar to Liverpool, returning home in disgrace.

Chapter 18

But fortune, in a very strange way, was smiling on Clarke. The German navy was about to save his career. It would do it by trying to drown him.

Clarke was travelling on the merchant steamer *Ariosto*, part of convoy HG-75, which was largely carrying iron ore. The *Ariosto* had done this route several times before, and its luck had run out.

Trailing the convoy was Wolfpack Breslau, a group of six U-boats coming to the end of a month-long patrol that had taken them out into the middle of the Atlantic and now down to the coast of Spain. They had been waiting there almost a week for a chance like this.

Just after midnight on the Thursday night, one of the U-boats fired three torpedoes, hitting an escort vessel, HMS *Cossack*. Much of the forward section of the ship was destroyed, and she caught fire. The convoy steamed on. Six hours later, a second U-boat fired five torpedoes. The first three exploded in columns of fire ten seconds apart from each other. The other two were heard to hit three minutes later. The *Ariosto* was one of three merchantmen holed. Six of the crew were killed, but Clarke, along with 44 other survivors, made it onto a lifeboat. His week was not, on the face of it, going well.

Most of the passengers were picked up by another merchantman in the convoy, but Clarke was rescued by HMS *Lamerton*, a destroyer. And here came an extraordinary moment of good chance. The next day a British plane spotted an Italian submarine and bombed it, preventing it from submerging. *Lamerton* was ordered to finish the submarine off, which she did after a long gun battle. But now low on fuel, *Lamerton* turned back to Gibraltar.

Which was why on Thursday, 30 October, just over a week after he had put to sea, Clarke cabled Dill to say that he was back in Gibraltar and ask whether he should still try to come back to the UK. The chief of staff saw his moment. 'Clarke has been delayed by about a week by this mischance, and as sailings from Gibraltar are irregular, there may still be further delay,' Dill wrote to Churchill. Meanwhile Clarke was 'urgently required' in Cairo.

Wouldn't it be better, Dill suggested, to have Clarke questioned on Gibraltar and, if his story seemed 'reasonable' and he was 'sound in mind and body', send him on his way? The release of Clarke by the Spanish police, the lack of further incident and the passage of time had done their work. Churchill consented.

The man who would decide Clarke's future was Lord Gort, the governor-general and commander-in-chief of Gibraltar. He'd had an outstanding record in the Great War, culminating in a Victoria Cross for an action in which he'd crossed open ground under fire, while wounded, to lead a tank in support of his battalion. Promoted between the wars to Chief of the Imperial General Staff, his weaknesses as a general had been exposed in France, and like many of Britain's other failed commanders, he'd been shunted off out of the country. There was not much love lost between Gort and Dill, but like Clarke, the governor-general was an army lifer.

Clarke's defence was, according to cables sent to MI6, that the 'incident in Madrid was carefully calculated' and 'nothing (repeat nothing) whatever compromised'. Whether Gort believed that or not, he clearly agreed that Clarke's fitness to serve was a matter for Auchinleck, not the Foreign Office or indeed the prime minister. A Force's cross-dressing leader was told he could proceed to Cairo.

It would be nearly a month before Gort's report arrived in London. It was, Dill told Churchill, 'of such length that you certainly should not be bothered to read it'. That may have been the intention. Clarke, Dill told the prime minister, 'showed no signs of insanity but undertook a foolhardy and misjudged action with a definite purpose, for which he had rehearsed his art beforehand.' The result was that 'he gravely risked undoing some of the excellent work already done in UK and en route there'. Gort had concluded the incident had given Clarke 'sufficient shock to make him more prudent in the immediate future.'

Churchill, though, still had a question. 'What was his purpose?' he scrawled on the bottom of Dill's note.

Eighty years later, the question remains. Not so much why Clarke went to Madrid – his explanation, that he wanted to build up channels for passing disinformation, seems plausible – but why he stepped out on a Friday night in a floral dress and heels.

Clarke's friends always resisted the idea that the lifelong bachelor was anything other than a heterosexual man who had simply failed to meet the right girl. Products of their time, they felt that his character needed to be defended from suggestions to the contrary, and they pointed to the way he was always surrounded by beautiful women. There must have been some reasonable explanation for the Madrid escapade, they said, without ever suggesting one.

Clarke's goddaughter didn't know him well, but assumed he was bisexual. Her mother, who had worked with him during the war, described him as the kind of chap with whom a lady could enjoy an evening around town without worrying that he was going to try anything on the way home. And even the nickname Clarke's friends gave the women around him, 'Dudley's duchesses', carries a hint that his intentions towards them weren't sexual.

It certainly seems that Clarke enjoyed dressing as a woman. At staff college a decade earlier, he had written the class pantomime, casting himself as 'Volga Olga, quite the Worst Woman in the World'. Olga, described in the stage directions as 'an exotic figure', is a seductive spy who speaks in double-entendres and in the final act sneaks into a senior officer's bedroom dressed as a maid. Clarke kept photographs and a sketch of himself in the role. On its own, that means nothing: lots of straight men have acted in drag, and it was certainly in character for Clarke to take a scene-stealing role that had the potential to bring the house down.

But Clarke's own attitude to his arrest suggested he viewed it as a scandal, rather than a cunning ruse. When he came to record the activities of A Force, he was generally happy to discuss failures and mistakes, especially if they had a funny side. But he wrote almost nothing about his Spanish trip. His report of the 'Collect' disinformation campaign says that he tried to put the story that there would be no desert offensive before Christmas over to the German military attaché in Madrid, 'but this had to be abandoned'. It was not a week he wished to record for posterity. The angry defensiveness of his friends likewise suggests they knew this wasn't really a caper that had backfired.

So there was probably truth in what many people in London clearly believed: Clarke was a cross-dresser who, coming off the high of his triumphant trip to London, had been tempted to indulge in a secret pleasure in a city where no one knew him.

But that may not have been the whole truth. As ever with Clarke, there are other intriguing possibilities.

According to Dill, Clarke had told Gort that his arrest had been part of a plan. He'd 'worked up contact with certain German or German-controlled elements, with a view, later, to their providing a channel for the dissemination of false information'. It would be understandable to dismiss this, but what if it were true?

First, there is the question of how Clarke managed to get out of prison. For all that Britain's diplomats in Madrid were happy to take the credit, MI5's Guy Liddell had a different explanation.

'His speedy release can only be explained by the Germans having intervened on his behalf,' Liddell told his diary. 'It will be remembered that he made contact with a man he believed to be a German agent in Lisbon. This man was in Spain at the time and, believing Dudley Clarke to be an important agent who was ready to assist the Germans, intervened with the Spanish police.'

If this story is true, then it is quite a coincidence that a German who was willing and able to help Clarke out of trouble had travelled from Portugal to Spain at just the right moment to do so. Indeed, Clarke's claim seemed to be that it wasn't a coincidence at all: that the pair were in Madrid as part of his effort to secure his relationship with his German contact.

In Clarke's narrative, this German believed Clarke – presumably under his cover as a British journalist – was a potential Abwehr source. And Clarke said his Madrid 'disguise' was part of building that relationship.

When he'd spoken to the Twenty Committee in London, Clarke had claimed that he'd created an 'imaginary young woman in Lisbon' who was 'offering her services to the Germans'. Was this fictional woman in fact Clarke in a dress?

It's unlikely that even a very gullible German spy would have believed Clarke to actually be a woman. The Spanish police certainly weren't taken in. But that may not have been the intention. In both London and Berlin in the 1930s, there was a fair amount of cross-dressing at underground gatherings of gay men. Was this the point of kinship that Clarke had developed with his German contact? Had the two men travelled to a city where they were unknown in order to indulge in a little role-play? Is this why Clarke believed that letters from 'Box 563' would be accepted – because of a shared secret?

Clarke's great-nieces and -nephew tell a story they heard from their grandfather, Clarke's brother Thomas, that Great Uncle Dudley had been decorated by the Germans, who had believed he was working for the Nazis. It's tempting to dismiss this as a family myth. Both brothers were, after all, well able to spin a yarn. Or it may be a garbled reference to an A Force double agent codenamed 'Axe' who was awarded the Iron Cross by controllers who believed him still to be loyal. Clarke certainly left no record of personally receiving such a medal, but he did keep some details of his activities out of his later accounts. The entire Madrid episode shows a man willing to keep his masters in the dark about risks he was taking. Might he have had a German contact that he kept off the books?

If that was the case, it raises again the question of whether the German agent did believe Clarke was working for him, or whether he knew that Clarke was passing disinformation and was willing to help. Was this one of the intelligence officers that Clarke had got to know during his 1939 holiday in Berlin? That had once been, like Cairo, a city famous for its permissiveness.

It all sounds far-fetched, but then so does a senior British officer getting arrested wearing a dress. Perhaps it is simpler: Clarke had got carried away with his previous adventures in espionage and, remembering his triumphant stage appearance, wanted to see if he could pull the disguise off for real. His explanations were simply fabrications to get himself out of trouble. It's not like Clarke had a problem making things up. 'It may be,' Liddell said, 'that he is just the type who imagines himself as the super secret agent.'

Churchill seems to have settled for the explanation Dill gave him. Perhaps the prime minister accepted that dressing as a woman was just the sort of thing a chap had to do if he wanted to get alongside a German. Perhaps he felt a little eccentricity was a price worth paying for a creative thinker who was clearly highly valued by his superiors.

Indeed, a private life that had to be kept hidden would offer insight into Clarke's facility with concealment and false narratives. He had a couple of stories he would tell about women he had loved and lost, one a mysterious Russian fleeing the Bolsheviks, and the other an English girl who married a fellow officer. These tales might have been true, but if not they contained just the right amount of detail to be memorable without being verifiable.

There remained, of course, quite a lot of sniggering in private.

The naval attaché in Madrid, a friend of Churchill's, got hold of more copies of the pictures of Clarke after his arrest and sent them to one of Churchill's assistants. 'I promised them to the prime minister and thought you might like to see them too,' he wrote.

As for Clarke's assurance to Gort that he was carrying no compromising papers, this is questionable. Clarke was a habitual diarist. In the early part of the war he made longhand notes of his adventures, and from 1942 at least he was keeping notes of his appointments and travels in a small pocket diary, including information that, if nothing else, revealed him to be a person with the very highest levels of access. He kept all these diaries until his death, but for 1941 there is nothing in his files. It's unlikely that he wasn't keeping a diary. Did he discard it during his arrest? Was it the notebook with names of people in London found by the Spanish police? Perhaps it went to the bottom of the ocean on board the *Ariosto*. The only thing that's certain is that, whatever lessons Gort believed he'd learned, Clarke went on keeping his diary.

He did become more cautious in other ways. Around this time, Clarke began using aliases in his communications. He went through several, but the two most enduring were 'Colonel Croft-Constable', for messages relating to operations, and 'Major Galveston' for intelligence communications. On no account were messages referring to deception to use the name 'Clarke'. However relaxed Clarke pretended to be about his arrest, he must have realised the danger he'd have been in if German intelligence had realised his significance. As he was sure that an organised intelligence service would keep a list of senior enemy officers, the less his name appeared, the better. Some of his more distant A Force operatives don't seem to have learned his real name until years later.

There is a final postscript to the story. The following August, Madrid sent another cable about Clarke to Cadogan. This time it was from the ambassador, Sir Samuel Hoare.

'I have received anonymous letter saying that police photographs of Wrangel Clarke when arrested in Madrid for masquerading as a woman are shortly to be published in a leading Berlin daily newspaper,' he wrote. The warning was passed to MI6 with a note from one of Cadogan's colleagues: 'Unless C has views, I think we can only await developments in a spirit of calm and resignation.' The reply came back: 'C entirely agrees.'

The Assistant's Revenge

October 1941–February 1942

The Magician restrains an assistant with chains in a frame and then draws a curtain around the frame. As the Magician disappears behind the frame, the assistant appears, now drawing the curtain back and revealing that the Magician is restrained.

Chapter 19

While Clarke was sitting in a police cell in Madrid and Churchill was mulling his fate in London, back in Cairo, Cheese was about to send his controllers a juicy bit of intelligence from his new South African military source.

'Very important news,' his signal began. 'Piet is desperate for money. He visited us yesterday.' Wavell, Cheese went on, had paid a secret visit to Cairo the previous day, flying in from Tbilisi, the capital of Georgia in the Caucasus. It went on: 'Auchinleck under pressure from Churchill has consented against his better judgement to send one armoured division and three infantry divisions to help the Russians in the defence of the Caucasus. Wavell is going back to Iraq immediately to make the necessary plans for their reception.'

This was high-level stuff, bound to be attractive to a scoop-hungry Abwehr officer: a secret meeting between two generals under pressure from the interfering prime minister, that had led to a significant troop movement towards Russia, the direction that would most concern German high command.

It also had clear implications for the Libyan front: troops heading for the Caucasus weren't going to be available to relieve Tobruk. A week later, that was exactly the word that Cheese passed on from 'Piet': the weakened British, fearful of German offensives, had been putting about false dates for their own attacks. The signs of a coming attack in November were just the latest example of this.

The hope was that Cheese would have bought his way into the Abwehr's good books by telling them the truth about deceptions past, which would make them more likely to believe the deception he was now trying to sell. In London, there were eyebrows raised at the cleverness of all this. 'It is difficult to know what is going on by way of deception in the Middle East,' complained Guy Liddell at MI5. 'While we were given to understand that the impression should be created that we are not in a position to attack, *The Times* and other papers publish long articles showing our strength and active preparations.'

Clearly less impressed by Clarke's operation after the Madrid high-jinks, he observed: 'There is so much deception and counter-deception going on that it will not be surprising if our troops land up in the Arctic dressed in crepe-de-chine.'

As the launch of Crusader neared, camouflage artists were ordered to find a way to hide the railway depot that was being used to unload supplies for the attack. They realised there was no way of concealing it, but that extending the line might lead the enemy to attack the wrong part. The sight of men working on it would also lend credibility to the idea that no British attack was imminent.

The question was whether the Germans would buy any of this. Within SIME and A Force, there was growing anxiety about Renato Levi, the supposed recruiter of Cheese, who had returned to Italy in the summer. There had been no word from him for months. Was he dead or alive? Had he become a triple agent, revealing all?

They would have been even more worried had they known the truth: that Levi had been arrested by the Italians months earlier, and had for weeks been undergoing a series of interrogations aimed at proving he was working for the British.

The Italians, it turned out, had always had their doubts about Levi. They'd known about his visit to the British embassy in Yugoslavia before he set off to Cairo, and had been troubled by it. When he returned from Egypt to Italy, they raised it again. Why had Levi gone? Who was he working for?

The double agent affected injured innocence. Had he not just risked his life, travelling behind enemy lines to build an intelligence network for them? Of course he'd made contact with the British before setting out on this mission: he needed to build a picture of himself as a refugee from persecution. But Italian intelligence had another card to play. They said they'd been told Levi had been working for the Allies when he'd gone to Paris in 1940. Again, Levi denied everything.

It seemed, at first, to have worked. That July, the first Cheese message from Cairo was received, to general delight. The Germans, who were now running Levi's case, made a plan for him to return to Egypt in August. He would take cash, and a list of alternative contacts sympathetic to the Nazi cause.

But then, just as he was preparing to set off, the Italians arrested him. He was thrown into a prison in Rome. The wireless set he'd left behind in Cairo was operating under British control, his interrogators said. If that was true, Levi replied, he knew nothing about it. Perhaps the network he'd built had been caught.

For two months, he was held in solitary confinement, interrupted only by questioning sessions. Sometimes his interrogators were sympathetic, saying that they believed him and that he'd be released shortly. Sometimes they were aggressive, telling him he'd be shot. And here Levi proved his value as a secret agent. He might not have been a good son or husband, but he was a terrific liar. He must have sensed that his only safe route was to stick to his story. To confess that he'd been lying would surely mean death.

Finally at the end of October, apparently unsure what to make of him, the Italians sentenced him to five years imprisonment for unspecified crimes against the state.

Levi's German handlers don't seem to have been very happy about all this, but neither did they do much to help him. They were in communication with the network he'd apparently set up in Cairo, and unlike the Italians, they had confidence in it. They took complete control, moving the radio contact from Italy to Athens.

The codebreakers of Bletchley Park were still wrestling with Enigma, but at the start of November they broke a German army message that suggested Rommel wanted fuel and ammunition in place for an assault by 20 November, after the date Auchinleck was planning to launch his own attack. What was Rommel's target? Subsequent messages requesting multiple copies of photographs of Tobruk and its defences were a pretty big clue. Crucially, there was no evidence in these messages that Rommel was expecting the Auk to attack.

As Clarke, delayed both by Gort's inquiry and then the difficulty of finding transport, finally flew back to Cairo on 18 November, he could see the RAF's bombs exploding as they attacked enemy airfields at the start of Operation Crusader.

'Collect' had been a complete success. Rommel had been so relaxed about the possibility of an attack that he was in Rome in the days before it began. Focused on Tobruk, he refused to take the Allied assault seriously for nearly forty-eight hours. But though spies and deceivers can give their side an advantage, they can't win wars. When it came to the fighting, Crusader exposed the flaws of the commanders on both sides.

The opening days of Crusader were characterised by confusion, as the armies chased each other around the desert, seeking advantage. At different moments, each side thought it was on the point of victory. The British continued to pay the price for not thinking seriously about armoured warfare in the years before 1939. With many of his tanks destroyed, the commander on the ground wanted to retreat, and Auchinleck was forced to overrule and then replace him, insisting his troops fight on.

The Germans meanwhile were helped by their commander's brilliance at tank command. Before the assault, Auchinleck had warned his senior officers that 'our friend Rommel is becoming a kind of magician or bogeyman to our troops, who are talking far too much about him.' He urged them to remember that 'he is by no means a superman'.

Although the early phases of the battle had done little to dispel that idea, Rommel ended up risking everything with an impetuous and nearly disastrous drive into Egypt that became known as 'the dash to the wire'. That gamble failed to deliver for the Axis and Rommel saw he had little alternative but to try to retreat to safer ground faster than the British could pursue him. On 10 December Tobruk was finally relieved.

The Desert Fox had been beaten, but he was still in the fight.

Chapter 20

If the news in the desert was good, Clarke was finding that the news at headquarters was anything but, at least as far as he was concerned. He had been out of the country for three months, far longer than intended. In his absence, A Force had drifted. Shearer had taken over 'Collect'. Worse, Clarke was told that there was now a Chief Deception Officer – and it wasn't him.

Ralph Bagnold had served in the trenches in the Great War and then become a desert explorer. He'd experimented with ways of driving over dunes, writing a book on the physics of sand, and developed a sun compass that wasn't affected either by the metal in vehicles or by the iron ore deposits often found in deserts.

He rejoined the army when war broke out again, and in 1940 offered his skills to Wavell: he could take scouts across parts of Libya reckoned impassable by regular soldiers, perhaps to carry out raids far behind enemy lines. Wavell, typically, was supportive, and the Long Range Desert Group (LRDG) was born. It would go on to make the sands of Libya its own, monitoring enemy troop movements and ferrying the SAS.

But after a year in command of the LRDG, Bagnold had become conscious of the toll it was taking on his health. He decided it was time to hand the unit to a younger man, and headed back to Grey Pillars. There he seems to have been at a loose end, because in October 1941 he proposed the creation of a unit for 'planning and development of deception units and schemes, and the control of camouflage'.

This may not have been intended as quite the land-grab of A Force's turf that it appeared to be. Few people at headquarters knew what Clarke was doing, and the success of the one bit that many of them knew about, the dummy tanks, had created a demand for more deception efforts along similar lines.

But it might not have been an entirely friendly move, either. It's possible Bagnold was encouraged by Shearer, with whom he'd worked on the LRDG. The intelligence chief, who was definitely aware of Clarke's role, seems to have disliked and resented him. Years later he described his appointment as a mistake, and claimed that he had done very little while in Cairo – an idea clearly contradicted by files from the time which show not only Clarke's frenetic work rate but his regular contacts with Shearer.

Bagnold was appointed to the post on 20 October, the day of Clarke's arrest. With it came a promotion to colonel. While Clarke was sitting in a Madrid police cell, at the other end of the Mediterranean it looked an awful lot like someone had just taken a big chunk of his job away.

When he finally made it back to Cairo a month later, Clarke was outraged. He had, after all, turned down a promotion in London so that he could continue running A Force, and now he had been usurped. He was assured this wasn't the case. He would still be in charge of 'strategic deception' – misleading the enemy high command about Allied intentions – while Bagnold would handle 'tactical deception' – the stuff done by units actually in contact with the enemy.

Clarke replied that while this sounded fine in theory, it was hard to draw the line between the two in practice. He had other objections: deception was supposed to be a secret. 'A Force' had tried to conceal its very existence, and almost no one knew what it really did. To Clarke's mind, calling yourself 'Chief Deception Officer' was like putting 'Liar' on your business card: it rather suggested that you hadn't thought things through.

Was Clarke being sidelined? He certainly thought so. It may have felt like a punishment for his foolishness in getting arrested. Things were not going his way.

But at least the news coming from the front was good. As British forces advanced into areas that had been held by Rommel, they captured not just ground but also documents. For intelligence officers, these offered important clues about their enemy. For the deceivers, it was a chance to mark their work. What had been believed?

Here there was much that was encouraging. The 38th Royal Tank Regiment, fitted out with new light M3 Stuart tanks – in reality models built of wire and sailcloth – had been deployed to bolster forces defending the far southern end of the British line. They were listed as real in a captured German intelligence summary. Other dummy tank units had filled holes in the British line at critical moments, giving the impression that Auchinleck had more armour at his disposal, and providing targets for German aircraft. It wasn't safe work: one of them was overrun and taken prisoner during the dash to the wire, only to be freed when the battle turned.

In terms of 'Collect', there was pleasing evidence of success. In September, Axis intelligence had reported that 'two different sources, whose reliability it has not been possible to prove' had suggested an attack would begin against Rommel's forces in Libya in the second half of October. This was in line with the moves in 'Collect' to cry wolf.

By 11 November, the Germans' assessment had changed. 'There are no apparent signs of preparations for an attack,' it read, seven days before the attack began. That partly reflected the RAF's success at keeping reconnaissance planes at bay, and partly the work of the camoufleurs in suggesting that the supply railway was still incomplete. But there were signs it was informed by other things Axis agents were hearing.

'Taking into account the much improved German and Italian armies, any attack in Cyrenaica by the English must be preceded by considerable reinforcements, especially as regards armoured vehicles,' the next paragraph read. The British commander 'must also consider that for such an attack he would be obliged to commit strong forces in Cyrenaica, which would not for some time be available for transference to Syria or the Caucasus.' That was precisely the line that Clarke had agreed with MI5 in London, and that he had pedalled himself in Lisbon.

Even better, the briefing contained information from a new Abwehr intelligence source. 'There are also differences of opinion between Generals Wavell and Auchinleck concerning strategy,' the report went on. 'Wavell advocates an attack into the Caucasus.' 'Piet's' message had made its way from a Cairo transmitter to a Nazi intelligence document.

All this was greeted with delight in Cairo. Maunsell wired MI5 in triumph. 'Have been officially informed that Lambert was the main source by which successful deception recently achieved, resulting complete strategic surprise at outset of western desert campaign,' he wrote, using MI6's original codename for Cheese. 'Without Lambert the main theme of deception plan which was put over on 20th October and 27th October could not have reached the enemy before 18th November. This very satisfactory.'

This had come at a cost, though. In London, Liddell was taking great care with MI5's network of double agents, anxious not to do anything that might reveal that they had been turned. Cairo had been rather more careless with the reputation of Cheese, using him to put over a story that had been shown to be false.

The channel, Maunsell noted, was 'still in touch but I doubt future utility'. The team running it had, unsurprisingly, noted a 'noticeable change of tone' from the German controllers with the launch of Crusader. SIME had understood this risk. Shearer, running 'Collect' in Clarke's absence, had judged helping Crusader to be worth the cost.

Among the plundered documents was an Italian assessment of the defences of Cyprus. Clarke was delighted: 'It is really the first chance we have had of discovering in any detail how much of the stuff we put across really achieves the desired effect.' There was even a map, which showed the Italians estimated the British had two divisions on the island, one more than was really there.

A British intelligence officer in the headquarters on Cyprus was asked to compare the Italian assessment both to reality and to the deception story that had been put over. 'It is difficult to regard this map as a completely serious document,' he replied. Before the war this officer had been a schoolmaster, and it came across in his withering write-up. 'It seems the sort of work which might be produced by a staff officer who, after filling in the little he knew to be true and exhausting what his common sense told him was, in the nature of things, probable, found the picture unconvincing and filled in further details at random.'

The German intelligence analysis also offered insights into the audience for whom A Force was putting on its show. For a start, a close reading revealed the occasional strange gap in German knowledge. Noting that, at the beginning of November, Alan Brooke had replaced John Dill as Chief of the General Staff, one document went on: 'Reliable reports indicate that the reason for this replacement was the removal of the focal point of the war to the Middle East, with which area Dill is not believed to be well acquainted.'

German spies might not have been expected to know that Churchill had grown tired of Dill, whom he viewed as insufficiently gung-ho, but the idea that Brooke knew the Middle East better than Dill was a strange one. Both men's service histories, which showed that Dill had recently commanded British forces in Palestine, while Brooke had never served in the region, were a matter of public record. Even if the Abwehr had somehow not compiled basic dossiers on enemy commanders, they were available in the Army List that the British government published twice a year. Had no one in Germany thought to procure a copy before the war? Or had whoever compiled the briefing not thought to check?

This rush of captured documents told Clarke that he had an ideal audience, one that was keen to buy the stories he was selling. Indeed, the Italian assessment of Cyprus showed evidence that it was telling itself stories. The map estimated 5,000 troops around the city of Paphos at the western end of the island, four times the real number. This wasn't the result of anything A Force had put across. But the city had been the target of repeated bombing and reconnaissance over the summer. 'The Italians obviously regard the area as of great importance and assume we must have garrisoned it strongly,' the British intelligence assessment concluded.

Rommel's retreat in North Africa was only one of the areas where Germany was facing setbacks that winter. The invasion of Russia had ground to a halt outside Moscow, as Hitler's troops and their weapons froze.

Then in December, on the other side of the world, Japanese planes launched a surprise attack on the US Navy at Pearl Harbor. The war had spread to the Pacific, where the British Empire and dominions faced a new enemy in Japan. But they had also gained a powerful ally in America.

Clarke had now been a deceiver for a year, a period that had also seen him play the spy, sit in a police cell, escape from a torpedoed ship, and turn down a move back to London and a likely promotion. The early months had seen more failure than success, but there were signs that some of the tricks he was performing were starting to fool his audience.

'We felt, in fact, on the eve of 1942 that we were beginning to know how to plan deception, and that at last we had a well-oiled machine available to implement our plans,' he wrote later. 'The organ was now built, its stops were ready for us to pull at will, and all we had to do now was write the music and gain a little more practice in playing it.'

There was a final observation from the captured material. The German estimate for the strength of British forces in the Middle East at the start of November was 24 divisions. The reality was 17. Perhaps, Clarke thought, there might be a way of putting those extra divisions to work.

Chapter 21

At the start of 1942, the British were back where they had been eleven months earlier, at the far side of the Cyrenaica desert, once again at the extreme end of their supply lines. 'The year opened,' Clarke later recalled, 'with bright prospects.'

But Auchinleck was learning, as Wavell had before him, that North Africa rarely got first call on resources. There was always somewhere else that was more urgent. The previous year had ended with Japan and the USA entering the war. In the long term, that would mean more American tanks, planes and men to help fight Germany. In the short term, it meant troops were needed to defend Britain's Empire in the Far East from the Japanese. Meanwhile, Germany's advance into Russia had stalled. This was good news, of course, but it meant Allied tanks were being sent to the Eastern front, rather than the desert.

The Soviet Union's ability to hold German forces had surprised the other Allies. Unfortunately, it was proving harder to do the same to the Japanese. Hong Kong had fallen on Christmas Day 1941. They'd taken Manila a week later. Singapore fell in the middle of February. It was an advance as stunning as that achieved by the Germans in 1940.

Suddenly the Australian government was worried about its own defences, and demanding the return of the soldiers it had sent to North Africa. So A Force's first job of the year was to provide cover for the redeployment of 60,000 Australians from Syria to the Far East. Clarke had little confidence that the movement of so many people from a place where the Axis had so many informants would stay secret for long. His main hope was that the enemy could be misled about where they were going. Again, this would be tricky: with the Japanese making gains around the Pacific, anyone could see where men were needed.

Further complicating matters, there were lots of other places that the commanders didn't want the Germans to think that troops were being sent. Auchinleck was hoping to advance further into Libya, so didn't want to give the impression of excessive strength at his front with Rommel. The navy was moving a convoy through the Mediterranean, so didn't want the U-boat packs out hunting for troop ships heading towards Malta. In the end, they'd settled on a story that they were going to be used to retake Crete. Clarke felt a bit hopeless about it, especially when the Australian prime minister gave a speech making it clear that the country's young men were now going to be fighting much closer to home. But the story turned out to be sufficiently plausible for the Germans to reinforce Crete in haste.

Over on the Egyptian border with Libya, there was a thorn in the British side: the Axis garrison at Halfaya Pass. In the summer, Wavell's Battleaxe assault had failed partly as a result of the German 88mm guns dug in at Halfaya, which wrought havoc on the British tanks that had tried to capture the pass. Auchinleck's solution had been to sweep round to the south of these strongholds, but now they had to be dealt with.

No one relished the prospect of another assault on Halfaya, christened 'Hellfire' by Allied soldiers. The terrain was ideal for defenders, who could stay in protected positions and pick off exposed attackers as they climbed the winding road uphill through the pass. One option was to wait the Germans out: they were cut off, and their army was now 300 miles away. But their continuing presence was a significant problem, making it harder for the British to move supplies up to the forces at the front.

In an effort to persuade the defenders to surrender, A Force turned to one of its more unusual recruits. Eric Titterington had lived in Cairo for two decades. He'd gone to school in Cambridge, before becoming apprenticed to a pharmacist. He'd served in France in the Great War and then had moved to Egypt to become private chemist to the king, a job he'd held ever since. One of his responsibilities was preventing poisonings, which explained his nickname: 'Titters the Taster'.

Maunsell had grabbed Titterington at the start of the war to work in his censorship bureau. Officially, his work there was testing letters for secret inks. Unofficially Maunsell and Clarke used him to fake documents. Titters had recruited a Polish forger to help him with that, and at the end of 1941 the team formally joined A Force, in what would become known as its 'Technical Unit'. The bulk of the forgery was creating fake identity cards and travel papers for MI9's work helping prisoners of war to escape, but sometimes, as now, it meant creating fake orders.

Specifically, Clarke asked Titterington to fake a letter from Rommel to the commander at Halfaya, giving him permission to surrender. Military intelligence had been unable to pick up wireless signals from Halfaya, and the hope was that the defenders no longer had a functioning radio.

Almost the moment the plan had been signed off, it ran into problems. By the end of the war, Titterington would have built up a stock of 1,200 different types of paper, but at the end of 1941 he was still missing crucial elements. Rommel's force had months earlier been upgraded from the 'Afrika Korps' to 'Panzergruppe Afrika', but Titters only had samples of the old headed notepaper. Hoping the commander would assume that Rommel was being thrifty and using up his old stock, the deceivers went ahead and produced a note on the old paper, complete with Rommel's signature. It praised the men of Halfaya's 'heroic resistance' and said there was no need to 'demand more sacrifices'.

Titterington's team faked a German army seal, and used captured rubber stamps to mark the message urgent and secret. Unable to use a captured German aircraft as they had hoped, the deceivers resorted to dropping it at night from a British plane, and hoping no one on the ground noticed. Operation Gripfix, as the mission was called, was relying on a lot of hope.

Reality didn't deliver. Although the German radio was broken, the Italian one wasn't, enabling the German commander to check his orders. The plan, Clarke said later, 'might well have worked' were it not that, the same morning the fake message arrived, a real one came from Hitler 'saying that Halfaya was assisting the battle considerably by its resistance and appealing to its defenders to carry on as long as possible.'

It was more than two weeks before the Halfaya garrison did eventually surrender. Afterwards, its commander was heard telling one of his fellow officers that he'd thought it odd Rommel had used the old notepaper.

Meanwhile Bagnold's attempt to build a deception empire was causing Clarke more and more irritation. The newcomer had been persuaded to change his job title to 'Camouflage', which was something. But although he had great plans for his new outfit, and was already taking on responsibilities in the field, he had no staff. And so Clarke was told that, while Bagnold found recruits and trained them, A Force would fill in for him.

The argument had run through December and January, with Clarke insisting that it was impossible to separate the different elements of deception, and that it should be tightly controlled by someone who knew what they were doing – him – and his superiors telling him he needed to support Bagnold, and even train his team.

Just as Clarke's temper reached boiling point, the argument was settled by Rommel.

Chapter 22

Four days after Halfaya surrendered, on 21 January 1942, a British lookout on the other side of the Cyrenaica desert spotted a group of tanks approaching from the direction of the front line. His assumption, that it was a friendly patrol, was swiftly reassessed when it opened fire. The pendulum of the desert war was about to swing back.

This may sound familiar. It was an echo of events a year earlier. In 1941, troops had been pulled away from North Africa to defend Greece. This time they'd been summoned to the Far East. In 1941, Wavell hadn't believed Rommel would attack before his forces were all ready. This time, Auchinleck hadn't believed the Germans would be ready to counter-attack so swiftly after their retreat. And, just as in 1941, a British advance westwards was suddenly followed by a hasty retreat east.

As Rommel pushed forward, it quickly became clear that he had, unconsciously, been running a deception operation of his own. The German commander's complaints to Berlin about the weakness of his forces and their lack of supplies had been intercepted, decrypted by the Bletchley Park codebreakers, and passed on to Cairo. This 'most secret' intelligence, codenamed 'Ultra', was becoming an increasingly reliable source of information about the Axis, but it had to be handled with care.

'Nothing is easier than self-deceit,' the ancient Greek statesman Demosthenes said. 'For what every man wishes, that he also believes to be true.' It was unfortunate for the Auk that this was true of his intelligence chief. Ultra material had mentioned that Rommel was getting new tanks. The scouts of the Long Range Desert Group reported seeing them. But Shearer, who preferred to deliver optimistic reports, refused to accept this evidence.

Out in the desert, Auchinleck's hope at the start of the month that he might drive the Axis forces out of North Africa altogether had been rapidly abandoned. On the evening of 2 February, having returned from a visit to the front, the Auk and Shearer summoned Clarke to Grey Pillars.

The pair painted a grim picture of the situation. Rommel had advanced 200 miles in ten days. Benghazi was cut off. The troops holding the front line were thinly spread and there was little to stop a further German advance if they decided to make one. What Auchinleck badly needed was time to establish a new defensive line. Could Clarke persuade Rommel to hold off his attack, by making him think that the forces ahead of him were stronger than they were?

The request, to Clarke, illustrated the difficulty with trying to split tactical and strategic deception. It was bound to mean trying to make the forces facing the Germans look stronger than they were. That was surely tactical deception. But it was also likely to involve persuading the enemy that Auchinleck's army had not been stripped of soldiers, and that he had some sort of plan to fight back – strategic deception. It was hard to imagine that Clarke wouldn't need dummy tanks, but the dummy tanks were now under Bagnold's command.

Clarke flew out to the desert at dawn the following morning, but before he left he dictated a blistering memo setting out what he saw as the idiocy of the new structure.

Britain's force in North Africa had been formally named the Eighth Army towards the end of the previous year. Its commander was General Neil Ritchie. He'd been appointed in crisis the previous December, when the previous commander had proved out of his depth during Crusader. But Ritchie too was struggling. He had little experience of tank warfare – few British commanders did – and none of handling such a large force. His immediate subordinates both seemed to feel they'd do better without him. Clarke landed to find him in the midst of another retreat. 'Dense streams of vehicles were flowing back,' he wrote, 'and the Eighth Army Headquarters was being rapidly packed up in a blinding sandstorm.'

The Auk's orders were already out of date. Rommel would soon pass the place where Clarke had been asked to hold him. Ritchie was moving his own base back inside the Egyptian border. Clarke asked him what he wanted.

Getting generals to be precise at moments like this took skill. They wanted lots of things. Often, as Wavell had done in his early deceptions, they would talk about what they wanted the enemy to think. Clarke eventually settled on asking them to imagine that they could make a phone call to Hitler and ask him to issue an instruction: what would that order be?

What Ritchie desperately wanted was time. 'Stop the enemy attempting any further advance for the next three to four weeks,' he said. That would give him a moment to gather his forces and build a defensive line.

This too was an echo of the orders Clarke had received a year earlier. Then, he had tried to threaten the German supply lines, and learned that this was ineffective against Rommel. Another approach might be to imply that a British counter-attack was imminent. But, Clarke said afterwards, 'with people like Rommel, if you suggested you were going to attack, his first reaction would be to try and attack first.' What else was there?

Clarke found a corner amid the chaos of the headquarters and set to work, writing out his thoughts in pencil on a piece of thin paper. 'Object,' he printed at the top. 'To dissuade the enemy from continuing his advance.' He put down possible 'factors which will tend to dissuade him in any case'. It was not an entirely hopeful list: British troops putting up more of a fight; evidence that Tobruk was being fortified; and finally 'any suspicion that he is being led into a trap'. He paused to sharpen his pencil, and looked at what he'd just written. That might do it. 'This we must work on heavily,' he added.

Next he listed the thing that would encourage Rommel to push ahead: back at the Egyptian border, Ritchie was building a defensive line to which he could retreat if necessary. If the Germans realised what it was, they might conclude that there was no plan to defend Tobruk. They would be right: Auchinleck had decided that the port wasn't worth it: the cost of keeping it was, he judged, higher than its strategic value. The works on its defences were stripping them for use elsewhere. So the border work, likely to be visible to reconnaissance flights, was a problem. 'The story we use must provide some reasonable excuse for this,' Clarke noted.

'Suggested story,' he wrote, and underlined it. 'We are about to resume the offensive in the near future and the whole of our strategy is designed to place Rommel in the worst possible position.'

The story needed to fit the observed facts, chief among them the speed of the German advance. 'We have been surrendering ground fairly easily in order to extend his communications to the utmost,'

Clarke scribbled. 'This giving of ground will stop only when he gets near Tobruk.'

The port was 'being rapidly converted from a defended fortress to an advanced base, and the whole defence layout (now well known to the enemy in detail) is being altered.' Perhaps that might plant another doubt in Rommel's mind.

Finally, there was the question of the defences being built on the Egyptian border. 'A mobile striking force is getting ready near the frontier,' he added, before finishing with a call back to his deception of the previous month. 'An attack against Crete is also being prepared.'

Having set out the situation for himself and a possible story across two pages, Clarke began to think in more detail about how he could tell this story. The second draft of his proposals ran to seven sheets of paper.

His uncle Sidney would have recognised the structure of the note. A magic trick has two components: the effect – what the audience believes it has seen – and the method – what the performer actually did. Conjurers generally started with one and then worked out the other. One of Sidney's contemporaries had been so keen to develop novel effects that he'd offered to pay people for suggestions of new impossible tricks he could perform, confident he could work out the method himself.

Clarke had now worked out the effect he wanted his audience to see: a British force that was only pretending to retreat in chaos, while it was actually luring the enemy out so as to defeat him. Next he needed to devise the method.

Amid the fighting in the desert, the deceivers and their audience were in constant and unplanned direct contact, with patrols on both sides probing defences. The Luftwaffe flew overhead, and the German intelligence officers listened closely to Allied radio communications. Signals sent in Morse code were encoded first, but even so they revealed the location of transmitters, and the quantity and frequency of messages gave an indication of the size of the unit that the operator was attached to. Worse, there was no way of encrypting spoken radio communications, used by frontline forces with urgent information. All the Germans needed to do with those was listen.

So Clarke was going to have to deploy several techniques at once. He listed seven deductions he wanted German intelligence to make, and then set out how each would be put across. There was the now-standard request for dummy tanks, guns and aeroplanes to be brought up to fill gaps left by real equipment that was being pulled back or repaired. There were also whispers to be spread by Maunsell's team and in Istanbul and Lisbon.

More than this, he wanted signs close to the front warning that areas had been mined. Were the enemy listening to wireless chatter? He wanted 'indiscreet' radio conversations among the forces ranged there, first complaining about unmarked minefields, then discussing the strength with which different positions were held.

In Tobruk, Clarke wanted camouflage officers to make the port look like it was going to be the base for a major attack. The 'cages' set aside for prisoners of war should be enlarged. Roads should be made to appear as if they were under repair. Work on a railway line and jetties should continue.

While he'd been in London the previous year, Clarke had agreed a list of codenames that would be used for future deception operations. It was a neat way of hiding the meaning in a message: if he assigned one of these codewords to an operation, London knew it was a deception. Four days after he arrived at Ritchie's headquarters, he deployed one of them in a signal back to Britain: 'Code word BASTION has been allotted to the despatch of reinforcements to TOBRUK and other Eighth Army destinations now in progress.' A lot of information was hidden in those twenty-one words: A Force was running a new deception, and its story was that Tobruk was being reinforced.

The next day, he began his third draft of the plan. Cairo had come to his aid: two real divisions were now moving up from the Nile Delta. 'We must suggest greater strength of armour and much more rapid reinforcement than in the actual programme,' he noted. But he was worried that it was still too obvious that commanders were preparing to evacuate Tobruk. His description of the supposed trap had become more sophisticated: 'We are ready for the counterstroke against Rommel, but are waiting until he gets his main forces well forward, so as to give us a chance of cutting them off and destroying the lot.'

Clarke needed to put this story over and fast. Using his standard format for telling people what stories he wanted spread, he drafted messages to London – 'Please counter suggestions that ROMMEL is advancing into a trap set specially by us'; 'Please counter leakages regarding arrival tank reinforcements TOBRUK' – and Istanbul – 'Please counter rumours that substantial reinforcements have now reached Eighth Army' – and Lisbon – 'Please counter leakages that British have a big surprise in store for ROMMEL.'

He also considered other methods of getting his story over, including 'losing' a document where a German patrol might find it, setting out the idea of a trap. This was an intelligence ploy so well-known that it had its own name: a haversack ruse. It dated from the previous war, when, in an effort to deceive the Turks, a British officer had ridden to within sight of one of their patrols and waited for them to open fire. He'd then slumped in the saddle as if shot, and dropped a bag containing fake attack plans, before riding away.

But haversack ruses were tricky to pull off. Intelligence officers were often suspicious of documents that fell into their laps. At the very start of the war, a German light plane was forced down in Belgium, carrying a staff officer who failed to burn the papers he was carrying setting out his army's plan to strike west through the Ardennes forest and head for the Channel ports. The British and French both dismissed the genuine papers as an obvious plant.

While he pondered that, he learned there was a snag with another part of his plan, to deploy dummy tanks at the front. He needed at least 300, but 'there was nothing like enough dummies for this in the whole of the Middle East'. It was time for some creativity.

Chapter 23

Even the best magicians make mistakes. They call the accidental exposure of part of a secret move – the glimpse the audience gets of the rabbit as it goes into the hat – a 'flash'. But sometimes what seems like an accident can be deliberate misdirection. One of Rommel's own deception tricks was to hide his armour under the cover of Bedouin tents. RAF reconnaissance flights had got used to watching out for Arab encampments surrounded by tank tracks. Sensing an opportunity, Clarke requested Cairo rustle up a load of canvas dyed to resemble the black tents of the Senussi clan, who lived in the area.

In the course of one night, the dummy tank teams set up 150 tents in the desert. Four tents were given dummies 'just showing sufficiently to look as though the tentage had been accidentally torn or blown aside'.

'By morning the whole area was also covered with track marks, while fires and other signs of habitation were arranged and the unit's wireless sets put on the air,' Clarke recorded. 'At noon three German aircraft attacked the encampment and dropped twelve bombs in the middle of the tents.' More attacks would follow, until the dummy team returned and adjusted the tents to look as though they had been abandoned.

To tighten up security in Tobruk, Maunsell loaned Clarke an officer on his staff, known as Major Dominic Macadam-Sherwen. The name was, Maunsell explained, made up. In reality he was a Frenchman, distantly related to Wavell. Determined to carry on fighting after the French surrender, he'd appealed to his relative, who'd found him a spot at SIME. His real name was Dominique, Vicomte de la Motte.

His English was perfect, Maunsell later recalled, 'but he succeeded in being intensely French'. This seemed to mean that he started a lot of fights. At one point, arrested as a 'suspicious individual', he responded by threatening to arrest the person who had arrested him if he wasn't immediately freed. 'It was, however, usually possible to save him from arrest by explaining that he was French,' his commander recalled.

In reality, the most impressive thing about Macadam-Sherwen is that his story was more or less entirely false. It was little surprise that he spoke perfect English. He'd been born Thomas Sherwen, middle names Burton Macadam, in South Africa, shortly after the death of his father, a doctor from Cumberland. His mother had moved back to England with him, and brought him up in Epsom, just outside London. By the 1930s, he was living in the Caribbean, working as a planter, and had added one of his middle names to his surname. By the time he joined the British army in 1940, he'd added two more names, to become 'Thomas Birton Dominique Marie Macadam-Sherwen'. Precisely when he started telling people he was a French aristocrat is unclear, as is whether he had any real connection with Wavell, but his colleagues at SIME were all taken in. His habit of integrating French military kit into his uniform completed the effect.

Would Clarke have cared if he'd known the truth? He too was finding in war the opportunity to live a richer, more exotic life than peace had offered. As for Macadam-Sherwen's colleagues, it's clear from the way they recalled him that they were delighted by his colourful history and his antics, and would have found the true story a huge disappointment.

It was not, of course, ideal that Maunsell's counter-intelligence team was completely fooled by a fake Frenchman who didn't even bother to put on an accent, but from another perspective, it was the ability to pull this sort of thing off that made Macadam-Sherwen an ideal recruit for SIME. Maunsell, who was very comfortable saying so if he thought a subordinate wasn't up to scratch, was highly complimentary.

Clarke, escorting Macadam-Sherwen to Tobruk, explained his mission to him. He was to keep people away from the dummy tanks and spread rumours in the port, especially among the ships' crews: 'Tobruk is being held at all costs'; 'Tobruk is full of tanks'; 'we are trying to entice Rommel forward'.

But Macadam-Sherwen quickly found this kind of story was hard to sell on the ground. Auchinleck had decided that he didn't want another siege of Tobruk. If Rommel reached the port and surrounded it, the defenders were to evacuate. On the ground, the troops knew this. Staff officers had been overheard talking about it. An order to this effect had been dropped at a post office. Sailors at the dock discussed the huge naval cost of keeping the port supplied during the previous siege. Worse, reporters arriving from Cairo were confident that there were no plans to hold on. The Auk's intelligence chief, John Shearer, was responsible for briefing reporters, but he'd got into trouble before for revealing more than he was supposed to. Had he done that again?

Back in Cairo, Maunsell was trying to start his own rumours. For well over a year, he'd been waging a campaign to have the Egyptian government expel neutral and hostile diplomatic missions. The Vichy French delegation was about to leave, and he wanted it to take some misinformation with it. He had, of course, someone on his payroll who was friendly with the diplomats, and he sent them to a farewell party the group were holding to spread the idea that retreating British soldiers seemed oddly 'anxious to advertise their weakness' and had 'some surprise in store for Rommel'.

The next day a message came back, signed 'X', in French: '*J'ai accompli la mission que vous m'avez confiée.*' They had identified two diplomats to plant the story on, one of them a man who was '*furieux*' with the English because he was convinced – correctly, of course – that they were behind his banishment from the delights of Egypt.

'It was very easy to suggest the idea,' Maunsell's agent reported. 'He discussed it for a long time. It is absolutely certain that through him the information will be transmitted to the pro-Axis members of the group.'

For a moment in mid-February, it looked as though 'Bastion' was going to be too late. Axis tanks advanced towards the British lines. Ritchie told Clarke that every intelligence indication was of an imminent offensive. And then, Clarke said, 'a strange thing happened'. With Allied soldiers hunkered down in their positions, preparing to hold out as best they could against a force that had already pushed them back hundreds of miles, the Germans stopped. For a whole day they stayed more or less where they were, and then that night they returned to their original line. 'What explanation lay behind this strangely un-German manoeuvre, we never discovered,' Clarke wrote later, 'and it still remains a mystery – though some of us would like to think the Deception Plan had played a part.'

It's not inconceivable that 'Bastion' had helped introduce an element of doubt into Rommel's mind, but his letters home suggested he had always planned to halt his advance in the middle of February. He was having supply problems and had far exceeded his orders by counter-attacking at all. That said, had he understood the state of the British camp, he would surely have been tempted to press home his advantage and see if he could capture Tobruk.

One frustration for Clarke out of the operation had been the uselessness of the London Controlling Section, the body tasked the previous year with coordinating deception worldwide. His requests that stories be put over had been refused. In March, an apologetic note arrived: 'It is on our conscience that we have been able to do nothing to help. Our conclusion is that the plan was essentially local with all the evidence local, which means that "leakages" here would have appeared unnatural.'

This was maddening for Clarke. Months earlier, he had sat with the Twenty Committee and been told about their amazing ability to put information over to the Abwehr, but when he needed it most, he was told there was nothing that could be done. 'It is a source of real worry,' he wrote back, 'to have to depend time after time on our local sources, particularly those in Turkey, which we are working far more than we should.'

If 'Bastion's' effect on Rommel was uncertain, its impact on Clarke was entirely positive. For a start, it helped him see off Bagnold. While Clarke was at the front drawing up his plans, Auchinleck agreed that it made no sense to split the deception operation. It may not be a coincidence that at the same time he dismissed his intelligence chief. The Auk had reluctantly accepted that Shearer's overconfidence and inability to admit mistakes had become a problem. Clarke had seen off an influential enemy at headquarters.

Bagnold was sent on his way to the signals section. The men he'd recruited were absorbed into A Force. Clarke, in sole command, was promoted to colonel. Less than five months after his arrest in Madrid, he was respectable again.

The Miser's Dream

February–June 1942

The Magician shows their hands are empty, and then proceeds to pluck, from the air, coin after coin, noisily dropping each into a metal bucket as they go.

Chapter 24

Clarke now had a free hand to bring in his own recruits, including three men he'd known for years. The first was Noel Wild, a small, elegant old Etonian who'd had a frustrating war, trying and failing to get to his old unit, the Eleventh Hussars, who were at the front. Instead he was stuck behind a desk at Grey Pillars, and miserable about it. One of his few comforts was discovering that his old friend Dudley was also in Cairo, doing something characteristically mysterious. Clarke was one of the few people who got on with Wild. He rated his abilities and liked him a lot, but no one else much liked him at all, finding him arrogant and, unlike Clarke, humourless.

Dropping into Shepheard's to cash a cheque, Wild was told that Clarke was looking for him. When he found his old friend in one of the bars, Clarke raised his glass. 'To your promotion,' he told him. Wild was baffled. Clarke told him he was to become a lieutenant colonel, and his deputy. Wild wanted to know what the job was. Clarke was as evasive as ever, saying simply that he wanted someone he knew. The evening carried on like that until Wild was drunk enough to accept. His current boss was furious, and accused him of wanting an easy war. As far as he was concerned, Clarke was running a racket.

Some recruits were easier to persuade. One friend from before the war, frustrated in his role in Palestine, wrote to Clarke asking if he knew of any interesting jobs going in Cairo. Clarke replied in much the same way he'd approached Wild, that he could offer a job, but couldn't explain what it was. 'Knowing Dudley I accepted with alacrity, and have never regretted it,' the officer recalled decades later. 'And I am certainly as fond of my service under him as of anything else I did in the war – or in my life, come to that.'

Then there was Tony Simonds. He'd returned from his adventures in Ethiopia and had been struggling to find a role. Clarke brought him into A Force to take care of the MI9 work, running escape lines through Turkey and training troops in North Africa and the Middle East in how to avoid capture. Simonds then brought in his own recruit.

Camouflage was becoming a big business, and Geoffrey Barkas had reorganised his team. Part of that involved shutting down Jasper Maskelyne's Camouflage Experimental Unit, which hadn't lived up to early promise. Simonds ran into a dejected Maskelyne, who was feeling under-appreciated, and offered him a role as an MI9 lecturer. The magician knew how to hold a crowd, and would be ideal for demonstrating some of the secret gadgets that the unit manufactured to help soldiers escape: concealed compasses and saws, maps inside playing cards and board games. Maskelyne divided his time between putting on magical entertainments for the troops and these more secret lectures. He was rather good at it, and to soldiers who doubted whether the Germans would really be fooled by buttons that unscrewed the wrong way, the Maskelyne name was a stamp of confidence. Many believed the master magician had invented the gadgets himself, an idea that he was happy to encourage.

Clarke saw the advantage of this, too, and would use Maskelyne's name freely when he thought it might help to persuade a dubious senior officer of the plausibility of a deception plan, or to get out of an awkward situation. When the navy issued a furious complaint that they had spent the day hunting for a submarine that had been reported off the Egyptian coast only to realise, just as they were about to bomb it, that it was a dummy, they got a light-hearted reply: 'I am credibly informed that Captain Maskelyne is stationed there and it is therefore possible that a rapid transformation may occur at any moment.'

Joining Simonds on the MI9 side of A Force, at least at first, was Michael Crichton, of Eton and the Desert Rats, as the 7th Armoured Division had come to be known. Crichton had expressed little interest when Clarke approached him: he wanted action, not a desk job. But there was something else in Cairo he wanted, too.

The roof garden of the Continental Hotel was home to a cabaret, compered by an American blonde who would announce each act and then finish off the evening with a solo number, each evening prefaced the same way: 'And now, introducing myself, Betty to you, in a rumba', or whichever dance she'd chosen. Although she'd been

The master of deception:
Dudley Clarke, drawn in 1945 by Patrick Edward Phillips.

Clarke as a boy . . .

. . . a soldier . . .

. . . and a spy: a wartime false passport, in the name of Derek Wilson Carter.

Claude Auchinleck (left) and Archibald Wavell both appreciated Clarke's genius.

The first deception: Troopers Smith and Gurmin flash their wings as members of the then-fictional SAS.

A fake Ethiopian paratrooper in a picture released to the press. Note the spiked Arab Legion helmet in the background.

The Desert Fox: Erwin Rommel's ability to spot opportunities and take them inspired his men.

Teacher: Bernard Montgomery understood that his soldiers needed confidence in their orders and commander.

Double: Clifford James's uncanny resemblance to Montgomery was crucial to one of the most famous deceptions of the war.

Clarke in the outfit which prompted
Madrid police to arrest him . . .

. . . and after he had been allowed to
change back into a suit.

It wasn't his first time in drag.
At the Staff College panto he
played Volga Olga, 'quite the
Worst Woman in the World'.

Dummy tank units, improved by Geoffrey Barkas's team of artist-camoufleurs, filled out the British lines.

And dummy gun emplacements, obviously fake up close, looked plausible in reconnaissance photographs.

Ewen Montagu, a difficult colleague to the deceivers, enjoyed his post-war fame.

Johnny Bevan, head of the London Controlling Section, accountable to 'God and history'.

David Strangeways, who rewrote the D-Day deception 'entirely'.

Jasper Maskelyne made a lot of false claims about his war work, but he made a big contribution ahead of the British attack at El Alamein.

His 'Sunshield' design turned a tank . . .

. . . into a truck, from a distance at least.

born in Wabash, Indiana, as Alice Sims, she was known in Cairo as 'Betty-to-You'. Crichton was smitten.

He wasn't the only one. Betty's after-show soirées in the lobby of the Continental were a destination for plenty of officers back from the front. Clarke was fond of declaring that the best way to find out what was going on in the desert was to buy Betty a drink and ask her. He got on well with her, of course. He was ideal company: entertaining but unlikely to make unwelcome advances. 'One of our favourite people,' Hermione Ranfurly, a young Englishwoman working in Cairo, wrote in her diary of Clarke. 'Quite small, brilliantly clever and imaginative and always on the edge of laughter.' When her sister needed a job, she sent her to work for him – 'she will not have a dull moment'.

Seeing the effect Betty had on Crichton, Clarke asked her to send him along to the A Force office, and before he knew it, the Desert Rat had realised that he wanted a desk job after all.

If people felt an instinctive dislike for Wild, the opposite was true of Crichton. He was kind, charming and funny. Having worked with the Long Range Desert Group in 1941, he joked that he was now part of the Short Range Shepheard's Group. Aristocratic by birth – his father had been equerry to the king – he had no trace of snobbery. In Cairo full-time, he began an enthusiastic courtship of Betty.

Clarke's approach to his staff was relaxed. He selected people he trusted and then let them get on with their jobs. He was just about to turn forty-three, but to his younger officers he seemed impossibly old. Here was a man who had been in uniform for twenty-five years, longer than some of them had been alive. He had an assured manner – 'quiet and authoritative', as one of them put it. The war in the desert was advances and then sudden retreats, months without movement and then hundreds of tanks wiped out in a couple of days. Amid this chaos, Clarke's even temper, sardonic humour and air of unconcern reassured those around him that even if things looked tricky now all would, in the end, be well. 'If you made a mistake you were either fired or forgiven,' Wild recalled years later. 'And there it ended.'

The crisis of 'Bastion' had helped Clarke to clarify in his own mind some of the principles of his work. On his return to Cairo in February, he went to lecture the new recruits on the basics of deception.

The first thing a deception plan needed, he told them, was 'one straightforward, perfectly simple object'. This was harder than it sounded. 'What you will have to do is to help the Commander to get the object paragraph absolutely right.'

Clarke was still getting to grips in his own mind with what he would come to see as one of the most important principles of military deception. It was about the distinction between making the enemy think something, and making him do something. 'You will put down as the object not only what you want them to believe – it is better to put down that you want to stop them attacking before a certain date, or something like that.'

Later, putting his thoughts in writing, he would expand on this. 'It is important to appreciate from the start that the only purpose of any deception is to make one's opponent act in a manner calculated to assist one's own plans,' he wrote. 'In other words, to make him DO something. Too often in the past we had set out to make him THINK something, without realising that this was no more than a means to an end.' This, he now realised, had been the problem with his very first deception for Wavell, Camilla: the Italians had thought what Wavell wanted them to think, but had reacted precisely as he hadn't wanted them to react.

The distinction between belief and action had other subtleties. An enemy commander might feel obliged to take precautions against a threat even if they had private doubts about its plausibility. Or they might be too stretched to act against something they completely believed in. 'Fundamentally,' Clarke wrote, 'it does not matter in the least what the enemy thinks: it is only what line of action he adopts as a consequence of his line of thought that will affect the battle.' If you wanted the enemy to move troops, you had to threaten a point in his defences that was so vulnerable and so important that he had no choice but to respond as you wanted him to.

From here on, A Force officers would ask commanders what they wanted the enemy to do. Only then would they start working out what they wanted the enemy to think. This Clarke described to his trainees as a 'story' that the enemy would be allowed to discover, and that would induce him to act as hoped. 'Unless you have the story clear beforehand, all fitted together, you will not have a reasonable explanation ready for anything that might happen,' he said. 'The story must be complete enough to have a clear picture in your mind of what everybody is doing in the imaginary plan.'

'Bastion' had also shown that deception needed time to work. 'There is a lot of loose talk in Cairo but it is not easy to get it out,' Clarke said. 'I always like to allow three weeks for any information to reach the enemy.' (Stories moved a bit quicker from Palestine and Syria, he added, and even faster from Aden.)

Finally, 'Bastion' had been a deception carried out while in constant contact with the enemy. 'Up to date we had been relying far too much on the planting of false information to implement a plan,' he wrote. 'Bastion had showed us vividly that we had to deceive not only the ears but also the eyes of the enemy. We decided that for the future a deception plan must never rely upon implementation by one method alone.'

'What is seen is usually believed,' Clarke told his recruits. Visual deception was, he told them, hard work, but sometimes there were shortcuts. Just as a novice magician learns to clench their fist in a way that suggests they're still holding a coin or ball that has long since made its way to a pocket, A Force's recruits were encouraged to think what they could do to give the impression that something existed when it didn't.

'One might want to pretend that a number of submarines existed,' Clarke suggested. 'Instead of building the submarines, one could get exactly the same result by drawing attention to some sort of shed or slip-way. On one occasion we suggested the presence of tanks by doing nothing more than making a prohibited area.'

In a similar vein, he quoted the promotion of the Cyprus brigadier the previous summer, when A Force had been trying to make Cyprus look better defended than it was. 'The number of major-generals,' he joked, 'is a fair guide as to the number of troops. This is a very cheap form of deception.'

Three days later, Clarke noticed a lorry driving past him in Cairo. Beneath the dust and grime that instantly attached itself to every vehicle in Egypt, he spotted on the front an insignia he hadn't seen before, an eye. Then he saw a car with the same mark, and realised a new unit must have arrived. An idea began to form in his mind.

Chapter 25

A basic job for any intelligence service is to maintain a picture of the enemy's 'order of battle': what troops he has, and where they are. When British intelligence officers had gone through papers captured during the Crusader advance, they'd come to some striking conclusions about their opposite numbers. 'The total strength of the Middle East forces is usually consistently over-estimated,' they concluded. Assessments of forces that had been in combat was 'fairly good'. But information about troops further from the fighting was 'very faulty'. The Axis estimated Auchinleck had 22 infantry divisions at his disposal, five more than he really had. Three of the imaginary divisions were ones A Force had invented. Its two dummy tank units were also listed as real.

This mattered because one of the biggest strategic problems facing the British was a shortage of troops. Germany had begun the war with over three million troops, more than four times the number Britain had. Over the course of the war, 27 million Germans and Italians would be mobilised, almost three times the number the British would summon up, even including her empire. Many of the German troops were tied up on the Russian front, and Clarke thought it might be possible to pin more of them down by making it look as though attacks were imminent in different parts of Europe. But only if those attacks looked plausible.

'Time after time,' he wrote later, 'we had come up against the unpleasant realisation that no deceptive threat to any chink in the enemy's armour can be made effective unless he is also persuaded that ample reserves are in hand to implement it.' It was no use London's double agents trying to put across a story about a plan to invade Norway as long as the Abwehr knew there weren't the forces in Britain to do the job, the ships to carry them, or the air force to protect them.

But over the previous year Clarke had shown it was possible to persuade the enemy of the existence of imaginary forces. Indeed the documents captured in recent months suggested a far greater willingness to believe in their existence than he had thought possible.

If the number of major-generals was one guide to how many troops an army had, might not the number of different unit insignia do the same job? He dictated a memo: 'I want to go into the question of doing a deliberate Order of Battle deception job by making use of the divisional signs worn on uniforms, and especially those marked on vehicles.'

Clarke had created false units before, but now he wanted to pull those operations together and expand them. 'Now,' he wrote, 'was the time to amalgamate all the efforts into one permanent comprehensive plan designed to convey to the enemy a complete version of the whole Middle East order of battle. But it was to be an Order of Battle so falsified as to give a margin of exaggeration which would leave sufficient surplus in hand to provide for any future deception requirements.'

This was the beginning of Operation Cascade. It had an immediate goal, to persuade the Germans that the Middle East was well-defended. This wasn't really true. It wasn't simply that Rommel was still looking dangerous in Libya. Troops were needed to fight the Japanese, now advancing into Burma and still apparently unbeatable. Meanwhile the improving weather in Russia meant fresh German advances in the south, as Hitler began a push towards the Caucasus mountains. Once again, Auchinleck's northern flank was a worry.

But Clarke had a longer-term idea as well. The previous year he'd told the chiefs of staff that the London deception operation should be working on a huge false jigsaw puzzle, 'a completely bogus plan for winning the war'. It was becoming clear to Clarke that the outfit wasn't up to the job, so he was going to start producing some of the jigsaw pieces in Cairo.

Much of magic depends on being one step ahead of the audience. A duplicate of the card the magician is going to force you to select was slipped into your pocket as you came on stage, or as you walked into the theatre. At the moment the audience thinks the trick is just beginning, the hard work has already been done.

In the same way, if A Force could persuade German intelligence of the existence of bogus units well before they were needed, they could then be deployed far more effectively as part of future deceptions. This would have distinct advantages. Clarke was keenly aware that the previous summer they'd put out a story of a real unit being sent to Cyprus, only to find it had been unexpectedly deployed to the Libyan border, where the Germans could see it, revealing that their intelligence was faulty. That wouldn't happen to a fictional division. Indeed, the very non-existence of these units would become an advantage: it is very hard to prove that something doesn't exist – even when that something is an infantry brigade.

In total, he planned to apparently increase the strength of Allied forces in the Middle East from five armoured divisions and ten infantry to eight armoured and twenty-one infantry. This wasn't quite as huge an increase as it sounded – there were tens of thousands of troops in the region who weren't allotted to any division – but it would still represent a 30 per cent exaggeration.

Two decades earlier, hoping to demonstrate magic on a new scale, Harry Houdini had made an elephant disappear on stage in New York. Now Clarke was proposing to conjure, out of nothing, over 100,000 men and hundreds of tanks in the Middle East.

How would he pull it off? As he drafted his plan, Clarke realised he would need more than fake divisional markings. Real armies generated other things, like radio signals, and paperwork. Those could be faked, of course, but it involved a lot of people and effort. A simpler and more elegant solution was to adapt Rodwell's fake promotion. There were already hundreds of thousands of soldiers in the region, and they all had headquarters units that were sending each other messages. A selection of these would be renamed.

For instance the Basra Base Area Headquarters, far from the fighting, would henceforth be known as the HQ of the 2nd Indian Division. Clarke's own A Force offices would be known as the HQ of the 18th Division. Messages sent to and from these 'headquarters' – messages that might be overheard by enemy radio, or glimpsed by Egyptians willing to sell information, or simply noticed by soldiers who might then mention something in the wrong company – would naturally imply the existence of the named divisions. In an age before computer databases, when the British army had rapidly expanded and information about it was classified, it would be very hard for anyone even in headquarters to establish that the 2nd Indian Division didn't exist.

It was going to be a lot of work. Each 'notional' – Clarke preferred that term to 'imaginary' – unit had a name, a badge and a command structure. Brigades were told that they were to pretend to be divisions, with commanding officers flying divisional commander flags from their cars.

This involved letting many more people in on the secret than Clarke liked to do. He tried to minimise the security risk by telling them as little as possible. Those officers who had to be in on the secret were told that the idea was to conceal the true order of battle. The analogy they were offered was the Royal Navy's practice of giving its shore bases the names of ships to confuse enemy intelligence – HMS *Armadillo*, for instance, was a country house in the west of Scotland, used as a training base.

Keeping track of it all became a major task in itself. A reference file at A Force HQ listed all the bogus units and their supposed activities, and the real units that were impersonating them. It would be, Clarke said, 'a long and tiresome process'.

All this reflected the reality of stage magic: amazing effects are usually the fruit of years of patient, tedious preparation – in the words of the modern magician Teller, 'spending more time on something than anyone might reasonably expect.'

Until now, Clarke had kept much of A Force's work in his head. 'He had the most all-containing brain of anyone I ever met,' one of his officers said. 'At any time, as well as complete deception orders of battle and battle plans for say two particular situations which were worked out all in detail on paper, there would be six embryo plans in his mind which could be translated to paper in 24 hours. I have never known a brain so full of stuff!'

But a larger team meant finding a proper way to keep everyone up to speed. Thus began the publication of a very unusual newsletter. The 'A Force Strategic Addendum' was a couple of pages long. It listed true information that the deceivers were happy for the enemy to find out, false information that should be passed to the enemy if possible, and finally the ideal false picture that Clarke hoped Axis intelligence officers were building up. It was sent to A Force officers on a very tight circulation list. After receiving the new edition, they had to destroy the previous one.

Clarke took the Addendum seriously, writing it himself. Explaining why, he described the role of a deception chief using a theatrical analogy. 'Only in doing so could he convey to others the essentials of the wide overall picture which he alone can see. He is to the actors the author of the play.' His staff were managing 'lighting, scenery, costumes and property', and together they would 'create from the written pages of a manuscript a living play which will carry in convincing fashion the message of the author to his chosen audience – in our case the Enemy.'

He was putting on a show, and all North Africa and the Middle East was his stage.

Chapter 26

While Clarke was creating his grand deception, painting tens of thousands of troops onto the map with a broad brush, one of Maunsell's officers was working on a quite different scale, filling in light and shade on a single fictional creation.

The assumption at the end of 1941 had been that the credibility of Cheese, the imaginary double agent Nicosoff, had been destroyed by his role in the Crusader deception. Surely, after passing such obviously false information to his German handlers, he would never be believed again? But one of the SIME officers working on the case disagreed.

Evan John Simpson was another unusual soldier. Before the war he had been an actor, playwright, novelist and historian. Recently converted to Catholicism, he had joined up determined to fight Hitler and, despite being forty-three, 'of no outstanding physique' and very short-sighted, had found his way by what he called 'unusual channels' into the Commandos, taking part in the raid on the Lofoten islands at the start of 1941.

On his return, he applied to the Intelligence Corps. With fluent French and a little Norwegian, he'd expected to be assigned to the European theatre, which showed how little he understood of the army's ways. Instead he was sent 'untrained and in haste' to the Middle East. As best he could work it out, this was because he'd once met Lawrence of Arabia at a tea party in Oxford.

And so he had wound up behind a desk at SIME catching enemy agents, a job that he thoroughly enjoyed. Although it involved a lot of paperwork, 'it dealt with human beings instead of bedding or ammunition,' he wrote. 'And though, in the flesh, no one can be more boring company than a spy, the tracking and sifting of material about their activities made one of the most fascinating paper-games in the world.'

In civilian life, having roamed across several creative fields, Simpson was regarded as respected in each but not outstanding in any of them. 'His lively mind refused to be confined,' *The Times* would write later. But Maunsell thought he showed great promise. 'Brilliant but unstable' was his assessment, noting that Simpson suffered from bouts of depression.

That lively mind had made Simpson the obvious choice to play the role of Nicosoff, the Axis agent working far behind enemy lines. His language skills turned out to be useful after all: Nicosoff communicated with his handlers in French.

In early 1942, Maunsell was handed something that suggested Simpson wouldn't need to work on the case much longer: decrypted internal Abwehr messages about a spy in Egypt named 'Roberto'. This, it was apparent, was the German codename for Nicosoff. In October, 'Roberto' had been rated 'credible' as he passed on information from his friend 'Piet' about British troop movements. There had been discussion between Berlin and Athens about how to get money to their man.

But three days after the start of 'Crusader', the tone had changed. 'The reliability of Roberto reports must be subjected to severe doubt,' one message read. He had reported a division of troops leaving Palestine for the Caucasus when the Abwehr knew it to be in Egypt. Their man's silence in the run-up to the attack 'is likewise very striking'. Even when 'Crusader' would have been common knowledge in Cairo, he hadn't mentioned it. By the start of December, they seemed to have reached a conclusion: 'Interference by the enemy intelligence service in the Roberto network is becoming more and more obvious.' Around the same time, SIME learned about Levi's arrest in Italy. The prospects for Cheese seemed bleak.

But Simpson wasn't willing to give the operation up. The Germans, he argued, might be persuaded that the problem wasn't Nicosoff but his source, 'Piet'. Nicosoff might yet be redeemed. He was given time to try.

Simpson approached the problem with a novelist's eye for character. He constructed a picture of Nicosoff fitted around the details which he knew Levi had given the Germans, and trying to avoid areas where the Italian might have invented new details he didn't know about. This wasn't straightforward. Levi had told the Germans that Nicosoff was born in Egypt to a Syrian family. But he had also, without consultation with anyone else, invented the surname Nicosoff. Some in SIME suspected this was a pun on 'knickers off', which given Levi's main interest in life wouldn't have been a surprise, but whatever the reason, the distinctly Russian-sounding name created a problem. 'He must be of Slav origin', a SIME officer decided.

Many of the notes on Nicosoff were in that vein, as though written by agents trying to establish who this man was, based only on his wireless signals. 'There is no positive evidence at the present time that he has any other profession than that of spy,' one said. 'On the other hand he apparently has enough money for his living expenses. He must have, or have had, some financial standing, in order to be able to borrow money at a time when he was – according to the evidence of the messages – absolutely on his uppers.'

Perhaps this was simply how the staff of SIME, who spent so much of their time trying to catch spies based on clues, were used to thinking. Or perhaps they were putting themselves in the place of Nicosoff's German handlers, trying to work out what picture they would have assembled of their agent.

His job was listed as 'unknown'. They toyed with the idea that he was a 'half-commission man' – someone who introduced clients to brokers, in return for a cut of the proceeds. 'He would frequent (at the upper end of the scale) such places as the bar of the Metropolitan; and (at the lower end of the scale) would not be out of place in a better-class Arab cafe or an other ranks' eating-shop. He would not mix socially with British officers, but might with Greek, Polish or Yugoslav.'

As for past jobs, he had to have learned how to operate a wireless transmitter at some point, though SIME couldn't quite decide how. 'If we place his age at about 45, he might have been a ship's wireless operator in his younger days,' they said, though they generally worked on the basis that he was between thirty and thirty-five.

Simpson was sure that Nicosoff could win the Germans' trust once again. He painted a picture of a man who had been deceived by a greedy source the previous year, and had since been abandoned by unreliable helpers. 'I am alone,' Nicosoff complained to his handlers, 'and without funds I cannot hire agents.'

Though he transmitted twice a week, the intelligence content of his messages was minimal. He had been abandoned by the rest of his spy ring. 'All the others, and all the sources of intelligence, have lost faith in the enemies' promises to send money, and have left him hanging on alone in the faint hope that such money may yet arrive,' Simpson explained. 'This is the burden of every message, and it is only varied by occasional and unimportant tit-bits of information such as anyone might pick up in Cairo.' In February, he reported having seen American troops in Cairo, and that he'd heard an aircraft factory was being built near the city. But when pressed on these, he offered little more detail.

Not that Nicosoff's handlers seemed to care much. Signals went unacknowledged. Replies, when they came, contained few questions on military subjects. As for the requests for money, there was the occasional reply that it was on its way, but also suggestions that perhaps he could come somewhere – Istanbul, say – to pick it up. SIME was suspicious of a trap. As Nicosoff, Simpson replied that he didn't have the cash to get to Turkey.

For months, Nicosoff and his German handlers maintained these half-hearted exchanges. Could he locate the 23rd Infantry Division? the Abwehr asked. 'No money,' came the reply. 'No agents to collect information.' Agent 'Roberto' barely appeared in internal Abwehr signals.

To Simpson, the problem with the character of Nicosoff was that this apparent mercenary had been working for nearly a year without pay. This ought to make him suspect in German eyes. With no sign of any money on its way, he played Nicosoff as sulky. He sent a message threatening to sell his wireless to pay off the debts he had run up in his service of the Axis. When still nothing came, he grew sarcastic. Whenever a promise of money arrived, he was immediately enthusiastic.

The aim was to leave the Germans with the impression of a potentially useful agent who was losing faith in his controllers. Simpson's main worry was that the Germans would lose patience first. They certainly didn't seem very bothered about their man in Cairo. That lack of interest should have been a clue to SIME that they had a security problem. The reason German intelligence wasn't bothered about its man Roberto was only partly because he had misled them over Crusader. The other, bigger reason was that they had a far better man in Cairo.

The Cut and Restored Rope

June–July 1942

The Magician holds up a rope and a pair of scissors, and proceeds to cut the rope in half. They tie the two halves together
and then slide off the knot, revealing the rope has been made
whole again.

Chapter 27

Colonel Bonner Fellers, US Army, had been a fixture in Cairo since late 1940. In his mid-forties, still handsome despite his concerns about losing his hair, he was the military attaché at his country's legation. For more than a year, he had been his country's main observer in the only place the British army was actually fighting. His reports were read by the president.

With America supplying so much equipment, his good opinion was vital to the British, and as a result they let him go where he wanted and see whom he pleased. It helped that he had a great deal of charm. 'An original and delightful person,' Hermione Ranfurly wrote after meeting Fellers in Cairo in early 1941, 'who seems to say exactly what he thinks to everyone regardless of nationality or rank.' When her husband, an army officer, went missing during Rommel's first advance, Fellers had wired to the American delegation of the Red Cross to see what they could find out. A fortnight later he rang to pass on news: 'Ranfurly captured. Last seen in good health.'

His motives may not have been entirely altruistic. The Countess of Ranfurly, as she was formally known – her imprisoned husband was the sixth earl – was a useful person to cultivate. She worked for the Special Operations Executive, and knew everyone. She was no mere socialite, either. By mid-1941, concerned at the way SOE was operating, she was sneaking documents out of the office in her bra each evening to pass to Wavell. Her subterfuge led to a restructuring of the troubled organisation that summer.

Fellers wasn't aware of all of that, but he was formidably well-informed, and his reports back to Washington reflected it: troop movements, plans, the opinions of the most senior officers were all in there, along with Fellers' own often caustic observations about the British position. Which made it all the more unfortunate that in early 1942, Rommel was reading them within hours of their dispatch.

The previous September, Italian intelligence had stolen codebooks from the US embassy in Rome and then copied and replaced them before their absence was noticed. Axis spies were now reading all sorts of US diplomatic traffic, but none was valued as highly as that of Fellers. Here was the man in the room, passing on the details of every discussion. He was the ideal spy, touring battlefields with a soldier's eye for what mattered. In January of 1942 alone, he had told his masters – and Rommel – of the transfer of 270 aircraft from North Africa to the Far East, and given them complete details of the British tanks in the theatre, including their location and state of repair. He opened February with a report on forthcoming Commando operations.

'Personnel losses of the British are fairly light but loss in materiel heavy,' began one long report at the start of June. 'It is estimated at 70% of British tanks engaged were put out of action and at least 50% permanently destroyed. The air ground liaison was poor and the RAF repeatedly bombed own forces.' The next day he sent more detail. 'It is believed that the Southern Brigade of the 50th Division has been completely destroyed,' he wrote, before going on to give the locations and strengths of specific units. It was all, one of Rommel's intelligence officers marvelled, 'stupefying in its openness.'

In Germany, information from what was known as 'the Good Source' was rushed through the system, translated, re-encoded and transmitted to Libya with the goal that Rommel, at lunchtime, would know where Allied troops had been the evening before.

There was nothing quite like it. When Allied codebreakers read German messages, they had to go through a process of interpretation, working out who was talking to who and deducing, from the content of their messages, the location, status and intentions of different forces. Rommel had none of these problems. He was reading a report on his enemy's situation, written with complete frankness by one of the US Army's best intelligence officers. It was the assistance he needed as he drew up plans to resume his attack.

That April, as he went through the samples of decrypted German communications – known as 'Ultra' – that were placed in his daily box, Winston Churchill noticed something odd. The Luftwaffe had received an urgent warning that the British knew the location of its secret desert headquarters. Churchill scrawled a note to Menzies, the head of MI6: 'Please report on this. How did they know that we had told the Army in Egypt where it was?'

It was a good question. Menzies replied that an investigation was underway, which was surely true when he said it, even if it hadn't been before then. It was looking for security weaknesses at Grey Pillars. It was hardly surprising that senior British officers quickly settled on the American in their midst: it's always easier to blame an outsider. On this occasion, though, prejudice delivered the right answer. Bonner Fellers had indeed been the German source.

In April, this was simply a guess. But it led Auchinleck's staff to begin drafting new rules for what the American could see. It was a tricky area: he was the representative of the ally that was sending them the tanks they badly needed. It wouldn't do to offend him. No one wanted him to know that he wasn't being told things. But they wanted to stop telling him things.

They also sat him down for a chat about his security measures. They didn't tell him why, but Fellers was no fool, and he started to wonder what was wrong. As it happened, he had his own doubts about US codes. In February, he'd asked Washington for assurances that the codes were secure. Of course they were, came the reply.

In May, the staff at Grey Pillars settled on new rules of engagement for Fellers. They asked him to show them anything potentially compromising before he sent it. He promised he would. He didn't. In early June, Churchill's box of Ultra decrypts included one with an alarming cover note: 'Another long report to German Army in Africa from "Good Source" concerning British morale, training, supplies and intentions, evidently based on the Good Source's visits to British units.'

For the previous two months, MI6 had been hunting the Good Source. At Bletchley Park, they'd collated clues from the messages they'd been able to decrypt. They realised the term wasn't a descriptive evaluation that could be applied to reliable intelligence, but a reference that applied to a specific channel. But who? Where? One message, complaining that the British were wasting US aircraft and spare parts, sounded like things that had been said by American manufacturers who'd visited the Middle East. Could the Good Source be in the US War Department in Washington?

The message in Churchill's box nailed it. Menzies wasn't sending the prime minister another piece of the puzzle to infuriate him, but instead its solution. Included in the signal was the final clue. The Good Source had visited the front in North Africa, and reported back: 'Training inferior according to American ideas.'

The Good Source was in North Africa, with access to Grey Pillars, able to visit the front line, and his point of comparison was the US Army, which he naturally assumed to be superior. It wasn't much of a mystery any more. 'I am satisfied that the American ciphers in Cairo are compromised,' Menzies wrote in a note to Churchill included in the same box. 'I am taking action.'

That was even more sensitive than it might have seemed. There is a certain delicacy involved in telling your closest ally that they are the victim of a security leak. The job was given to Bletchley Park, who began an exchange of messages with their counterparts in Washington, the Signal Intelligence Service.

But as well as warning the US that its codes had been compromised, Bletchley had to protect its own work. The British knew that the Germans were reading the American code because the British were reading the German code. If they acted too clumsily, there was a danger that the Germans would start assembling their own puzzle, and realise that someone was doing to them what they were doing to the Americans. The message to Washington contained a plea to say nothing at all to Cairo.

For several days, the two sides consulted, hampered by time differences and delays as the Americans considered pieces of evidence that were being sent piecemeal in transatlantic cables. Despite what Menzies had told Churchill, both ends of the conversation were aware that there were other ways in which Axis intelligence might have read Fellers' telegrams. An enemy agent might have access to the unenciphered messages, either in Cairo or Washington.

In the US, there was reluctance to believe what they were being told. The implications were too awful. If the code was compromised, US communications from all their diplomatic outposts were being read. Who knew what other secrets had been blown in messages from their embassies?

As for Fellers, Bletchley Park was still compiling evidence about what the Good Source had been giving the enemy, but in Washington, a flick through his cables over the previous six months would reveal that, if he were indeed the leak, he had been giving them everything.

And while they delayed action, he carried on giving. Even as the discussions were going on, he wired Washington about imminent plans for Commando raids on nine Axis airfields. At Bletchley Park, reading Good Source warnings based on that cable, they were apoplectic. 'Further information from Good Source reveals our future plans,' read one cable to Washington, 'and matter becomes of extreme urgency.'

Even as the Bletchley Park analysts read the Commando message, they knew there was little they could do. Too blunt a warning to Cairo that the raids were expected would risk all their work. All they could do was tell Cairo that the Germans were increasing security at airfields. It was, in any case, too late to get a message to the Commando units far out in the desert.

The news from the raids would take days to arrive. The SAS claimed to have destroyed up to forty planes. German reports the next day suggested the number was ten. But it was clear that the raiders had been expected: one group trying to sneak onto a base found themselves surrounded by German soldiers. Only one of those men made it home.

Meanwhile Fellers was still sending his dispatches, unaware they were being read. And now Rommel was closing in on Cairo.

Chapter 28

At the end of May, his strength consolidated, his picture of the British defensive line better than anyone in Cairo realised, Rommel had launched his assault.

He used deception techniques of his own, sending forward trucks mounted with aircraft engines on his northern flank, to blow up a dust cloud that looked like it had been caused by a fleet of tanks, while at the southern end of the line his real force pushed forward, overrunning the surprised defenders.

The Eighth Army – with more men and more tanks than the Afrika Corps – fought back, and at times came close to winning, but while its commanders failed to exploit opportunities, Rommel, short of fuel and ammunition, managed to squeeze his way out of trouble again and again. The men on the ground fought bravely, desperately, but by the middle of June British forces were in full retreat, trying to get to the defensive line on the Egyptian border ahead of their pursuers. 'The battle has been won,' Rommel wrote to his wife. 'The enemy is breaking up.' He saw the possibility of a victory by the following month so total that he would be able to get home. 'Perhaps we will see each other in July after all.'

As for Tobruk, its defences had fallen into disrepair. The South African troops occupying it had never seen battle, and neither had their commander. On 20 June, Rommel attacked. The defenders surrendered the next day.

While the strategic value of Tobruk was debatable – the Auk, clearly, didn't think it was that great – the loss of the town was a huge blow to morale. All through the previous year it had been viewed as a symbol of British resistance, and now it had been swept away in a moment. 'No news has shocked us more since Dunkirk,' Hermione Ranfurly confided to her diary.

With the Japanese advancing across the British Empire and the Pacific in the Far East, and the Germans advancing in Russia and now the desert, 1942 was turning into another bad year for the Allies. On the Eastern front, the German army was turning towards Stalingrad, to consolidate its gains in southern Russia. If the Soviets couldn't hold their ground, the British in the Middle East would find themselves with another German force on their northern flank, ready to strike through Iran and Iraq. In the Far East, Japanese forces had captured the Philippines and Burma. They were now on the Indian border. Only in the Pacific was there good news, with the Japanese navy defeated at the battles of the Coral Sea and Midway.

For Churchill, the sting of Tobruk's loss was magnified by the humiliating way in which he learned of it. On a visit to Washington, he was in the White House when a messenger handed Roosevelt a slip of paper bearing the news. The president looked at it and then silently gave it to the prime minister. 'I did not attempt to hide from the president the shock I had received,' Churchill recalled. 'It was a bitter moment. Defeat is one thing. Disgrace is another.'

His feelings were shared by ordinary Britons. It was not just that the port had fallen, but that it had fallen so quickly, after holding out so long the previous year. What was wrong with their soldiers? It was a question the prime minister asked too. His commanders had asked for tanks and men and guns, and had got them, and still they couldn't win.

When he returned to London, Churchill faced a motion of censure in Parliament. Replying, he made no effort to play down the defeat, suggesting what was happening in the Middle East was a 'disaster' on a scale with the fall of France. Though he won the vote overwhelmingly, a substantial number of members of parliament abstained – a warning that support for him was not unlimited. Labour's Aneurin Bevan had claimed to speak on behalf of ordinary soldiers, noting 'the prime minister wins debate after debate but loses battle after battle'.

Meanwhile Rommel's army was advancing, over the Egyptian border and on towards Alexandria. Soon he would reach the Nile Delta, the fertile triangle of flood plain that spread out as the great river approached the sea. Auchinleck looked for a place where the invaders could be held. He identified a spot where the gap between the sea in the north and the impassable desert to the south narrowed to 40 miles. Here he would make his stand, just a few hours' drive from Cairo. There wasn't really much on the map to identify it, but he ordered his army to make a defensive line south from a railway station on the coast named El Alamein.

In Egypt, there was uproar. Rommel was unstoppable, only days away. Mussolini had flown to Libya, accompanied by a white charger that he planned to ride into Cairo for his victory parade. British forces streamed back from the front, battered and beaten. At Alexandria on the coast, the Royal Navy, fearing both land and air attacks, suddenly weighed anchor and departed.

For those who had arrived in Egypt having fled the Nazi advance through the Balkans and Greece, this was all familiar. These refugees had learned one important lesson the previous year: if you think the Germans might come, don't wait around to see if they do. The difference between escaping and not might be the difference between the morning and the afternoon train.

So Europeans fled, piling into cars or trains and heading east. (Not all the Europeans, of course: there was a report that some fascists among the Italian population had sent their party uniforms off to be cleaned.) Queues formed at banks, for money, embassies, for visas, and the railway station, for trains. The British authorities tried to be dismissive, by calling it a 'flap', but also set about getting soldiers' families, female staff, and anyone judged likely to be targets for the Gestapo out of the country.

The fear was real at the highest levels. Though the British ambassador, Sir Miles Lampson, affected nonchalance, going shopping with his wife and dining out, he knew that a train had been laid on to carry them both to safety if needed. At Shepheard's, officers joked darkly that if they wanted to slow Rommel down, they just needed him to try and get served in the bar.

If the many Europeans in Egypt were terrified, the Egyptians themselves seemed less troubled by the prospect of invasion. In Alexandria, shopkeepers put out bunting for the Germans, and women ordered dresses for the victory ball that they expected the conquerors to hold. Down the street from A Force's headquarters in Cairo, a shopkeeper created a display of trunks and suitcases, which was taken as a hint of what he thought the British ought to be doing. Fearful of civil unrest in support of Rommel's army, the Auk's chief of staff ordered all officers in the city to carry revolvers at all times.

Maunsell, though, was doubtful that the Egyptian behaviour reflected genuine animosity so much as indifference. 'The Arabs seemed to view the struggle with the Axis in much the same way as Americans might view a test match at Lords,' he wrote. Taxi drivers joked with their British passengers in that spirit: 'Today, I drive you to Groppi's,' they told them. 'Tomorrow, you drive me!'

And other parts of Cairo life carried on as they always had. Foreigners making their way down the street, considering if they should leave, and if so how, were still pestered by sellers of fountain pens, and fly swats, and dirty pictures.

As the British were wondering whether they could hold Rommel back, in Washington they were still debating what to do about Fellers. There was a reluctance to give up on their man. Some suspected an MI6 plot to remove him. And as they dithered, Fellers was revealing to Rommel the full extent of the British weakness in Egypt. In fact, he was doing more than that.

For all his congeniality with Hermione Ranfurly, Fellers was generally unimpressed by the British military and the commanders he had encountered in Egypt. There was, obviously, some justification for this, but also a certain naivety in his belief that the US Army, which had yet to face the Germans, would have more success when it did.

After the fall of Tobruk, Fellers composed a furious memo complaining that despite superior numbers, the Allies had failed to defeat the Axis. His aim was to make the case for the immediate dispatch of proper, American troops, whom he was confident would be able to push the enemy back. He had little success persuading his own commanders, but did rather better at convincing the enemy. Unable to get accurate figures from the now cautious staff at Grey Pillars, Fellers estimated that the British were down to 100 tanks in Egypt. 'If Rommel intends to take the Delta,' he wrote, 'now is an opportune time.'

Rommel never needed any encouragement to go after a big prize. Having pushed the British back across Libya, he was sure they were close to final defeat, and sure he was able to deliver it. Fellers' words were music to his ears.

At the start of July, the Axis forces tried to break through the El Alamein line. As the Eighth Army attempted to hold them back, staff officers at Grey Pillars in Cairo took the prospect of defeat seriously enough to begin burning their papers in four huge bonfires. The first of July became known as 'Ash Wednesday', as the air around the headquarters turned black with smoke. It went almost comically wrong: some of the documents were lifted up by the heat of the fires and blown out of the compound before they were destroyed. In the days afterwards, soldiers buying peanuts from street vendors found they came in little cones made from half-charred classified documents.

A Force held its own bonfire, burning documents for two solid days. There was no time to think about deception plans now: Cairo would be held or lost by hard fighting, not tricks and illusions. The most precious files, and those that were still needed, were loaded onto a train to Jerusalem, with two secretaries and one of Clarke's subordinates, under instructions to set up a new headquarters.

But Clarke wasn't planning to join them. He was clear that if Cairo fell, he would stay. Partly this would be in his capacity as head of MI9, helping the many soldiers who were likely to be hiding out in Egypt, separated from their units, to evade capture and make their way back to the British lines. But he had bigger ideas than that. He was going to become a guerrilla, waging a war in the Nile Delta against the new occupiers.

For most people, war really is hell: boredom and discomfort interrupted by intense periods of terror. In Egypt it was too hot in the day and too cold at night. The sand got everywhere, the water tasted terrible and the food might poison you. But for some people, war was a chance to break rules and live out fantasies. Dudley Clarke was one of them.

His plan was of a piece with that. Where would a man of action put himself? Where would Richard Hannay have wanted to be but hiding out behind enemy lines, rescuing his fellow soldiers and making life dashed difficult for the Hun?

As Hannay would, Clarke picked his friends to stay behind with him: Simonds – an obvious choice as an MI9 man who'd already fought one guerrilla war in Ethiopia – but also Wild and Crichton. Clarke told them to get ready. They'd need hideouts, transport and supplies, all ready to go at twelve hours' notice.

But first Crichton had a piece of business to attend to: he told Betty that they should marry at once. Persuaded, she fought her way through the panicked crowds outside the American consulate to get the documentation that a US citizen needed to marry. When she told the consul what she wanted, he was astonished, and after recovering himself, he jumped on the table. 'Look at this lady!' he told the crowd. 'You're all frantic to get out, and she's not trying to get out, she's staying and getting married!' Betty and Michael Crichton were married by a military judge at Grey Pillars, and then the groom had to get back to work. 'I may not see you for a while,' he told her. It was a line David Niven himself couldn't have delivered better.

His marriage settled, Crichton returned to his office-under-a-brothel to look over Clarke's plan. Even by the standards of unconventional warfare, it was unusual. Clarke's vision was that he would gather thousands of scattered soldiers who had escaped the advancing Germans, and form them into a guerrilla force to fight 'under almost ideal conditions'.

The heavily irrigated Nile Delta, he reasoned, would offer poor going to German tanks kitted out for desert fighting. British intelligence had concluded that, even with what he would be able to plunder in Cairo, Rommel would run out of supplies if he was prevented from using the railways to Alexandria for four months. Clarke believed he would be able to deliver exactly that, carrying out hit-and-run attacks, luring enemy armour into traps, and spreading false rumours.

For the past year, a unit of troops designated 'K Detachment, SAS Brigade' had, far less excitingly than their name suggested, been assembling dummy gliders for display to the enemy. Now Clarke wanted them to do something rather more SAS-like, operating as a demolition squad. There would also be dummy tanks and a forgery team, complete with its own printing press.

His experience of combat had been inauspicious to this point: sheltering from gunfire for hours in Norway, and then nearly getting his ear shot off by a stray round on the first Commando raid. But now he hoped to have the chance to prove himself in battle, as he had dreamed of doing ever since the start of the Great War. What was more, it was going to be hit-and-run, irregular warfare, exactly the kind of work he'd envisaged for the Commandos, and that he'd fantasised about with David Stirling and the other bright young men of Shepheard's.

For a week, A Force worked frantically to set up its hideouts: one in a workshop on the edge of the city, one in a school building five miles north, and then finally a place deep in the Delta, near the only location they reckoned it would be possible to land a light plane. All were stocked with food, petrol and ammunition.

In Cairo, a bookshop and a perfume factory were identified as shelters for soldiers trying to evade capture. The team bought a laundry van to move round the city, and paint to disguise their military vehicles. One of Clarke's officers popped down to the Muhammad Ali Club one lunchtime and stole a collection of number plates off cars parked outside. Somewhere they'd got hold of a captured German car, and stocked it with enemy uniforms and weapons. On the Nile, Clarke secured a yacht and some barges to facilitate escapees, and promised a space to Betty-to-You, the new Mrs Crichton.

A Force identified civilian volunteers who promised to help, including the Freemasons, who committed to run escape centres in every village. Meanwhile the ease with which police and smugglers agreed to work together to run escape lines out of the country suggested that the British government may not have been the only organisation supplementing law enforcement incomes.

If the general mood in Cairo was terror that the Germans were going to arrive, at A Force headquarters on Sharia Kasr-El-Nil, there was at least one man who was rather looking forward to it.

Chapter 29

While Clarke was preparing for life as a guerrilla leader, Rommel was discovering that even the Good Source had its limits.

Fellers had prepared his reports in good faith, based on what he knew, but thanks to Bletchley Park's interventions earlier in the year, he was being told less now than he once had been. Like spies through the ages, he had filled in the blanks with educated guesses. In particular, he was wrong about how many tanks the British had at their disposal. When Rommel made his attempt on the El Alamein line, there were 400 more of them waiting for him than he expected. And, in a development that should have pleased the patriotic Fellers, the US-made Grant tanks turned out to be far more effective than either side had realised they would be.

Fellers had, unconsciously, lured Rommel into a trap, changing trades from inadvertent spy to inadvertent deceiver. And having done that, he went quiet. The Americans finally changed their code on 25 June, two weeks after Bletchley Park had first alerted them to the leak. In the midst of the battle, Rommel had lost his Good Source.

Within days he suffered a second blow, as his wireless intelligence unit, which had done sterling work gleaning information from radio chatter at the front, was overrun and captured. He was, one of Rommel's intelligence officers said, like 'a man accustomed to going around at will and in broad daylight but suddenly forced to grope around in the pitch dark.'

There had been another change: the Auk had taken personal command of the Eighth Army. The Afrika Korps now found itself facing an enemy that was going to fight creatively. Attack after attack was repulsed, while artillery and bombers pounded the German and Italian positions.

Once again, the calculus of the desert was taking its toll: Rommel's supply lines were long, while Auchinleck's were short.

Taking Tobruk hadn't helped: the Royal Navy still threatened the sea outside it; the port wasn't designed for unloading merchant ships; Allied bombers were constantly attacking it. The Auk had been right: the port's military value wasn't actually that high.

Even if supplies could get to the ports, they still had to travel from there to the front, in trucks that were constantly breaking down. To make matters worse, the vast bulk of German transport vehicles had been captured from the British, which made it much harder for Rommel's mechanics to source spare parts.

Days of hard close fighting, involving forces from across the world – Italians and Germans facing Britons, South Africans, Indians, Australians and New Zealanders – turned into weeks, and it became clear that a breakthrough wasn't imminent. The Afrika Korps had nearly made it, but it had finally been held.

Back in Cairo, the Flap gradually subsided. For most, the response was relief. For Clarke, it was mixed with disappointment that he didn't get to try his hand at being a guerrilla. It would have been a great show.

He did get one compensatory performance. Once it was clear that the Germans weren't coming, Michael and Betty Crichton decided to have a proper wedding, at a little Cairo church. Clarke gave the bride away.

There were other changes afoot. Fellers, no longer trusted by the British staff, was recalled to Washington. His departure under a cloud was understandable – his hosts saw him as someone who had been high-handed about their abilities while unconsciously sabotaging their work – but also a little unfair. He had been rude about the British, but he'd made the case for equipping them. He had informed Rommel, but also misled him.

Fellers hadn't told the enemy everything. He hadn't been told that the German codes had been broken, and he doesn't seem to have known about Clarke's work. While other private armies in Cairo worked at self-promotion – the SAS in particular – A Force kept its secrets tight. Clarke knew that Fellers' job was to gather information and pass it on. It probably helped that he disliked Americans almost as much as Fellers disliked the English.

And the silencing of Fellers meant that another months-long Cairo courtship was also bearing fruit. On 2 July, a week after Fellers went off the air, the Abwehr sent a signal to its agent 'Roberto', as it knew Cheese: 'Be very active these days. Good information will be well rewarded. From now onwards we are going to listen in every day for your signals.'

For Evan Simpson, Rommel's advance had provided the perfect excuse to revive Cheese's enthusiasm. It was no longer improbable that an unpaid Abwehr agent in Cairo would be hard at work. Simpson had played Nicosoff as a man who saw himself as the future hero of Rommel's victory, the good and faithful spy who had risked much for his masters, and now hoped to share in their triumph.

None of this on its own had been enough to persuade the Abwehr to take him back. But it had meant that when they discovered they could no longer break the American code, they grabbed onto Nicosoff with enthusiasm. At the start of July, the Abwehr began grading his reports as 'credible'. German agents were known as 'Vertrauensmann', meaning 'trusted man', or 'V-Mann' for short. By August, Abwehr reports were sourcing information from the 'Reliable V-Mann Roberto'.

Objectively, this makes little sense. The Abwehr knew he had passed them false information the previous year. If an agent was compromised in 1941, it was implausible for him to uncompromise himself in 1942. The staff of SIME, though happy about the break-through, were surprised that it had happened. The Germans, they felt, should be better than this.

This is a persistent view. Ever since the end of the war, there has been a theory that German intelligence was riddled with anti-Nazis who were deliberately passing on poor information in order to hasten the fall of Hitler. Much of the evidence for this comes from the success that the Allies had at putting over their deceptions. Surely, goes the argument, these clever and efficient officers couldn't have been so comprehensively taken in.

It's certainly the case that many Abwehr officers were accused of plotting against Hitler. The service's chief, Admiral Wilhelm Canaris, was among those killed in the wake of the 1944 attempt on the Fuhrer's life. And within A Force there were staff who were sure that Clarke had been able to put his 'stories' over so effectively because he'd been helped from the other side.

But there is a simpler explanation for the failure of German intelligence. While it was natural for the British to believe that the enemy who had beaten them so often was fearsome and powerful, in fact parts of the German war machine were in terrible shape. And its intelligence service in particular was a disaster.

All intelligence agencies face similar pressures: to answer questions with more certainty than they should; to conceal mistakes; to put too much trust in the sources that they have; and to belittle internal or external rivals. Allied intelligence was subject to each of these, as shown by the weeks of tense discussion over changing the code used by Fellers. In the middle of 1942, MI6 was still refusing to share much of the information it gleaned from Bletchley Park with either MI5 or SIME.

But whatever problems there were within Allied intelligence were nothing to the difficulties on the other side. The Abwehr was a part of the German military, but one that was regarded as a career dead end, so it struggled to recruit high-calibre staff.

Canaris was a schemer and a climber, rather than an administrator or an organiser. He built no system for cross-checking information or assessing its quality. The men who prospered underneath him were often scoundrels, charmers who saw a chance to spend the war living large in a neutral city at someone else's expense. 'He chose worthless officers,' an MI6 report observed, and then allowed them to do as they pleased.

Those officers, in their turn, recruited poor agents to do their spying. Some, like Renato Levi, were planning to betray the Germans from the moment they were approached. Other Abwehr agents included people who had been blackmailed into becoming spies with threats against their families, or who agreed to do the work to escape prison. In some cases they took the job to escape Nazi territory, and with the intention of handing themselves in to the Allies the first chance they got.

Having selected substandard agents, Canaris's men trained them badly. Captured Germans were found to be confused by British currency and military structures. These were, fundamentally, not good spies.

But in the early years of the war Canaris had won favour by giving the impression that he had eyes and ears everywhere. The last thing he wanted to do was encourage people to start questioning the reliability of those eyes and ears.

Hitler's government was a court of competing factions, all seeking the Fuhrer's approval. The Abwehr, responsible for military intelligence, had a vicious rival in Department VI of the Reich Main Security Office, the foreign intelligence service of the SS. Canaris knew that to admit a mistake was to give ammunition to his internal enemies. His officers likewise had no incentive to think critically about the quality of their own work. Quite the opposite. An ideological and murderous regime like Nazi Germany is not a place where people flourish by asking difficult questions or speaking truth to power.

Maunsell took a straightforward view of why the Germans had been deceived. 'Because the Abwehr was a thoroughly corrupt organisation, careless, dilettante and foreign to exact administration which is essential to good intelligence work,' he recalled after the war. He believed they were more interested in being able to show evidence of their work than in being honest about its quality: 'The whole organisation was permeated with "pins in the map syndrome".'

Some Abwehr officers did suspect that some of their agents had been captured and were operating under British control. But they also suspected, probably correctly, that saying anything would put their own necks on the line. According to MI6, Abwehr officers who were perceptive enough to see the necessity of a proper system of intelligence assessment 'were corrupt enough to see the necessity of preventing it'.

The Abwehr had also failed to grasp something about their enemy. Both the German and Italian models of total war placed great emphasis on the army. The British and Americans had a different approach, putting men into industry and air and naval forces. Nearly four-fifths of the German military was in the army, compared to three-fifths of the British forces. But Axis intelligence services never understood this. That explained why Clarke had found it so easy to persuade them that the British army was larger than it was: they were already looking for the troops they were sure must exist somewhere.

The national stereotypes of the war are of ruthlessly organised Germans facing English gentleman amateurs. In the deception battle the opposite was the case. German intelligence was chaotic and poorly controlled, while A Force's rigorous, tedious bureaucracy of deception, patiently building the stories of notional units over months and ultimately years, helped the deceivers to keep their story straight and to steadily pass over small jigsaw pieces of mutually reinforcing misinformation that carefully led the recipients to the wrong conclusion.

Between them, Italian and German intelligence knew quite enough to render Cheese suspect. The channel had been handed to them by Renato Levi, who was sufficiently tainted that the Italians had him in prison. It had been used to pass bad information. There were other question marks. Abwehr officers in Athens noted that when atmospheric interference had stopped most of their wireless stations from successfully transmitting, their man 'Roberto' had stayed on the air. This was a clue that he was better equipped, or a better radio operator, than they'd been led to believe.

But with no other sources in Cairo, and superiors who only wanted to hear about successes, the best course was to silence their doubts and keep on believing.

The counter-intelligence officers at SIME would get a sense of the Abwehr's problems in late July, when they picked up two German spies. Almost everything about the men's story was glamorous: they had got to Egypt by crossing the desert from Sudan, under the guidance of a renowned explorer, Count Laszlo Almasy. Once in Cairo they had taken shelter with a belly dancer, and then set themselves up in a houseboat on the Nile. Even the name of their mission was first-rate: Operation Condor.

The one part of their story that was disappointing was the actual espionage. This they had found difficult. They couldn't get their radio to work – not their fault, as the unit that was supposed to be listening for their signals had been captured – and they weren't especially good at finding things out.

The pair spent their afternoons at the cinema and their evenings at nightclubs and casinos. They had been sent with plenty of money, but the wrong sort: they had British pounds, which weren't legal in Egypt, and they'd had to change them on the black market. Their hope was that British officers, bought enough drinks, would reveal things they shouldn't. In reality the spies found that while nightclubs were fun, they were burning through their cash without anything to show for it.

Then they'd had a stroke of luck. They'd made contact with some Egyptian army officers who wanted to help Rommel. One of them, a signals officer, offered to try to fix their wireless. His name was Anwar al-Sadat.

And just as things seemed to be looking up for the pair, their adventure ended. At dawn the next day, the police arrived, guided there by SIME. One of the people the spies had approached for help had hinted to the British that he knew something. SIME, not an outfit to beat about the bush, had kidnapped him and promised not to shoot him if he told all he knew. The spies were imprisoned, as was al-Sadat, who had a much brighter future in front of him than was obvious in the summer of 1942.

As they looked into the case, the SIME officers got a very mixed picture. At one level, Condor was a sophisticated operation that had successfully infiltrated two spies into Cairo, where they had in turn made contact with useful sources in the shape of disaffected Egyptian officers. At another, it was a mess. The men had been sent with the wrong currency – a failure of the most basic preparation – and not much in the way of a clear idea of what they were to do when they got there. They had spent a huge amount of money for no result, and been picked up within weeks. The military wireless unit that was listening for their signals had been allowed to go somewhere where it was caught, and there had been no backup plan for communication.

There was however a clear upside for Simpson as he continued building up Nicosoff. At the start of August, he was able to signal to the Abwehr that two German spies and a number of civilians had been arrested in Cairo. He was their only source in the city, and they decided they had better trust him.

Chapter 30

When Nicosoff had last enjoyed the status of a reliable Axis source, the previous autumn, Shearer had treated him as a disposable asset, one that could be used in order to help deliver a surprise for Crusader, and then abandoned. But since then Clarke had sat with the Twenty Committee in London and seen how a double agent could become a long-term property. His deceptive ambitions had also grown.

Starting that July, a committee chaired by Clarke would meet each day at A Force headquarters to decide on the day's message, which would be transmitted that evening. To explain Nicosoff's increased output, he was given a new network, starting with a girlfriend, 'Marie'. In messages to the Abwehr, she was Nicosoff's 'amie'. A Force gave her the codename 'Misanthrope'.

The Cheese messages suggested that Nicosoff was far from the only man in Cairo who was beguiled by 'Marie's' charms. She seemed to have a wide acquaintance among the city's military circles. She also served as an insurance policy for Cheese. Warrant Officer Ellis, the original wireless operator playing Nicosoff, had been replaced by a Sergeant Shears, but he too was becoming worn down by the work. Wireless transmission styles are distinctive, and the team feared using someone else in place of Shears: at one point he'd had to be brought from hospital on a stretcher in order to transmit a message. Now 'Marie' would be able to send signals, allowing them to use another operator.

One of the rules adopted by the Twenty Committee in London was that the double-cross agents it ran should live the lives they described to their German controllers. If they were told to go and look at a factory, they made the journey, and tried to find as much as they could. Clarke imported that rule to Cairo. As Nicosoff was supposed to be spending his time hanging around Cairo chatting to soldiers, the team was able to describe his life without difficulty.

But he was now going to be sending 'Marie' on missions, and they needed someone to play her.

SIME found the perfect woman in its Greek section. Evangeline Palidou was twenty-nine years old, a Cretan whose experiences under German occupation had left her with a loathing of the Nazis. She had an impressive effect on the men of SIME and A Force, especially when they discovered that she carried a miniature revolver in her handbag and knew how to use it. She was rumoured to have shot a man, or, in another version, pushed him off a roof. Clarke's mind was never far from Hollywood, and he saw in Palidou something of the femme fatale. Though she was a brunette, he christened her the 'Blonde Gun Moll', and the name stuck, with references to 'the BGM' appearing throughout the Cheese files.*

Palidou was asked to keep notes of the badges and vehicle signs she saw in her daily life, just as 'Marie' was doing. When 'Marie' was sent to Alexandria to find out about the feelings of the French sailors who remained loyal to the Vichy government, it was Palidou who went in reality.

But if Rommel's advance into Egypt had given Nicosoff a reason to stay on the air, his failure to break through in July took A Force back to an earlier problem: how could they plausibly explain the agent continuing to work when he wasn't being paid? In June, Nicosoff had told his controller he needed £1,000. In July, he said it was now £1,400, and complained that he wasn't able to borrow any more. Clarke and his team began to worry. How long could they keep things going if the Germans didn't start paying?

Then, at the start of August, a Royal Navy destroyer, HMS *Sikh*, on anti-submarine operations to cover a convoy at the eastern end of the Mediterranean, picked up a suspected U-boat. For ten hours the *Sikh*, joined by three more destroyers, hunted its prey, before finally U-372 was forced to the surface. Though the submarine quickly

---

* In theory, British intelligence practice is to remove the names of agents from declassified files. In practice, the files are confusing and sometimes the censor will miss something. It looks like Palidou's name, which appears once in the files, slipped through. An alternative reading of the file is that Evangeline Palidou too was a fictional creation, to be the 'real' identity of Marie. If this is the case, the level of detail about her life story suggests that at least one lonely SIME officer had spent a little too long imagining her.

sank again, the crew were rescued. One of them was an Arab, carrying bundles of notes in different currencies totalling roughly £1,400, which he said he'd been told to deliver to a 'Paul' in Cairo.

This was welcome proof that the Abwehr believed in Cheese, but it didn't solve Nicosoff's money problem. He could hardly admit to knowing about the U-boat and its courier. Instead he continued to complain ever more vociferously. In October, his controllers replied that they were trying again, and asked for a place in Cairo where he could be given money. This presented A Force with several problems, chiefly that Nicosoff didn't exist.

One option would be to get someone to impersonate him, but that would mean finding someone who could pull off playing a Middle Eastern Slav. If that weren't challenge enough, they didn't know what kind of physical description the absent Renato Levi might have given of his recruit. It would be safer, they decided, if he sent his girlfriend 'Marie'. Enter, once again, the BGM.

For a month before the proposed rendezvous, Palidou was drilled on the story that Simpson and A Force had written for her. It told the whole story of how she had met the imaginary 'Paul Nicosoff', how he had gradually inducted her into his secret life and then made her his partner in espionage. It offered particular details that Nicosoff had attributed to her in previous messages: her real trip to Alexandria, and her imaginary sighting of more than 100 tanks crossing one of the Cairo bridges.

'It will be her role not willingly to reveal information about herself or Paul, but rather to be constantly on the defensive,' wrote one of the SIME officers on the case. 'This will be naturally explained by the extreme nervousness of both herself and Paul. She will refer more than once to the recent execution of five spies at Aleppo; she may also mention the arrest of the two German spies on a houseboat, and the spate of arrests they brought in their train.'

The next question was where to hold the meeting. SIME had taken a flat in Cairo for exactly this purpose, but when they considered simply sending the address to the Abwehr, they realised that this might allow the enemy to put it under surveillance. Better to have the meeting in a public place. Palidou identified a cafe, and sat waiting in it on the arranged date, wearing a white dress with a red belt. Outside a SIME man masqueraded as a taxi driver, with two of his colleagues lurking within sight. No courier came. The following evening they tried again, and again no one showed up. Nicosoff sent a plaintive message to his controllers. 'Do you think this is all so simple?' came the grumpy reply.

If he had thought that, the following months would have disabused him. The Abwehr promised to deliver the money to a different address, concealed in a bottle of milk. It never came. More deliveries failed. At least once, it was clear that the courier had done a runner with the cash.

By the middle of 1943, A Force had concluded that Nicosoff was only going to get paid if they arranged it themselves. In one of the odder moments of an odd war, Clarke found himself dispatching a courier to Istanbul to transport money on behalf of an enemy spy agency, to pay a non-existent agent who was betraying them.

In all this, Clarke saw the funny side. There was a fashion in Cairo at the time for writing limericks about the city's notables. Clarke produced his own Most Secret effort:

> Nicosoff's a Russian name
> And not what you might think,
> A form of Oriental vice,
> Or buggery, or drink.
> A scion of this noble house,
> An unattractive sod,
> Was Stanislas P. Nicosoff
> Of Nizhni Novgorod.

The Abwehr weren't in on the joke. Bletchley Park's codebreakers had picked up an obvious change in the way the Germans were talking about 'Roberto', as they called Nicosoff. In the first half of 1942, mentions of his reports were picked up only twice. Then, in July alone, he appeared in Abwehr signals fifteen times. At the start of July, his name was accompanied by a warning: 'Reliability of agent not yet fully proved.' Within days that had changed. His reports were suddenly 'credible', and he gave information 'reliably'. By the end of the month he was 'trustworthy'. The Athens Abwehr station set up a direct link with Rommel's army, to pass 'Nicosoff's' messages on faster.

Clarke often described himself as someone who was producing a show. The best way of assessing how he was doing, he said, was 'by

the reactions of the audience'. In his first year in the job, those re-
actions had come sporadically, in the form of captured documents.
Now he was starting to receive a steadier flow of information on
the Abwehr's thinking from an intelligence source codenamed
'Triangle' – in reality decrypts of the traffic from the Athens
Abwehr to Rommel.

What Clarke didn't know was that he was missing a much richer
seam of intelligence. So closely guarded was the secret of Bletchley
Park that he was still unaware of how comprehensively German
communications were being read. More surprisingly, they were also
unaware of him. Somehow, it hadn't occurred to anyone in London
that these two parts of the secret world might be able to work together to help each other.

Simpson's insight in reviving Cheese had been that what the
Abwehr needed was an excuse to believe in him. By blaming
'Nicosoff's' unreliable source, 'Piet', he had provided that excuse.

Any magician performing a difficult trick makes sure they have
an 'out' – an alternative way of ending it so that the audience won't
realise it's gone wrong. Simpson had turned that round, giving the
audience the 'out' – a way to tell themselves what they wanted to
hear, that their man was still trustworthy. From here on, A Force
would ensure that each deception contained such an 'out', a plausible reason why the enemy had got things wrong. The jigsaw pieces
they passed over could always be assembled in different ways, so
perhaps the information had been correct but the interpretation had
been mistaken. Or perhaps the interpretation had been correct, but
the plans had changed at the last minute: a popular one with A Force
was that an attack which they had persuaded the Abwehr was going
to be a feint had been so successful that commanders had decided it
should become the real attack. Such things, after all, happen in war.

Clarke, too, took a lesson. He had been operating on the assumption that his audience was a suspicious one, and that if it realised it
had been fooled, it would be harder to fool it in future. Perhaps that
wasn't the case.

But that summer, as the Eighth Army held the line barely sixty
miles from Alexandria, the priority was to fool the Afrika Korps.
Auchinleck wanted to dissuade Rommel from launching another
attack until he'd had time to bring up reinforcements and dig in.
Clarke proposed suggesting that there was a trap waiting for the

German commander behind the El Alamein line, in the Nile Delta, where networks of concealed anti-tank guns were waiting to blow his vehicles to pieces as they advanced.

Cheese would play his part, as would the Turkish intelligence channels, but Rommel, so closely engaged with his enemy, was going to pay less attention to reports from unknown spies than to what his men were reporting they could see.

That meant that deceptions were going to have to rely on Geoffrey Barkas' camouflage experts. To Barkas, this was the moment he was finally getting called up for a starring role. Over the previous two years he'd become passionate about the possibilities of camouflage, but he'd struggled to interest his commanders. Both the artistic and military sides of his personality were intensely frustrated to see forward bases that were improperly camouflaged, his men ignored when they tried to suggest improvements.

Barkas was proud of his camoufleurs, and convinced that their talents weren't recognised as they should be. He spent a lot of time trying to get them that recognition, and trying to educate ordinary soldiers about the things they could do to conceal themselves. Both of these put him in a different position to Clarke. Where Clarke was a military insider whose work depended on as few people finding out about it as possible, someone with access at the very highest levels, Barkas was at heart a civilian, leading a group of very unmilitary artists, keen to explain his work to everyone.

He felt, too, that the deceivers of A Force didn't take the camouflage men seriously enough. They had, Barkas pointed out to Clarke, run deception during the siege of Tobruk with no help from A Force. They had come up with and implemented the dummy railway plan before 'Crusader'. They might not dabble in the mysterious world of spies, but they knew all there was to know about fooling the eye.

Now, finally, they needed him. 'This was balm to the soul,' he wrote later. 'We had been sent for at the start of something big and given a chance to help the fighting men.' The task was not simply to hide real things but to display fake things. Barkas and his team were determined not to blow their big break. Clarke was surprised and impressed at how quickly the camoufleurs built fake camps, with smoke rising from the cook tents and clouds of dust rising from the tracks that connected them to the main roads. Peter Proud, who the previous year had made a building at Tobruk look as though it had been bombed, had worked out how to stitch fabric into a net that, stretched over posts, looked from the air just like a gun emplacement. To these were added trenches and fake tanks, 'all of which,' Clarke noted with satisfaction, 'were carefully photographed by the watchful Boche'.

The audience was looking where he wanted it to.

The Shell Game

July–October 1942

The Magician places three shells on the table and then places a ball under one of them. When the audience is asked to guess where the ball is, it is revealed to have moved to a different shell.

Chapter 31

At the end of July, Rommel was where he'd been at the start, with Cairo at once close and beyond his grasp. The supplies he needed were in front of him and he couldn't get to them. He needed somehow to break through the 40-mile defensive line that ran directly south from El Alamein railway station. To the north was the sea. To the south, the Qattara Depression, a low area of desert impassable to most vehicles. There would be no daring flanking manoeuvres here. His men were exhausted and short of everything.

The Allied forces, on the other hand, were fragile – a month earlier they had thought they might lose Egypt – but stabilised. And now they were getting new supplies. They were also getting a new commander.

Churchill had, as was his way, lost patience with Auchinleck after the loss of Tobruk. The stand at El Alamein had made no difference: the prime minister wanted generals who could win, rather than simply not lose.

The Auk was furious to learn he was being sacked, and refused to accept a demotion. He decided instead to return to India. General Harold Alexander was to be his replacement. But more significant was the announcement of a new commander for the Eighth Army.

Lieutenant-General Bernard Montgomery hadn't been the first choice for the job. That had been William Gott, one of Auchinleck's subordinates who'd built a reputation as someone who understood how to use tanks. But his plane had been shot down just as he was preparing to take command, and he was killed. So, in the end, the War Office sent for Monty.

He was a small, thin-faced, difficult man, entirely confident of his own genius, and untroubled by the feelings of others. 'Here we will stand and fight, there will be no further withdrawal,' he told his staff on his appointment, as though Auchinleck had been planning another retreat. He would later claim this was exactly what the Auk had in mind if Rommel had attacked again, something that outraged many of those involved in holding the Germans that July.

But if his ego was monstrous, it was what his troops needed. The Eighth Army would, he told his officers, 'hit Rommel for six right out of Africa'. And listening to him, they found they believed it.

Six days after Montgomery took command, Clarke travelled out to his headquarters. Montgomery was no Wavell. He wasn't a man of deep imagination, and he wasn't especially interested in deception. It is hard to see him having commissioned a deception unit out of nothing. But he found a fully functioning one when he arrived, and he was happy to use things that worked. It didn't hurt that A Force was a secret unit, so there was no danger of it being publicly associated with Montgomery's predecessors. Clarke found, possibly to his surprise, that Montgomery was very good at briefing him, because he knew exactly what he wanted the enemy to do. He knew what he wanted everyone to do.

Montgomery had set himself up in a captured wood-panelled caravan that had once belonged to an Italian general. There, over his desk, he installed a large portrait of Rommel, in his desert gear, to gaze at as he contemplated how to conduct the coming battle.

First, he wanted time to impose his will on his new command. His question to Clarke was whether A Force could persuade Rommel to hold off attacking for two weeks. Clarke knew well the difficulty of trying to get Rommel to do anything, but he was keen to please the new commander. The best route seemed to be to continue the story started under Auchinleck that the Germans were being lured into a trap.

Urgent messages were dispatched to Wolfson in Istanbul and the defence attaché in Ankara, listing reasons why the Eighth Army might want the Germans to attack. Nicosoff began sending messages describing the armoured cars and troops heading to the front, along with a report that the British had no intention of attacking – that they were waiting for Rommel to come to them.

Montgomery got twelve of the fourteen days he'd asked for: Rommel attacked at the end of August. Clarke sent a message to the general's chief of staff, explaining what he'd tried to do. 'I hope perhaps it may have helped to give you a few extra days,' he wrote, a little nervously, before explaining that usually they needed more time to be effective.

As it happened, the man he wrote to, Brigadier Freddie de Guingand, had pulled off a trick of his own ahead of the battle. A protégé of Montgomery's, he'd just been named chief of staff to the general. Unofficially, this meant it was his job to smooth the feathers ruffled by his boss. Where Monty was austere – neither a smoker nor a drinker – and rude, de Guingand was a bon viveur and charmer. When Churchill, visiting the front, had needed refreshment, de Guingand had overseen efforts to obtain Egyptian brandy – generally known for its potency rather than its quality – and put it into French bottles in an effort to fool the prime minister.

As the Eighth Army waited for Rommel to attack, de Guingand considered what could be done to put the enemy at a disadvantage. He knew from Ultra that Rommel's forces were desperately short of fuel. Tanks were gas-guzzlers, and both sides went to great efforts to eliminate waste. In the desert, that meant creating 'going' maps, which showed where the terrain was hard, allowing tanks to move quickly and efficiently, and where deep soft sand would see them wallowing, burning fuel without making progress. But the Axis forces were now far further forward than they had ever got before, so they knew next to nothing about the ground ahead of them.

Montgomery, helped by Ultra decrypts, knew Rommel planned to attack at the southern end of the line, as close as he could get to a flanking manoeuvre, before turning north and moving into the British rear. De Guingand asked the cartographers of the Royal Engineers back in Cairo to work through the night to produce a false going map of the area. It was accurate except for the grid squares east of the British lines. There, ground that had been 'firm and fast' was now labelled 'generally impassable'. An area that on the original map was marked 'reconnaissance essential before movement, continuous low gear' now read 'fair going'.

Scuffed and stained with tea, this map was shoved into a rucksack. A small team drove a scout car to a minefield on the edge of the German lines, where they blew it up, left the rucksack, and jumped into a truck to escape. The next day, the car had been ransacked and the map taken.

They did it just in time. Rommel's attack came within days. It almost immediately went wrong. He had expected light minefields and little resistance: neither assumption was correct. Having got through the minefields, his tanks faced a choice. They could continue heading east, but on the British map they'd grabbed, the ground that way was marked as impassable. 'Vehicles stick,' the map said. Instead, they turned north towards a small ridge known as Alam Halfa, across what the map showed to be good ground.

The tank crews must have quickly realised something was amiss as their tracks began to lose traction in sand much softer than they had expected. But worse was ahead. 'Preparations,' one of the British officers involved wrote, 'had been made to receive them.'

Dug in at the ridge were anti-tank gunners of the Rifle Brigade, who held their fire until the enemy was just 300 yards away, before opening up with devastating effect. That night, the Germans considered whether they could launch a flanking operation, but their fuel supplies were too low.

As so often with deception, it was hard to know whether the fake map had made a difference. Prisoner interrogations suggested that the map had been found and believed. One captured German general said the soft sand had trebled the tanks' consumption. 'It looks as if it probably helped,' observed de Guingand.

The plan seems to have been his own. Clarke sought no credit for it. But de Guingand had been working on deception with Clarke for over a year. The previous summer, he'd arranged the dropping of dummy SAS parachutists. And in the months before he'd gone to the Eighth Army, he'd been Shearer's successor as Director of Military Intelligence in Cairo, working alongside A Force. That helps to explain why by August he was, in his own words, 'very deception-minded'. The gospel of deception had spread beyond its apostle, and taken on a life of its own.

Rommel's attempt to break the British line, in what became known as the Battle of Alam Halfa, had failed. Now it was Montgomery's turn. Where Rommel was a free-wheeler, pushing ahead to keep opponents on the back foot, Montgomery was defined by his caution. He could have pursued the Afrika Corps immediately after their failed attack. Rommel, in his place, probably would have. Instead Montgomery waited. The successful defence had steadied the Eighth Army's nerves, and shown them that the Germans could be beaten. He set to work explaining how they were going to do it.

Chapter 32

On the German side of the lines, they knew the attack was coming. Rommel, aware of the greater British strength and of his own weakness and lack of supplies, was dismissive of what he saw as timidity. 'If I were Montgomery, we would not be here any more,' he remarked to Hans-Otto Behrendt, one of his intelligence officers, in September.

But all the things that had made the line at El Alamein the ideal place for the Auk to make his last stand made it a difficult place for Montgomery to break through. After two years of tank chases back and forth across the desert, there was now a static front. The Axis had used the time since July to get their own defences in order, laying minefields and digging in.

Behrendt's job was to answer three questions: what forces did the British have, when would they attack, and where? It was harder than it had been in previous months.

In July they had lost both the 'Good Source' – Bonner Fellers – who had provided such accurate, timely information, and 621 Radio Intercept Company. This signals intelligence unit had been adept at intercepting messages between British forces at the front, either by encrypted Morse or unencrypted voice traffic. Its young high-flying commander had liked to get close to the front, where the signals were strong, and the unit boasted it could put decrypted British messages into Rommel's hands while their intended recipients, further from the front and with less good reception, were still querying them.

But that ambition to impress had been his undoing. He had positioned his unit just a few hundred metres behind the front line, and been overrun in a sudden counter-attack. The unit commander was killed and his troops and their kit captured, along with records of their successful work. It was, Behrendt noted sadly, probably not a coincidence that the British had now tightened up their radio security.

Still, he wasn't completely helpless. Efforts were underway to reform the 621, and in the meantime he had other sources to guide him. He knew from air reconnaissance of the port of Suez that the amount of shipping there had increased in recent months. That was a reliable guide to the arrival of more troops and equipment. Prisoners captured in the reconnaissance skirmishes on the front line helped to build a picture of which units were where. A linguist, Behrendt would interrogate the men himself to see what they might let slip. Soon the reformed 621 Company began delivering, picking up signals from the Scots Greys, part of the 10th Armoured Division, an indicator that the division was now in the theatre.

Behrendt had known since August that XXX Corps was at the northern end of the line and that the southern end was held by XIII Corps. Direction-finding radio units had detected that the Eighth Army had moved its headquarters at the end of August. Captured soldiers revealed the changes of command.

A remark by another prisoner in late September had stuck in Behrendt's mind. The British, he'd said, had known in advance, apparently from an Italian officer, that the attack at Alam Halfa was coming. Decades later, when he read the story of Bletchley Park, the German realised this was a story told to cover the reality that the attack had been predicted by the codebreakers. Montgomery, characteristically, had used a different cover, telling his commanders that he had an intuition about the attack.

But the big question in Behrendt's mind in September and October was the location of the third large formation he believed to be in the area, X Corps.

The German was sure the British attack was imminent. He noted that the pattern in British radio signals echoed those ahead of previous attacks, pointing to the full moon period around 23 October.

His superior officers disagreed. The head of army intelligence, Ulrich Liss, visited North Africa on 21 October and said there would be no attack before November. He'd seen intelligence indicating a joint British and US operation somewhere at the start of the month. Rommel agreed that it was safe to leave things for a few weeks. His health failing after a year and a half in the desert, he left Africa in late September, to consult his commanders and recuperate.

The Axis commanders were confident they would have warning of the British assault. 'As assembly of the attacking troops and artillery will take at least one or two days, our own troops cannot be taken by surprise provided they keep their eyes open,' an intelligence summary concluded.

And they were doing just that. In early October, aerial reconnaissance showed an increase in the number of military transports behind the British lines, up to about 13,000. A colleague feared the number was bigger, hidden by camouflage. For two days in the middle of the month, the planes were grounded by violent sandstorms, but they were showing a build-up in the southern sector.

What was there to see? There were a lot of trucks gathered about 25 miles behind the northern end of the line, but they had been there for weeks. Well in the rear, in Wadi el Natrun, a valley outside Cairo, was what they assumed to be X Corps. Meanwhile, at the southern end, there were supply dumps building up. At the end of September, the British had begun laying a pipeline to carry water, running south-west. Three weeks later, it was barely halfway to the front. If the British were planning to use it for their attack, then their attack was some weeks off.

On 18 October an armoured brigade moved forward out of Wadi el Natrun. It was still well in the rear. On 19 October tanks, guns and trucks advanced towards the southern end of the line and set up camp, still 20 miles from the front. Behrendt's team, using signals intelligence, identified the 10th Armoured Division. They decided it must be part of the southern sector's XIII Corps, along with – though they weren't quite sure about this – the 1st Armoured Division.

He knew the British were trying to play tricks on him. At the start of October, 621 Company had identified an attempt to pretend units existed using wireless signals. They hadn't been fooled. On 15 October, the British also began setting up artillery along the southern front, but to the trained eye, they were clearly dummies: neither moving nor firing.

And the aerial reconnaissance was clear: everything was static. The units that had advanced on the 18th and 19th were still in place on the 22nd. The men attached to them were making camp.

Nothing looked imminent, but whatever was coming would come in the south. Rommel's deputy, General Georg Stumme, had announced this to his commanders at the start of October, and he confirmed it on the 20th: there would be a feint from Montgomery in the north, and the real attack would come in the south. That day,

British planes began three days of attacks on ground troops and airfields. They had done so ahead of the last full moon, too.

A week earlier, Behrendt had been sure the attack would come on 23 October. But when the 23rd came, the Luftwaffe told him the same thing it had said all week: 'Nothing to report'. The RAF was stopping it from getting planes over parts of the British rear, but it was clear that the 10th Armoured Division hadn't moved. It was at least two days away from being able to take part in an assault. The general report for the day was blunt: 'Enemy situation unchanged. Quiet all day along the front.' Had Behrendt got it wrong? Intelligence was an uncertain business. That was why his commander had advised him to be vague about dates in his final report.

And then, a little before 10 p.m. that night, the British guns opened fire.

It was an artillery barrage heavier than anything yet seen in the desert war: more than a thousand guns, firing right along the length of the front. First they aimed at the Axis artillery batteries and then they shifted their focus to the frontline positions. The noise was horrifying even to the troops firing the guns. To those on the receiving end, it felt like an endless hell. 'I saw a notebook,' a British reporter wrote afterwards, 'in which a German dispatch-rider had tried to jot down his impression of this barrage. Language failed him, as it inevitably must. All he could write was silly little blabbing phrases, repeated over and over again.'

As the Axis forces huddled for cover in their positions, or fled the storm of high explosive, communications on the front line were lost. At dawn the next day, no one in Stumme's headquarters could tell him what was happening. It wasn't clear what the artillery barrage meant. If the British were adopting tactics from the Great War, there might be a week of shelling before any advance. He decided to drive to the front to see for himself what had happened.

Over the previous month, Rommel had visited both Mussolini and Hitler, pressing the case for more support, and then travelled to the Semmering, a mountain resort near Vienna, to rest. He was supposed to be cut off from the world, but it was hard to relax. On the afternoon of 24 October, he was summoned to the telephone. The British were shelling his lines, he was told, and Stumme had gone missing. He began to make his preparations to leave. Shortly after midnight, there was another call. It was the Fuhrer, ordering him to return to Africa.

He was there by the following evening. The situation was bad. It was not simply shelling: the British had advanced through the German minefields in force. Stumme was dead, apparently of a heart attack after his car came under fire from Australian soldiers who had got far further forward than he'd realised.

Behrendt had little time to take satisfaction in being proved right about the timing of the attack. Too much was still unclear. There were reports of British tanks in the south and the north. Which was the main blow? Wireless listeners were picking up intense traffic at the northern end of the line. A captured British soldier seemed to confirm this. On the evening of 26 October, three days after the start of the attack, Rommel ordered a panzer division to move north to meet the attack.

There was more than a week of brutal fighting ahead at El Alamein, as Montgomery's forces tried to push their way through the line of dug-in defenders. For Behrendt, it was a chaotic, exhausting time, but there was a lingering question: how had the British managed to launch a surprise attack in a desert that didn't offer enough cover to hide a platoon, let alone whole divisions?

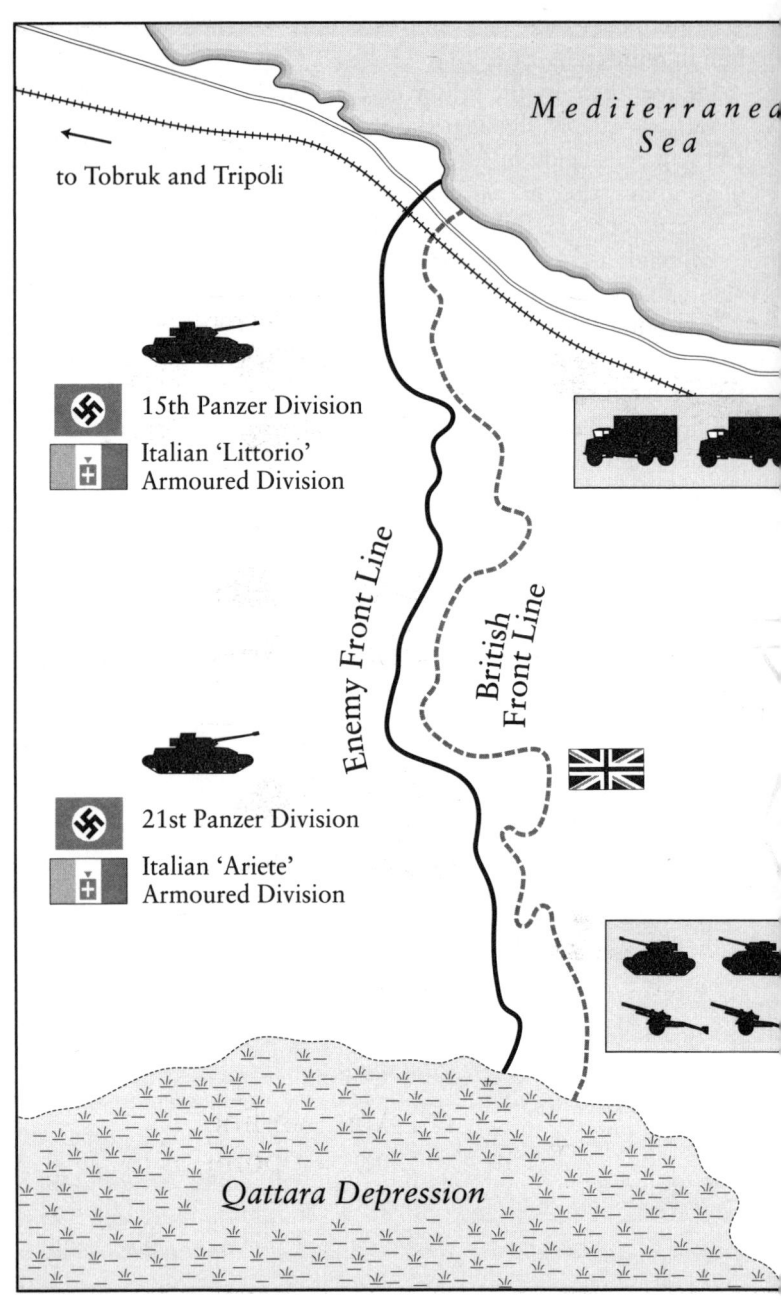

Mediterranean Sea

to Tobruk and Tripoli

15th Panzer Division

Italian 'Littorio' Armoured Division

Enemy Front Line

British Front Line

21st Panzer Division

Italian 'Ariete' Armoured Division

Qattara Depression

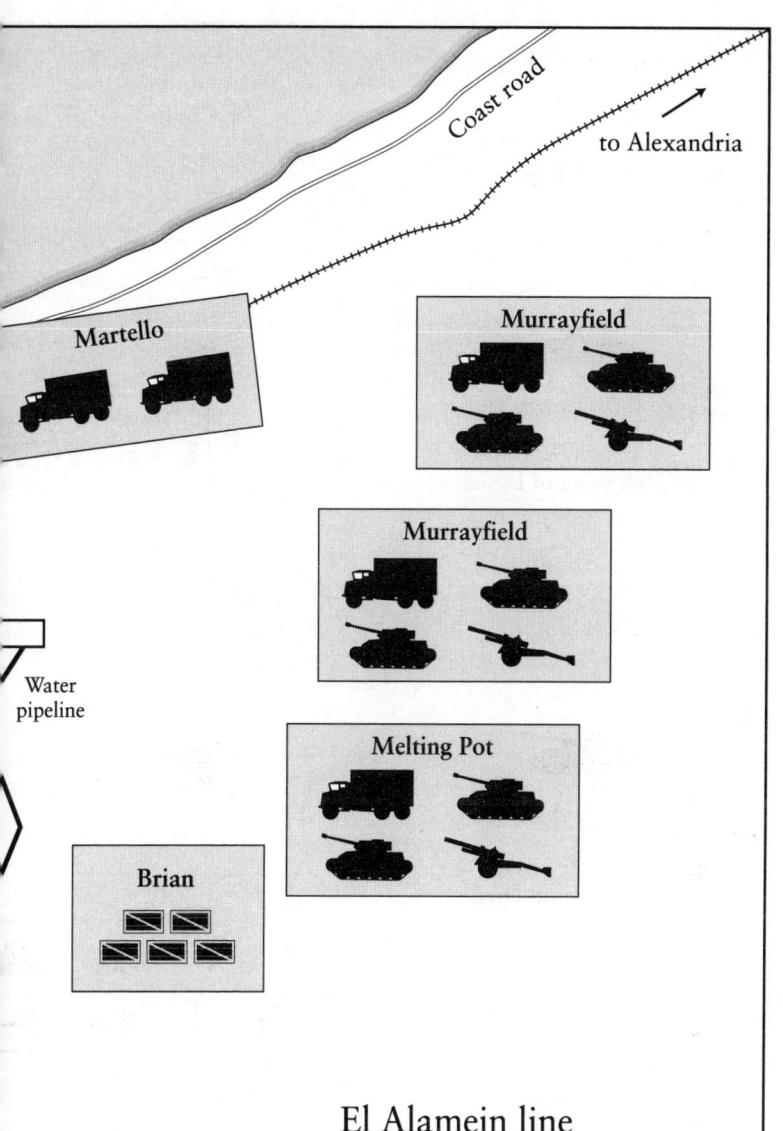

El Alamein line
From the German point of view

Chapter 33

Six weeks before his guns opened fire, and a week after the Battle of Alam Halfa, Montgomery had summoned Clarke to his headquarters again. This time, he gave him lunch. Clarke had met Montgomery before the war, on a course for Staff College candidates. The future commander had taught infantry tactics, something of which Clarke had little experience. 'Under Monty's teaching the whole thing suddenly became plain and simple to me,' he recalled. He was less of a fan of the brusque way that the general treated his senior staff, and privately resolved that he would try to deal with the Auk's replacement, General Alexander, where possible.

But if Montgomery's officers found him difficult, he had a knack with the rank and file. He recognised that he wasn't leading professional soldiers. His army was made up of civilians who had put on uniforms when their country had called. They needed to understand that there was a plan and that they had a part in it. And they needed to believe that they had a general every bit as special as the one the Germans had.

His tour of his new command veered well over into self-promotion. Here was a new broom, sweeping out the failed generals of the past. He admitted that it appealed to his vanity. But his troops wanted to have faith in the man who was ordering them to charge the enemy guns, and liked it that he loudly expressed his faith in them.

That September, a desert army that had come to look ragged over months of retreats began to take pride in itself once again. Shirts were tucked back into shorts. The new general demanded daily exercise, to prepare his men for what was coming. 'Ordinary fitness is not enough,' he told his commanders. 'They must be made tough and hard.' He wanted no one under any illusions about the battle ahead. 'It will be a killing match; the German is a good soldier and the only way to beat him is to kill him.'

Although Montgomery talked a great deal about morale and

self-belief, the force he was building was going to have other things that mattered just as much: equipment, in the form of new Sherman tanks from America; and training, with the troops rehearsing their roles in the coming fight. The armies of Britain and her allies had been in poor shape in 1939. For three years they had been losing. Now, at last, they were in a condition to start winning.

Montgomery knew he had no alternative but to make a frontal assault. He had vivid first-hand experience of the difficulties of attacking a strong defensive line. He'd been shot in the chest in 1914 while leading a platoon. He had been horrified by the waste of life in that war, and was determined not to repeat the same mistakes. His solution came in several parts: to ensure that his attack came with overwhelming force; to ensure that every unit understood and had practised its precise role; and to do what he could to take the enemy by surprise.

Which was why he wanted to see Clarke. It was a three-hour journey from Cairo to the spot where Montgomery had located himself, on the Mediterranean coast, and Clarke, never an early riser, arrived at noon. He was met by Lieutenant Colonel Charles Richardson of the planning staff. Richardson had drawn up details of the proposed attack, based on Montgomery's instructions, but he was worried that it involved sending the Eighth Army to exactly the place the enemy would expect them, at precisely the time when an assault was likeliest. He was conscious of his youth, having just turned thirty-four, and the responsibility of so many lives weighed on his shoulders.

Richardson liked Clarke, and was a little in awe of him. He didn't know the details of how he did what he did, and the senior man showed no inclination to tell him. Richardson explained his view, that the plan was 'horribly obvious', and they talked through some of the issues, and then Clarke took the opportunity to go for a swim in the sea. Swimming trunks weren't Army issue, so officers at headquarters swam naked, something that Churchill had joined them for when he visited, to widespread delight.

Then it was down to business, over lunch with the general. Montgomery set out his plan. He wanted to launch simultaneous attacks at the northern and southern ends of the front. The southern attack, by XIII Corps, would be a feint, designed to hold enemy forces there while at the northern end XXX Corps would break through the line, and X Corps would then follow up and draw Rommel's tanks into a fight. He was going to attack at night, to give his men the greatest chance of clearing the minefields and getting past the guns that covered the front. They would need a full moon to see what they were doing, and the next one was too soon, only a couple of weeks away, so they would go for the one after that, on 23 October.

'Every endeavour will be made to deceive the enemy as to our intentions to attack at all and, if this fails, as to the direction of our main attack,' the first draft of Montgomery's plan, published that day, read. The commander had a few ideas about that, but he wanted to know what A Force could offer.

Clarke set out the problems. Axis intelligence forces could hardly have missed the build-up of the Eighth Army. After the Battle of Alam Halfa, they'd be expecting an Allied offensive. If that weren't enough, they would have noted the arrival of a new commander and the visit by Churchill. They weren't going to buy the idea that the British would stay on the defensive for long.

Alam Halfa offered other lessons, too. It had been a night attack during the full moon. The Axis would hardly be surprised if Montgomery tried the same thing. And RAF reconnaissance planes had spotted Rommel's vehicles assembling before the attack. In the flat, featureless desert, it would be difficult to hide the men and vehicles moving up to the marshalling points.

Put like that, Richardson was right. Montgomery was planning to attack in the obvious place at an obvious time. Even his choice of the northern flank reflected his perfectly sensible desire to control the best road through the desert.

Montgomery was under no illusion at all that the battle wouldn't involve hard fighting. Indeed, that was his goal. His view was that one of Auchinleck's mistakes the previous year had been to allow Rommel to pull his forces back across Cyrenaica. This time, he wanted to keep the Axis army in place and destroy it. That was how wars were won.

But he didn't want to be a Great War general thoughtlessly throwing men into the meat-grinder. What did his soldiers have going for them?

Clarke pondered the question. It might be plausible to the enemy that the British were worried about events on the Russian front and a German attack through the Caucasus. He could put over a story arguing that the British were holding off until winter had set in. The longer the enemy waited for the attack to come, the more they might begin to doubt it ever would.

A Force had already had success over the summer suggesting that the Allies wanted to retake Crete. A large German force was standing by there to repel them. Carrying that story on would provide some cover for troop build-ups in Egypt, and have the added advantage of pinning the defenders in place.

There were things he could do about timing, too. A good sign that no attack was imminent would be the absence of generals from their headquarters. He would organise a conference in Iran for 26 October, with Alexander invited.

As for the question of which end of the line would see the real attack, Clarke suggested two magician's tools: concealment and misdirection. They would hide the troops in the north, and draw attention to those in the south.

With lunch over, Clarke talked through details with de Guingand, and then headed back to Cairo. He had things to be getting on with.

The following evening, Nicosoff sent a message to Athens: 'Believe English are worried about Caucasus and transferring troops from Africa. Some are already passing through Cairo.'

Clarke would not be able to run the operation himself. He had just been ordered to America, to induct the new allies into the ways of deception, and was departing that weekend. So the running of the plan would fall to his deputy, Noel Wild, in liaison with Richardson. But much of the work was going to involve what A Force referred to as a 'physical implementation'. This would fall to Barkas and his camoufleurs.

It was an exciting moment for Barkas. Three days after Clarke visited Montgomery, Barkas and one of his deputies, Tony Ayrton, made their way to Eighth Army Headquarters, and reported to de Guingand. The brigadier, with Richardson, took them through the plan for Operation Lightfoot, the codename given to the coming attack, and then asked what they could do to help. It was a daunting task. If the deception plan failed, Richardson pointed out, it would do more damage than no plan at all. Barkas tried his best to sound confident.

But de Guingand was asking for a lot. Barkas had a few hundred men at his disposal, and they had to hide tens of thousands, and all evidence of their passing, in terrain that was entirely free of buildings and vegetation, under the eyes of regular reconnaissance flights.

Years later, de Guingand would recall how he'd described the problem: 'You must conceal 150,000 men with a thousand guns and a thousand tanks on a plain as flat and as hard as a billiard table, and the Germans must not know anything about it, although they will be watching every movement, listening for every noise, charting every track.'

Barkas and Ayrton borrowed a typewriter and set to work. Two hours later, they presented the outline of a plan. De Guingand thanked them, and Ayrton set off to scout the ground where their illusion would be performed, while Barkas went back to Cairo to begin assembling his props.

Operation Bertram, as this exercise was codenamed, didn't look simple to anyone, but possibly no one involved grasped its full complexity. Clarke was on the other side of the Atlantic as Barkas worked out how to conceal men and equipment. Barkas was unaware of how Clarke was using Cheese and other channels to whisper misleading hints into the ears of the audience. And Clarke wasn't aware of how effectively Bletchley Park was able to check that the enemy really was fooled.

The illusion that the deceivers were going to pull off would be the largest performed to that date. But it would be based on a very small, very old one, perhaps the oldest one of all. You've seen it. It involves three shells and a ball.

Chapter 34

There are dozens of variations of the cups and balls routine, involving different numbers of cups and different sorts of balls in different combinations, appearing, disappearing, moving between the cups and in and out of them. 'There is no better test of a conjurer's skill,' Clarke's uncle Sidney had written a few years before. Looking at the earliest recorded tricks, he quoted an account by an ancient Greek writer, Alciphron: 'A man came forward and placed on a three-legged table three small dishes, under which he concealed some little white, round pebbles. These he placed one by one under the dishes, and then, I do not know how, made them all appear together under one.'

These days, we would call what Barkas and A Force were planning a 'shell game'. Genuine magicians don't tend to bother with it. You'll see it instead wherever tourists gather, and conmen want to fleece them. There are three walnut shells, or matchboxes, or bottle-tops on a crate. The ball goes under one, and you're asked to bet where it is. But however closely you watch the shells go round, the ball won't be under the one you pick. It's concealed between the conman's fingers, waiting to be placed where he wants it.

Bertram would follow the same principle, but instead of a ball, there would be X Corps, with its hundreds of tanks and guns, and tens of thousands of men.

First, they needed props: four hundred dummy tanks, a hundred dummy guns and close to 2,000 dummy vehicles. A Force's dummy tank units were already deployed, and there was nothing close to these quantities in storage. They would need to be built, and fast. Barkas' team quickly realised that the usual workshops wouldn't be able to produce close to what was needed. The camoufleurs would have to improvise.

One of Barkas' men noticed that the beds and packing cases the Egyptians made from palm trees contained standard shapes that

could be repurposed. The army began placing orders for unbeliev-
able numbers of bed parts, much to the delight and amusement of
the locals, and a production line of soldiers was tasked with assembling them into the required shapes, covering them with hessian and
painting them.

Next, they set up the stage. When the Eighth Army launched its
attack, it would need fuel, ammunition and supplies, vast amounts
of them. These needed to be brought up to the front and stored as
close to the men who would be doing the fighting as possible. But
growing piles of supplies were exactly the sort of clue the enemy
would be watching for. These dumps were, at the best of times, a
logistics problem. The petrol was a fire hazard, especially given the
army's standard four-gallon can tended to leak. The more mundane
supplies were a target for thieves.

Scouting the northern end of the line near Alamein station, five
miles behind the front line, Ayrton found dozens of slit trenches that
had been dug for defensive reasons the previous year and were now
unused. They were lined with brickwork, an army habit that, while
it definitely made the positions look neater, drove Barkas spare,
because from the air it meant clean lines with jet black shadows
that were easy to spot in reconnaissance photographs. But Ayrton
saw an opportunity. The Axis photo-interpreters would be used to
seeing the trenches by now, and so long as they looked the same, they
wouldn't pay any attention to them. He began experimenting with
stacking petrol cans inside the trenches, and discovered that, pressed
against each wall of the trench, they made no visible difference to
the shadows. By night, two thousand tons of petrol were sneaked
into the trenches, ready to refuel the advancing tanks. Even from
close-up, it was hard to tell the difference.

That left the question of the rest of the supplies. Sacks of sugar
and flour could be hidden here and there in shallow holes in the
ground, and covered with camouflage nets, but much of what they
were dealing with was in crates that were too large and too many to
be hidden. They would have to be disguised.

Over the course of four nights, a work party of 80 Australian infantrymen found themselves stacking boxes of supplies in the shape
of army three-ton trucks, and then covering them with camouflage
netting. Excess boxes went under small tents, and the result looked
from the air like soldiers making camp just back from the line. It

took 30 'trucks' to conceal close to 600 tonnes of supplies. The most coveted goods – cigarettes, sugar and milk powder – were in the centre of the stacks, to discourage pilfering.

Fifteen miles further back, 3,000 tonnes of ammunition was hidden under hessian sacking and sand in an existing ammo dump. Larger crates were again disguised as trucks. The stacks were covered with canvas painted to look like vehicles, complete with wheels. Barkas requested reconnaissance flights to check how all this appeared from the air.

While the real dumps in the north were being hidden, in the south another unit was working under the supervision of Brian Robb, a *Punch* cartoonist whom Barkas had found manning a searchlight in the Sinai desert, bored out of his mind. He was tasked with creating a fake supply dump in an area on the map simply marked 'Brian'.

The focus of the camouflage efforts was on hiding real equipment, so Robb had to work with what he could get his hands on. Much of it was 'two-dimensional', aiming to create something that would fool air reconnaissance. Without the manpower to dig real trenches, matting was laid along the ground the simulate the shadows they would create. Beds turned on their sides and covered with hessian and camouflage netting passed for petrol cans and crates of supplies.

More ingenious – and elaborate – was the water pipeline that snaked south and west towards the front. It too was a fake, built deliberately slowly to give the impression that the British were on a relaxed schedule. 'Construction', such as it was, involved digging a trench, with petrol tins beaten into the shape of pipe left alongside, and then filling it in at night and moving the fake pipe forward to the next 'section'. Every so often there was a 'pumping station', with scarecrow figures posed alongside. Real army vehicles going to and from the front were re-routed to travel alongside the 'pipe', to stir up dust and add to the impression of activity.

None of this was central to the big trick that Barkas, under Richardson's supervision, was performing in the desert, but all of it served to reassure the viewer of the false picture he was trying to show: a British force slowly getting ready to launch an attack at the southern end of the line.

On 18 October the grand illusion began, as X Corps began to move into position. A common misapprehension about magic is that sleight-of-hand relies on speed. In fact quick movements draw attention. It is the slowness of the hand that deceives the eye, by reassuring the audience that there's nothing suspicious going on. In the same way, the advance of X Corps was designed to put the Germans at their ease.

The stage that Barkas had set for Behrendt and his colleagues to watch contained, in mid-October, three visible elements. There were the dummy pipeline and the dummy supply dumps in the south, and, in the north, what seemed to be thousands of trucks, parked across the desert. These vehicles would definitely have been noteworthy to German intelligence. They would be essential in any battle to bring men and supplies forward. But to someone looking for signs of an imminent attack, they were secondary to armour and infantry. And they were just sitting there, as they had been for weeks.

The first change to that came with the move of the 9th Armoured Brigade, in daylight, to a staging area well in the rear, codenamed 'Murrayfield'. That was exactly the sort of thing Behrendt was looking out for. But what did it mean? That far back from the line, they might just be training. If it was a first step towards the front, they could go either north or south from that position. It was something to watch closely, but not an immediate threat.

That night, things got busy. The 9th Armoured moved north, to the area where the trucks were apparently sitting around. Far from being a random dispersal of vehicles that weren't needed, this was the part of Barkas's stage where most of the action was going to happen. It was codenamed 'Martello'. Days earlier, the tank crews had been taken there and shown exactly where each of them was to go. What was waiting for them was a genuine magic prop designed for them by a real magician.

The previous year, when Jasper Maskelyne had first been put in charge of experimental camouflage, Barkas had shown him a sketch, drawn by Wavell, of a tank with a cover over it that made it look like a truck. Could he make this? It was a task for which he was probably better qualified than anyone else in the army. This was a stage prop that hid something, and Maskelynes had been building those for three generations. Before he'd left the camouflage section he'd come up with a design that met the requirements.

Constructed out of steel tubing and painted hessian cloth, the covers came in two halves, one for each side of the tank. Lifted over the tank and bolted into place, they completely covered it. The result had tracks not wheels and the tank's gun barrel sticking through the windscreen. But from a distance, it looked like a truck. Aerial reconnaissance was asked to photograph it and give a view. 'Perfect,' was the response.

They called them 'sunshields' – a name chosen to hide their purpose – and there were hundreds of them now in Martello, each one numbered and allocated to a tank. The camoufleurs had rested them on barrels which, from a distance, looked like their wheels. They weren't going to fool anyone close-up, but a magician knows where his audience is, and Barkas would be keeping his well back.

The same storm that had grounded the Luftwaffe that week had ravaged Martello, demolishing sunshields and dummy trucks. But the Camouflage section had scrambled to repair and replace then, and when, on the night of 18 October, the 9th Armoured arrived, they found their sunshields waiting for them. Each crew lifted its cover onto its tank and secured it in place. It was plausible, especially if someone wasn't looking very hard.

Meanwhile the 24th Armoured Brigade had occupied Murrayfield, moving up in the darkness. When the sun came up on 19 October, everything looked as it had the previous evening. There were the trucks in the north, there was the brigade in the centre.

Perhaps if someone had looked very closely at the reconnaissance photos, they might have noticed changes, but there were more interesting things to look at that day. The 10th Armoured Division was on the move, and it was clearly moving towards the southern end of the front. It stopped behind the Brian false dumps, in an area the British codenamed Melting Pot. To someone who already thought an attack in the south was likely – hadn't that been the way Rommel had wanted to go weeks earlier? – and who expected to be able to see it in advance, this was a clear threatening move.

But nothing happened for two days. The Germans were allowed to relax. The 10th Armoured sat where it was. The pipeline slowly continued. Nothing was imminent.

Then, in stages at night between 18 and 22 October, an awful lot happened at once. All of X Corps, hundreds of tanks and thousands of men, moved to Martello, assembling sunshields over their vehicles in a scramble to ensure that when the sun came up they were hidden. Behind them, teams supervised by Barkas's camoufleurs hustled to assemble dummy tanks and vehicles at Melting Pot and Murrayfield.

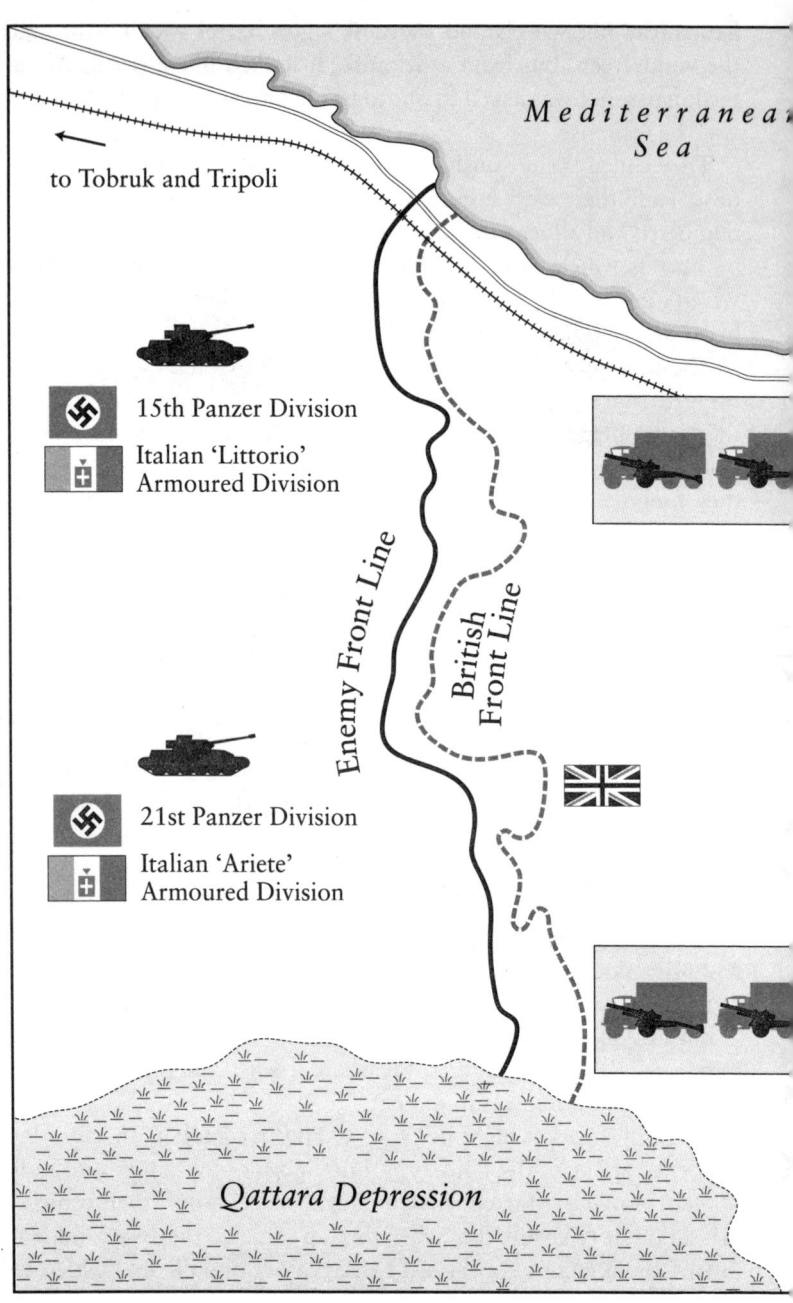

Mediterranean
Sea

to Tobruk and Tripoli

15th Panzer Division

Italian 'Littorio'
Armoured Division

Enemy Front Line

British
Front Line

21st Panzer Division

Italian 'Ariete'
Armoured Division

Qattara Depression

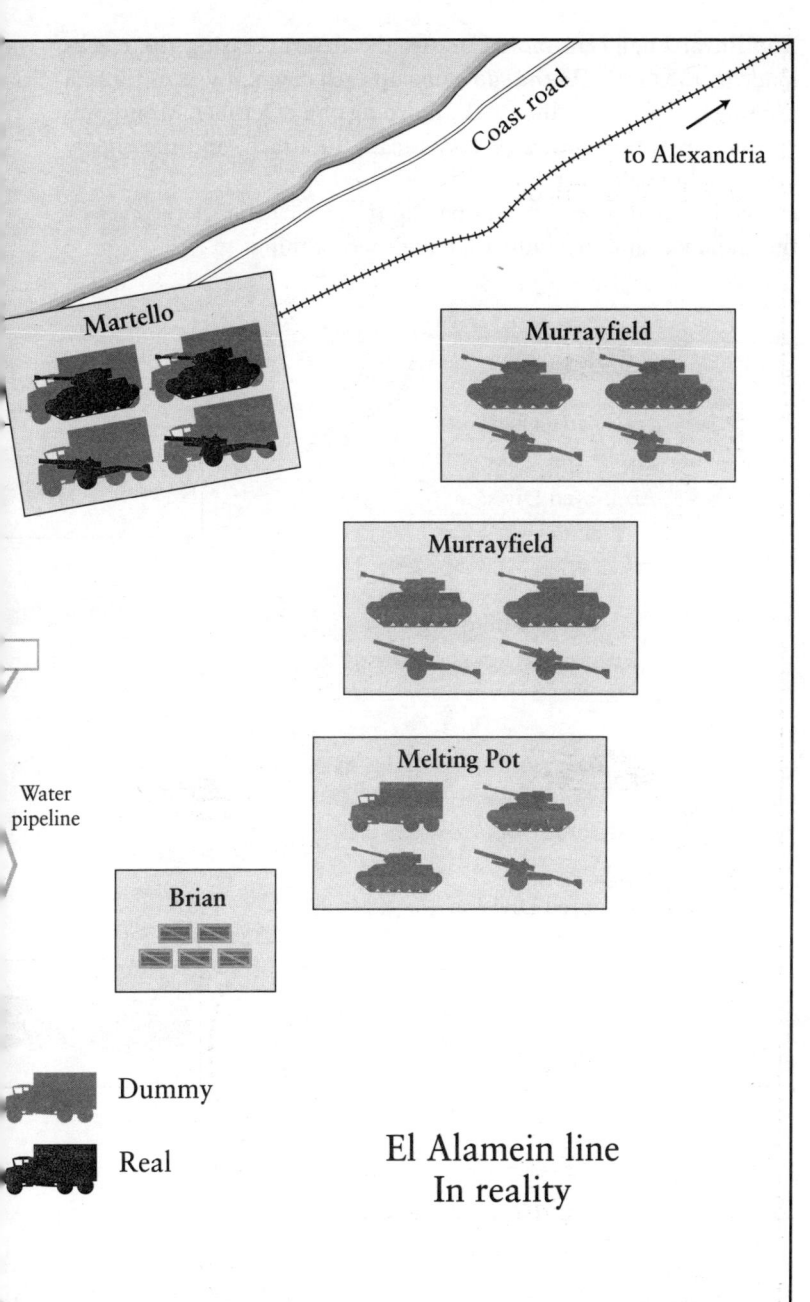

Coast road

to Alexandria

Martello

Murrayfield

Murrayfield

Water
pipeline

Melting Pot

Brian

Dummy

Real

El Alamein line
In reality

The Royal Engineers moved across the desert, erasing the tracks made by the tanks. As the sun came up each dawn, it was as though nothing had changed. But on the morning of 23 October, Montgomery had an entire armoured corps ready to attack, and the enemy knew nothing about it.

The ball had moved from one cup to another, under the eyes of the audience, and the audience hadn't seen a thing.

Chapter 35

While Barkas was manipulating the shells and balls in sight of the audience, Wild was delivering the magician's patter, telling the story over the top of the Eighth Army's manoeuvres: Monty was holding back; the generals were having a conference in Iran; the British were worried about the Caucasus.

The codename for this story-telling was 'Treatment', and Wild drew it up and ran it according to Clarke's instructions. From Tehran invitations went out to Wavell in Delhi and Alexander in Cairo for a conference on 26 October, and staff set to work arranging the logistics. Only the generals knew the meeting would be called off at the last moment.

At the front, senior Eighth Army officers sent messages back to Cairo reserving hotel rooms for the days after 20 October. The staff college at Haifa announced it was extending its current course, and wouldn't finish it before mid-November. Each of these was a clue that, with luck, would make its way in some form to the Abwehr, a jigsaw piece suggesting that the top brass wasn't expecting to be doing any fighting at the end of the month.

In Istanbul, Wolfson played his part, spreading rumours as instructed by Clarke, including placing a story in a Swiss newspaper that the Eighth Army was in a defensive posture, with forces being sent to protect the Caucasus. He sent a clipping of that to Clarke. 'In this particular one I thought it best to stress only the "defensive positions" part of your telegram,' he wrote, 'arranging for the "offensive postponed" to reach the enemy simultaneously, but through another channel, as being too obvious otherwise.'

In the desert, a stream of false radio traffic, both coded and in clear voice, was broadcast to give the enemy the impression of an army going about its business. German direction-finders would be able to see that these signals were coming from well behind the front line.

And in Cairo, Cheese was busy reporting sightings of troop transport boats in the harbour of Alexandria – perhaps getting ready to go to Crete – and numerous troops on leave from the front – just as leave was being stopped. At the end of September a question was passed on from Berlin: did he have any news about British plans to attack Rommel? 'When, how and where?'

Nicosoff didn't directly respond to that. 'So many rumours circulate about a forthcoming English attack in the desert that it is difficult to ascertain a definitive date,' he signalled in mid-October. He said he'd spoken to an American officer friend who was on leave. 'He is of the opinion that the attack will take place at the beginning of November.'

Anything more direct than that would have been a risk. He wasn't supposed to be someone with access to that sort of information. He was transmitting most days, messages as short as one sentence and rarely longer than ten: there was less traffic on the desert roads than there had been in August; he needed money; Greeks were always talking about attacking Crete; when would the money be arriving?

Clarke took the view that the best way to smuggle a lie was hidden amid a lot of truth. He told his subordinates that 90 per cent of what they sent to the enemy should be confirmable from other sources – although those sources might be the result of other efforts to mislead them, such as the fake divisional signs of the Cascade deception.

So a lot of what Nicosoff was sending was correct, but trivial – 'chickenfeed', the spies called it: the newspapers had reported the execution of five spies in Aleppo; locals complained about German bombing during Ramadan; there were Scottish soldiers in Cairo wearing an 'HD' insignia, which his masters would be able to identify as the 51st Highland Division. The impression was of a busy agent, developing sources among soldiers on leave and civilians in sensitive jobs, travelling back and forth between Cairo and Alexandria in an effort to gather information. Sure, he complained about money, but he was coming up with the goods. The 51st duly went into Behrendt's order of battle.

In the messages he drafted for the Cheese channel, Evan Simpson was telling two stories. The first was the one set out by Clarke, offering puzzle pieces that pointed to a large and expanding British force in Cairo, threatening Crete but not yet ready to move against

Rommel. The second was the tale of Nicosoff himself, an enthusiastic spy who was increasingly conscious of his own importance to his masters and required delicate handling. When he had been out of favour at the start of the year, Nicosoff had been humble. Now he was demanding. 'What happened yesterday?' began one angry message, after a communications failure. 'Impossible to work with your incompetent radio operators. My work is not worth the risk if communications are so uncertain. It has to be your best operator every night.' As for a request for specific information: 'Impossible to move without money.'

Had he been real, poor radio operation wouldn't have been Nicosoff's only complaint. Some of the information requests he received were, to put it mildly, ambitious. 'Try to find out if the British attack will be combined with a flank action,' read a request in mid-October. 'If possible also give the exact direction of this attack and the forces that will take part.'

The place the Abwehr believed this attack might come from was Northern Chad, a thousand miles away on the other side of the desert. It was not clear how Nicosoff's controllers imagined he would check to see who was on the march from there. Probably they were still yearning for the days when Bonner Fellers sent them detailed reports on British strategy. Like many masters of distant servants, the Abwehr wanted a lot but had only the haziest grasp of what was realistic.

As the date of Operation Lightfoot approached, the team at A Force headquarters considered the part Nicosoff should play. A year earlier, Shearer had been prepared, with Clarke's agreement, to destroy the Cheese channel as the price of success of Operation Crusader. But A Force was now more ambitious for their imaginary radio man. They wanted to keep him going as a supplier of false information to the enemy. The question was how best to maintain his credibility. Ideally, he would transmit something about the attack in advance, but what – and when? Usually Nicosoff went on the air around 7.30 p.m. – two hours before the operation was due to begin. De Guingand ruled out giving the enemy advance notice. Wild feared it would be implausible for the agent to go on the air two hours late.

Another option would be simply for him to learn of Operation Lightfoot at the same time as the rest of Cairo. That would be credible, but it would also undermine his value to the Germans as a spy.

Instead, A Force began drawing up a little playlet for the evening of 23 October, when the attack was due to begin. It became known as 'Cheese Cake', and they went through a couple of draft 'recipes' before they settled on the one they used. At 7.40 that night – two hours before the balloon was due to go up – Sergeant Shears began sending a normal Nicosoff message, noting that there seemed to be fewer troops on the streets and that General Alexander had cancelled his plans to travel to Iran.

Then, just before eight o'clock, he switched to Q codes, the unencrypted Morse shorthand used by radio operators across the globe to send immediate information. 'WAIT, WAIT, WAIT,' he signalled and went silent. A minute later, he signalled again: 'WAIT FIVE MINUTES. WAIT FIVE MINUTES.'

Five minutes later he was back: 'URGENT MESSAGE: WAIT TWENTY MINUTES PLEASE.' He asked for more time once more before, at half past eight, sending an encrypted message reporting that his girlfriend had called him to say she had urgent information she couldn't say over the phone. He was now heading to her flat, where she was entertaining an American officer. And then he went silent for an hour and a half.

At 10.17 p.m. he got back in touch. 'HERE. URGENT MESSAGE. WAIT 15 MINUTES.' He stalled twice more before, at 10.41 p.m., an hour after the offensive had started, sending his urgent news: 'My friend learned tonight from an American air force officer at her place that a British offensive is imminent. Will probably start early tomorrow or even this evening. All leave cancelled yesterday.'

Shears was given instruction about how to send his messages as though he were 'a man at fever heat of excitement with such news'. Nicosoff didn't usually make coding mistakes, but on this night he would: 'Errors can be made by switching letters round, e.g. EUKQB can be sent as EUKBQ, a mistake easily made by a man whose eyes are moving faster than his fingers.'

But when Shears sent the second message, 'revealing' Montgomery's imminent assault, there was no response. He stayed on the air for half an hour, but there was nothing. Perhaps the operator at the other end had got bored and decided that whatever it was could wait. Perhaps, with British artillery blazing away along the front, they had been called away to handle other traffic.

The next day, Crichton, now working on the deception side of A Force, considered how Nicosoff should respond to this silence. He wrote about the imaginary spy as if he were a real person. Having stayed up 'trying to put over the most important piece of news he has ever had' – and failed – 'he is very angry, discouraged and a trifle windy'.

He went on: 'He has probably had a bad night as a result of his troubles which by morning have probably magnified. He is nervous on account of our offensive, he is angry at not having scored his coup, he fears that his failure to warn his masters about the offensive may affect the question of his pay, and finally he is windy about his own security due to the fuss and bother he made over the air last night.'

Crichton drafted three messages of complaint that Shears would broadcast, depending on whether the Abwehr confirmed they had received the signal. But there was no response that night either. It wasn't until 25 October, two days after the beginning of the Lightfoot attack, that he got a response. It lacked any sense of urgency. Nicosoff was requested to change his hour of transmission to earlier in the day, and then asked if he could find out whether the British were thinking about attacking the island of Rhodes. 'Give every detail,' the message went on, 'like for the possible attacks on Crete or Rommel that you mentioned.'

It was a signal that would have had Nicosoff screaming, had he existed. The reply was suitably furious. 'What happened?' it began. 'I have been trying for two days to send you very important and urgent news.' The fake agent explained that the attack on Rommel was now 48 hours old, and rebuked his controller. 'These inaccuracies of yours discouraging and dangerous.' In reality, of course, the Abwehr's incompetence had worked out well for A Force, increasing Nicosoff's credibility without jeopardising Lightfoot.

As these exchanges between Cairo and Athens went on, in the desert the Battle of El Alamein was still being fought. Montgomery had been over-optimistic about his soldiers' ability to get through the German minefields under fire, and he was forced to revise his plan.

The battle would last more than a week, and when it was finally won, it was by soldiers and real tanks, not spies and wooden dummies. The fighting was as hard as Montgomery had told his men it would be. But weeks earlier, he'd said that surprise would be essential, and Clarke and Barkas had given that to him. If the Germans knew that an attack was coming at some point, they didn't know when or where. That uncertainty, Rommel's absence from the battlefield, and the conviction that the main thrust would be in the south, gave the Eighth Army space to establish a toehold.

At the end of 1941, Clarke had believed he'd built his deception machine, but hadn't quite got to grips with its capabilities. A year later he felt 'the machinery forged during 1941, and tempered in the fire of the summer battle, was now the finished product'.

El Alamein had shown what the machine could do. On the ground, Barkas had pulled off a stunt far beyond anything his former movie colleagues could have imagined. It was an amazing achievement, essential to the deception operation's success, but only one part of it. Operations Treatment and Bertram were together a vindication of the Clarke approach, that deception needed to be a complete project, from the dummies on the ground through the double agent passing false intelligence to the hotel rooms booked far from the line on the night of the attack.

The battle had combined tactical deception about the focus and timing of the attack with strategic deception about Allied intentions in the theatre. Every part of the performance had come together, to tell a complete – and misleading – story.

There was credit to go round. Barkas, keen as ever to show that camouflage worked, produced a report on his part of the operation which he sent to all and sundry. In Kasr-El-Nil, they were characteristically more discreet – the last thing they wanted was ordinary soldiers understanding what they'd done – but they had some private vindications. Wild's former boss, who had been so dismissive of A Force months earlier, now sought him out and apologised. As for Clarke, he had already enjoyed an even sweeter moment, a week before Montgomery attacked.

Almost a year to the day since his arrest in Madrid, which had seen Churchill demand Clarke be brought back to London to explain himself, he walked up Downing Street to do exactly that. But it was a moment of glory, not shame. The prime minister had recently mentioned in a note to General Alexander that the Ultra decrypts showed the Germans 'very nervous about Crete', and suggested this would help with the coming offensive. Alexander replied that

Churchill should talk to Clarke, who was about to pass through London: 'His work has created the nervousness you speak of.' Now Clarke was going to brief the prime minister on exactly how the trick was done.

Deception was no longer the province of a few oddballs sharing office space with a brothel in Cairo. It was now a weapon of war.

The Ingenious Confederacy

October 1942–February 1943

The Magician leaves the room and asks the audience to select a card in their absence. On their return, they're able to name the card, thanks to a helper in the crowd who communicates in code.

Chapter 36

Clarke was in London that October for the first global conference of Allied deceivers. It wasn't a big group: just three people, including Clarke, had been invited from outside Britain. That it was happening at all was a tribute to his success – and Wavell's persistence.

For A Force, the past twelve months had been relentless: Clarke's arrest, the torpedoing of his ship, the success of the 'Crusader' offensive and the subsequent collapse, the fall of Tobruk, the Flap and finally the arrival of Montgomery and the defence of Alam Halfa. The El Alamein deception was in its final stages, with the attack less than a fortnight away.

But elsewhere, strategic deception had struggled to get off the ground. The chiefs of staff had been enthused after hearing from Clarke in 1941, and had set up the London Controlling Section to coordinate deception work. But no one in it seemed to know quite what to do, and those higher up the chain didn't seem sure what this obscurely named outfit was actually for.

The result was stasis. Clarke's run-in with the LCS earlier in the year, when it had refused to help pass false information as Rommel advanced, had been typical. Its head, Oliver Stanley, had sent another apologetic note in April. 'I gather you feel I have rather let you down,' he wrote. 'I don't think you quite appreciate the set-up here. Now that we have lost (if we ever had) the strategic initiative, everything tends to become a series of improvisations designed to meet immediate crises.' You can't do strategic deception, in other words, when you don't have a strategy, and in April 1942, no one in London had a strategy.

It was true that the first half of the year had been very difficult for the Churchill government, with the Japanese advancing in the Far East and the fall-out from the retreat in the desert. But it had hardly been much fun for those doing the retreating. Clarke had found ways to make himself useful. He was unlikely to be impressed by Stanley's excuses.

Deception needed, as Wavell had recognised in 1940, a particular kind of character to run it, someone with imagination, military knowledge, connections and the kind of personality and charm necessary to win support for work that always risked seeming frivolous. It was part of Clarke's genius that he had made it all look so easy in Cairo. When others tried to follow his path, they found it wasn't so straightforward.

Stanley, who had served in the Great War with distinction and was a popular member of parliament, was a plausible choice of leader for the LCS. But he had been doing the job part-time while working with the planning staff, and the intense rivalries of London's various intelligence organisations had defeated him. He didn't mention it in his letter to Clarke, but the Twenty Committee had been reluctant to give him access to its double agents. He had, in any case, other things on his mind. His wife, just forty-one years old, had become seriously ill, and by the spring of 1942 it was clear that she had only weeks to live. Stanley disappeared on leave and after her death quit the army and returned to the Cabinet.

It wasn't just Clarke who felt let down by Stanley. From India, Wavell sent a cable directly to Churchill. 'I have always had considerable belief in deceiving and disturbing enemy by false information,' he began, before noting that while a deception section did exist in London, 'Have impression the approach is defensive rather than aggressive and confined mainly to cover plans for particular operations.' What was needed, he said, was 'a policy of bold imaginative deception'.

This was not the sort of thing Churchill needed to be told twice. Stanley had already told the prime minister that he wanted to go, and the chiefs of staff were ordered to give his section new vigour.

It got it from its incoming chief, Lieutenant Colonel Johnny Bevan. A 'rather frail-looking man of medium build with sleepy, pale-blue eyes and thin fair hair,' if his appearance suggested he lacked dynamism it was, appropriately, misleading. Bevan's approach to life was summed up by someone who had known him as a schoolboy: 'When things were looking pretty bad for his side at cricket, he would shuffle in, about sixth wicket down, knock up 100 and shuffle out again looking rather ashamed of himself.' He was a stockbroker and a stockbroker's son. His education had been Eton, Oxford and then the Western Front, where he had been an infantry officer for four years, earning the Military Cross and rising to the rank of major.

After the trenches, Bevan had joined his father's firm and become a pillar of the City of London, a place that operated on the motto 'dictum meum pactum' – 'my word is my bond'. Not everyone followed that rule, but he did, occasionally chided by another partner for being 'too honest'. He married Lady Barbara Bingham, the daughter of the fifth earl of Lucan. He enjoyed gardening, bird-watching, shooting, fishing and generally getting mud on his boots. He was an officer and a gentleman, and superficially an unlikely choice for a deceiver.

But he had relevant experience. At the start of 1918, he'd been given the job of working out the German order of battle and their likely intentions. His conclusions, presented to the top brass, were remarkably accurate. Churchill, then minister of munitions, had been sufficiently impressed that he invited the young officer to dinner. That was useful in itself, now that Bevan found himself briefing Churchill once again. But more important, he had learned the nature of military intelligence work, looking at clues and drawing conclusions from them. He was an intelligence officer set to trap intelligence officers.

Bevan decided that the inability of his masters to tell him what they wanted was an opportunity, rather than a problem: he wrote his own job description, and he pitched it wide. His work 'is not to be limited to strategic deception alone but is to include any matter calculated to mystify or mislead the enemy wherever military advantage may be so gained.'

Next, he turned his attention to his location. In Cairo, Clarke had moved A Force out of Grey Pillars because he hadn't wanted anyone to know what he was up to. He'd been relaxed about that because he'd had the ear of his commander. Bevan, leading a neglected team, took the opposite approach. He moved the LCS from its grand offices overlooking St James's Park downstairs into the underground offices of the War Cabinet.

Deep below the London streets was the place from which Churchill ran the war. It was stuffy, cramped, far from daylight, smelling of stale tobacco and sweaty humans. There were bedrooms and bathrooms alongside the offices. Though one of the LCS's wealthier members did his best to brighten up their corner, covering the linoleum floor with his own Persian silk carpets and bringing in Chippendale chairs, no one would have called the offices pleasant.

But Bevan understood the geography of power. The London Controlling Section was now working physically close to the planners. Its very presence in Churchill's underground warren implied importance.

It helped Bevan that he arrived just at the point at which there was something for the LCS to do. On entering the war, America had assumed that the Allies could invade France in 1942. The British, with a better sense of how difficult this would be, had refused, and suggested an attack on French North Africa instead. They had won out, and Operation Torch, a three-pronged set of landings in Morocco and Algeria, under the command of the US General Dwight Eisenhower, was set for November.

For the novice deceivers, it was no small challenge. They were, in the words of one of those involved, 'faced not only with the task of preparing a detailed deception plan to cover the greatest amphibious operation since the Spanish Armada, but also with the immense labour of thinking out scores of minor pieces of information which, suitably conveyed to the enemy, would give him the false picture we wished him to accept.'

The cover plan for Torch was complicated. It involved suggesting that the troops assembling in Britain were destined for Norway and northern France. When it became clear that they were sailing further south, it would be suggested they were going anywhere but their real destination: Sicily, Italy or Crete. To support the Norway idea, the RAF flew reconnaissance flights, and fake radio traffic was broadcast in Scotland.

But the big development of the Torch deception was that it saw the first whole-hearted use of the Twenty Committee's British double-cross agents.

This had been the source of controversy among the spies. Guy Liddell of MI5 seemed to have lost much of the enthusiasm for deception he'd shown the previous year. Perhaps Clarke's escapade in Madrid had put him off. He took the view that the purpose of the double agents was to help catch other German spies. 'Deception is merely a side-line,' he now insisted.

In the first half of the year it had also been blocked by Naval Intelligence's man on the Twenty Committee, Ewen Montagu, though for different reasons. He had taken a personal dislike to Stanley. Perhaps he resented the idea that someone else was in charge of deception. The son of a peer and one of the heirs to a banking fortune, Montagu had led a gilded life that hadn't taught him much humility. His successful career as a barrister did nothing to tame his arrogance. He was very clever, and he wanted to make sure everyone knew it. Montagu's boss, Rear-Admiral John Godfrey, had been interested in deception since the start of the war, and it's quite possible that he and Montagu, like Clarke, were unimpressed by Stanley. They certainly did nothing to help him succeed. They stopped him from joining the Twenty Committee, the main route for putting false information over to the enemy. Stanley was no fool, and knew about Double-Cross. He may well have had his suspicions about Ultra. In an effort to placate Godfrey, he had refrained from pushing for access to either.

Other members of the Twenty Committee had wanted to do more, and been approaching different parts of the military and asking for suggestions of false information they could put across. But the answers had been vague and unhelpful. The main concern of the forces was that the Twenty Committee not allow double agents to pass too much useful information back to Germany.

The arrival of Bevan allowed a reset. Montagu was supportive, at least initially. Here was someone with ideas about how to wield the weapon the Twenty Committee had built. Bevan was invited to join their meetings. He proved willing to make full use of his new tool. The Abwehr's agents in Britain reported troops massing in Scotland, as they would do if heading to Norway, and others preparing to set out across the Channel. It wasn't all straightforward. The most prolific Double-Cross agent, a Spaniard named Juan Pujol Garcia – codename Garbo – had, like Cheese, developed a network of imaginary sub-agents. His was far larger, and included one in Liverpool. Unable to think how they would explain his failure to report the embarkation and departure of the Torch force, the Twenty Committee killed him off. When 'Garbo' reported his death from sickness, his German controllers sent a letter of condolence. In Egypt, Cheese was playing his part, reporting that he'd heard rumours of an attack against Italy in November, though he'd also heard Crete was a target.

It wasn't just the enemy that was being misled. British troops were told they were going to the Middle East, the Americans that they would be training in the Caribbean.

It's not the plan Clarke would have drawn up if he'd been in charge. There was no clear objective except 'surprise', and no single story for the enemy to piece together. Some Axis intelligence reports did predict North Africa as a target, but others went for Norway or Calais or Sicily. This was the Allied operation that Ulrich Liss told Hans-Otto Behrendt he was expecting in early November.

Modern military theorists split deception according to whether it increases or decreases the ambiguity in the enemy's mind. Clarke had instinctively preferred what would now be called 'ambiguity-decreasing deception': persuading the enemy that the Allies were going to do one thing. The LCS had stumbled into the other version, and were about to demonstrate why it can be effective.

As Bletchley Park deciphered the Abwehr's signals, it became clear that the main result of Bevan's work was confusion. The contradictory false news drowned out the more accurate. Good luck and bad weather meant the convoy from Britain wasn't even detected until after it had reached Gibraltar. There it was impossible to prevent observers in Spain from reporting its entrance into the Mediterranean, so the job was to mislead about its destination. In Cairo, Cheese reported that an American pilot who was friendly with his girlfriend had told her about plans for long-range bombing missions, and speculated the goal must be Italy. The next day, Cheese reported he had 'very important news': the pilot thought the bombing target must be Sicily. He'd also heard the British wanted to know how Vichy France would react to an Allied invasion of Italy.

All this was faithfully passed up the Axis intelligence chain. As the Torch convoy neared its target, the conclusion was that its likeliest target was Sicily. Axis submarines and bombers were ordered to defend the island, and there they uselessly sat as, on 8 November, the troops stormed ashore in North Africa. The landings were, in the words of General Alfred Jodl, Hitler's chief of operations staff, 'a complete surprise'.

It was a success for a team that badly needed one. Bevan was promoted to colonel, and though the result was as much down to

German intelligence failures and confusion as of any deception triumph, it was a good start. Even Clarke found lessons. Bevan had proposed suggesting that the convoy was carrying troops to land close behind Rommel, but Clarke had vetoed that, saying it was implausible that the Allies would try to sail so many ships within range of the Luftwaffe bases on Sicily. As it turned out, Axis intelligence had been perfectly willing to believe they would try such a thing. 'If there is a firm lesson,' Clarke wrote afterwards, 'it lies perhaps in the readiness of an opponent to accept evidence which from a purely British viewpoint may seem quite implausible. It stresses once again the necessity for deception staffs to study and know their enemy until they are able to think with *his* mind.'

Working on Torch, Bevan had realised, as Clarke had before him, the difficulties of coordinating false plans across huge distances. Life was hard enough for a tactical deceiver, working on a single battlefield, as Richardson was at El Alamein. Clarke had been able to keep all the pieces of the Middle East command's deception, covering an area ranging from Istanbul to Khartoum, from Benghazi to Tehran, in his own head. That was going to be impossible for Bevan, whose responsibility was global and involved multiple interlocking real plans and units, as well as fake ones.

On top of that, the Americans were coming into the game. Although at this point, far from thinking about giving the enemy false ideas about their plans, they still weren't doing enough to keep the real plans secret. Perhaps it was because they were new to the war, or perhaps because Germany felt a terribly long way away, but their standards of military security were appallingly lax. In the run-up to Operation Torch there were a series of horrifying leaks. A US admiral overheard officers discussing the operation at a Washington cocktail party. His army counterparts were doing even worse: one estimate concluded that as many as five thousand people had some knowledge of the plans.

So Bevan had called the conference in London partly simply to agree how everyone would work together. But he was also keen to get some first-hand tuition from the man who had written so many of the rules of the game. In his first letter to Clarke, that August, he'd suggested he visit London – 'it would be invaluable'.

Gathered in the underground conference room on a dry October morning were the nine people responsible for trying to mislead

Hitler. As well as Bevan, the London representatives included the novelist Dennis Wheatley, whose supernatural shocker *The Devil Rides Out* had brought him fame and fortune. He'd spent the early part of the war as a civilian writing speculative papers. He'd tried to imagine, for example, tactics that the Germans might employ in an invasion. His connections meant these were circulated at high levels in government, although military professionals seem to have greeted them with eye-rolling, rather than enthusiasm. 'Too far-fetched even for Hitler,' was the response to one. But they had ended up getting him a post in the London Controlling Section, where until Bevan's arrival the greatest challenge seems to have been staying awake after lunch (a contact from another arm of intelligence didn't help on this, regularly inviting him for a meal accompanied by Pimm's, then absinthe, then wine and then port to finish).

From India there was Peter Fleming, a travel writer and novelist recruited by Wavell to run deception operations in the Far East. His younger brother Ian was in a similar line, working for Godfrey in Naval Intelligence – and gathering the ideas that would later help him to create James Bond.

But there was no question who was the star of the show. 'We had all heard so much about Dudley Clarke that we were most intrigued to see the "great deceiver" in the flesh,' recalled Wheatley.

Clarke talked the audience through his approach and A Force's methods. He set out the importance of knowing what you were trying to get the enemy to do. And as the deceivers compared notes on their different experiences and problems, he offered advice. The Americans should be chivvied to get on with things. Bevan should try to cut unnecessary people out of his chain of command. That advice was taken to heart: a colleague once watched Bevan begin implementing an operation before the chiefs of staff had signed it off, and asked to whom he was responsible. 'To God and history,' he replied. Clarke would have approved.

There had been talk, of course, about Clarke's many exploits, but also whispers about his Madrid misadventure. By the end of the conference everyone was utterly charmed. Clarke was courteous to a fault, deferring to his host Bevan, even though he outranked him and had far more experience. Wheatley was in awe: 'He won all our hearts.'

Chapter 37

Clarke's visit to London came after a week in Washington, explaining the concept of strategic deception to the new allies. The days were filled with meetings, but the evenings with meals, movies and nightclubs. On the weekend he'd caught the train to New York for Broadway shows, lunch at 21 and drinks at the Stork Club. Shopping, too, at Saks on Fifth Avenue: a wedding present for Michael and Betty Crichton, and items in short supply in Britain and Africa: hairpins, stockings and lipstick (it's not clear whether these were gifts or for personal use).

This was the America that Clarke appreciated: Hollywood, Broadway, cocktails and nightclubs. He was comfortable with Americans who were comfortable with these things. When it came to the rest, he was, frankly, a snob.

Alongside his meetings with the London Controlling Section that October, Clarke met one of the first US officers assigned to deception work. Lieutenant Colonel Carl Goldbranson was from the Mid-West, and represented an America in which Clarke had no interest. Unflashy, married to the same woman since he turned eighteen, a father of three, an actual Boy Scout leader, he was the kind of solid Iowan who built America. In civilian life a manager at the Union Pacific Railroad, he'd been a member of the Iowa National Guard since the 1920s, and had been on active duty since 1940. Now, as the Allies set about knitting their command structures together and learning each other's ways, he was assigned to liaise with the deceivers. A lot of them liked this likeable man, but Clarke sniggered at him behind his back. What sort of place was 'Council Bluffs', and who on earth came from there? Certainly not the sort of sophisticates who should be playing the great game of deception.

Deception was an unknown art to most Americans, but a few were applying themselves to it with gusto. Four days after Montgomery launched his attack at El Alamein, three hundred US troops began a night assault on the beaches of Sandy Hook, New Jersey, across the bay from Long Island. They were trying out a new weapon, built by a college professor and part-time theatrical designer named Harold Burris-Meyer.

There wasn't much about theatrical illusion and sound reproduction that Burris-Meyer didn't know. He'd worked with the New York Metropolitan Opera, the Muzak Corporation and Bell Labs. His design for stereo sound had contributed to the making of Walt Disney's *Fantasia*. When war came, he'd joined the navy, with thoughts of generating noises so loud they would terrify or even injure the enemy. Nothing came of that, but sonic deception looked more promising. That was what he was testing at Sandy Hook.

In an age before tape-recording and easily portable batteries, playing sound on the move was difficult, but Burris-Meyer had designed a bulky piece of equipment that could do it. One landing craft headed towards the south end of the three-mile beach, the loudspeakers blasting out a recording of small boats. The defenders rushed towards the noise and the bulk of the assault force landed unopposed at the other end of the beach. The navy got the point.

Asked what the purpose of his equipment was, Burris-Meyer had replied it was to 'scare the BeJeezus' out of the enemy. Colleagues quickly dubbed his outfit the BJs. When they were asked what it stood for, they decided they needed something a little more polite. America's first deception unit would be known as the 'Beach Jumpers'.

They were bringing a little bit of Hollywood magic to the war, so it was appropriate that their most prominent recruit was a bona fide member of American cinema royalty.

Douglas Fairbanks Jr had inherited his father's good looks and followed him into the movies. Fairbanks senior had played Zorro and Robin Hood in the silent era. His son starred in *The Prisoner of Zenda* – opposite Clarke's new friend David Niven – and *Gunga Din*. But he wanted real action, so he wangled a naval commission and got himself sent to Britain as an observer. There his celebrity was a great help: Lord Louis Mountbatten, who was now running Commando operations against Europe, was a friend and had invited Fairbanks to watch the men training and even go along on raids. He'd also been briefed on efforts by A Force to implement sonic deception, playing the sound of tanks in an effort to make the enemy think an attack was imminent.

Fairbanks returned to the US determined that his country, with its technological and cinematic might, should get involved in this side of the war. Seeing his enthusiasm, his bosses assigned him to the Beach Jumpers, and then to handle liaison with the British. They couldn't have picked a better man to charm Clarke.

If he was sniffy about Goldbranson, Clarke was delighted with Fairbanks. The A Force commander loved celebrities and movies, and here was a genuine movie star. As he had done with Niven, Clarke made sure to include the actor's first name in his reports, lest anyone be in any doubt about who he had in his team. What was more, Fairbanks's approach to stardom – dropping names and using his fame to open doors – was one of which Clarke clearly approved, especially when Fairbanks's former lover Marlene Dietrich joined the officers of A Force for a party in Algiers.

But in general the Englishmen of A Force struggled with their American counterparts. They were used to acting swiftly and on their own authority. Dealing with the US Army, they faced what one called 'this extraordinary chain of command' who 'made a great song and dance over the whole thing with masses of orders'. It wasn't only in military protocol that there was a culture clash. Visiting an American base, Clarke ordered a breakfast of 'eggs and bacon with marmalade'. The baffled cooks, uncertain what this senior officer wanted but unwilling to question an order, eventually spread the marmalade over the eggs.

Bevan had at least made sure everyone knew who was running which show. On a trip to Washington at the end of 1942, he warned about the dangers of crossed wires. In a series of meetings, he dropped vague hints that the British might independently use deception channels in South America. This idea so horrified the Americans that they swiftly agreed a demarcation: the US would run deception in North and South America, and the British would run it in Europe. Bevan's focus was on the action in Europe, so this suited him nicely.

It's hard to imagine anyone less American and more English than the man Bevan had sent to brief Clarke on the Torch deception plans. Lieutenant Colonel David Strangeways was a thirty-year-old infantry officer whose war had begun with his deployment to France. After the ensuing retreat he had got his men off the beach at Dunkirk by swimming out to an abandoned barge that he sailed back to England himself. Always immaculately turned out, Strangeways was resourceful, happy to speak his mind to his superiors and impatient with those who stood on their rank. You either found him insufferable or you liked him. Clarke liked him, and requested him back full-time.

At the start of 1943 it was clear that the Allies had broken through in North Africa, with the forces that landed as part of Torch advancing eastwards, squeezing the Axis troops retreating from Montgomery's forces who were moving westward through Libya. There was good news elsewhere, too. In Russia, the long bloody battle for Stalingrad had resulted in a decisive defeat for Germany. In the Pacific, the Japanese were close to defeat on the island of Guadalcanal. For the Axis troops, the story of the next two-and-a-half years would be slow, painful retreat.

Strangeways was assigned to the Allied forces advancing eastwards into Tunisia. It was now taken for granted, at least by the British, that a commander needed a deception officer. A Force was operating in sections. Clarke designated Cairo 'Main HQ', run by his deputy, Noel Wild. Algiers would be 'Advanced HQ', under Michael Crichton and the American Carl Goldbranson. And Strangeways, advancing through the desert, was running 'Tactical HQ'.

After a briefing from Clarke, Strangeways set about a series of tactical deceptions with enthusiasm. His work rate was frenetic: stunt after stunt as he tried to confuse the enemy about where the next blow would come, and make his team of a hundred sappers look like a threatening tank force. 'The object was to draw down whatever we could.' If it was scary to find that his unit of dummies now faced a real German division, he also found it exhilarating. 'You always had this strange contradiction within you,' he said. 'You couldn't tell the men why you were there, that the object of the exercise was for the enemy reconnaissance aircraft to spot you and photograph you. You had to have anti-aircraft fire to make yourself look important and threatening, but of course you were hoping like hell that at least one of the recce aircraft would get clear and back to base with his false information.'

Strangeways was, in his way, as difficult a character as Noel Wild, and the pair had a hearty mutual loathing. Clarke could see the value in both, and also in keeping them on opposite sides of Africa.

As the Allies closed in on Tunis, Strangeways realised there would be valuable intelligence material that would need to be grabbed before it was destroyed. Without consulting his superiors in Cairo, he formed a team, 'S Force', to do the job.

As soon as Strangeways got the word the Germans had collapsed, he led his team into the city, bluffing his way into the enemy head-quarters – Dennis Wheatley, probably using a novelist's licence, claimed he shot his way in – and blowing open the safe.

Wild was outraged, but Clarke was more indulgent, if concerned that the main job was being neglected. 'He said I was very naughty and I wasn't to go on operations,' Strangeways recalled.

Whatever his superiors in A Force thought, the commanders on the ground were impressed. Strangeways was awarded the Distin-guished Service Order, for his 'resourcefulness, determination and coolness in difficult situations', as well as his 'total disregard for his personal safety'.

The real sign of how completely Clarke had sold his weapon to the Allied command came at the end of February, when he was handed a document drafted by Bevan but signed off by the chiefs of staff in London and Washington. It was a comprehensive plan for deceiving the Axis powers in Europe in 1943. Nothing like it had ever been produced before in any war. Its target wasn't a captain trying to work out how to defend the ground ahead of him, or a gen-eral assessing where the enemy thrust would come, it was the Fuhrer himself. And it wasn't simply a discussion about how he could be taken by surprise, but of how he could be induced to assign units to defend against fake threats, effectively taking them out of the war. It was, in fact, close to what Clarke had urged London to produce eighteen months earlier – a bogus plan for winning the war.

Bevan proposed persuading Hitler that the Allies planned to attack three areas.

First, Norway. The British expedition of 1940 had ended in a humiliating retreat, as Clarke could testify, but the Germans seemed ready to believe that the Allies would want a rematch. Hitler himself was deeply concerned about the country, convinced this was where the war would be won, and the deceivers were to learn that it took little to persuade him that a threat to the country was imminent.

Second, France. The British had persuaded the Americans that a cross-Channel invasion in 1943 would fail, but at some point one would have to happen. The deception mission was to tie down troops by making the enemy think an attack would come sooner rather than later, with the Mediterranean coastline a possible target. Among the more creative ways the LCS came up with of generating such rumours came from the manipulation of a genuine committee that had been set up to protect ancient monuments and works of art from fighting on the continent. Neutral diplomats including the Spanish, who could be relied on to pass intelligence back to Germany, were asked if their countries would be willing to store works of art removed from France. It was even suggested that those countries could approach the French government and offer to store pieces.

And third there was the Balkans, another area of permanent anxiety for Hitler. With his forces struggling on the Eastern Front, deep inside the Soviet Union, an Allied thrust up through Greece was a real worry. It could cut Germany off both from its troops in southern Russia and from supplies of vital materials.

But the biggest difficulty in the deception plan for 1943 was in the middle of the Mediterranean. Once North Africa was secure, the Allies had agreed the next target was Sicily. The efforts to persuade the enemy that this wasn't the case would involve the most famous deception stunt of the war.

The Artist's Dream

February–July 1943

The Magician paints a picture of a person on a large canvas and then covers the painting. Suddenly the person in the picture steps out of the painting, brought to life by magic.

Chapter 38

Everyone agreed it was the obvious target. It was close, for one thing. Sicily, the island at the toe of the Italian boot, was barely 90 miles by sea from Tunisia. That was half the distance from Egypt to Crete, and even if you captured Crete, you had to cross another sea to get to the next bit of Greece. Take Sicily, and you'd be right next to mainland Italy. Malta, the island loyal to Britain which held out while virtually cut off the previous year, would feel a lot safer. Control of the Mediterranean would be yours.

It wasn't just a question of minimising the distance that soldiers would have to be transported across water. The proximity meant fighters and bombers flying from Africa and Malta would have longer in the air over the battlefield, enabling them to better protect the men on the ground. It was the obvious target.

And that, of course, was the problem. An amphibious assault on this scale had never been attempted before. Unlike North Africa, the beaches of Sicily would be strongly defended. It would help if the attack were a surprise. It would help even more if the island weren't heavily reinforced.

Was it possible to persuade the Germans and Italians that the obvious target was the wrong one? The Mediterranean was A Force's territory, so Bevan passed the problem to Clarke. The plan to invade Sicily was codenamed Operation Husky. The deception plan was Operation Barclay.

The flow of Ultra material had now improved. Bletchley Park had begun issuing reports titled 'German Appreciations of Allied Intentions', summaries of what they had divined from intercepted messages. The codebreakers, still unaware of A Force's existence, sent the reports to overseas commands in what they later described as 'the rather vague hope that someone on the operations or security side would find them of value'. Clarke certainly did.

Reading the first report, issued at the start of March, he must have felt like an impresario reading rave reviews of his latest show. At the end of 1942, the Axis powers had 'received a flood of reports from their agents in the Middle East announcing immediately impending attacks' on Crete and other Greek islands, it said. That was the story he'd been trying to put across.

Helpfully for the problem he now faced, the report concluded that in mid-February, German high command were 'seriously exercised about the possibility of an Allied invasion of the Balkans'.

'All cover plans should be based on what the enemy himself not only believes but hopes for,' Clarke told his subordinates. Fear isn't hope, but it would do. The Allies didn't have to make the Axis certain about their plans, simply make them think that something was a strong enough possibility that it needed to be defended against. If Hitler was worried about an invasion of the Balkans through Greece, he was already most of the way there.

Here too was evidence that A Force's regular stories about an attempt to retake Crete were working. None of these threatened invasions had materialised, but instead of making the Axis question them, the repeated use of the story seemed to have made it seem that the question was When, not If.

There was, Clarke knew, no point in trying to pretend that the Allies weren't planning to attack somewhere. It would scarcely have been plausible. So there would be no efforts to conceal the assemblies of soldiers and equipment. The deception would be over where they were going – and when.

The story he wanted to tell the Germans was of a plan to liberate Greece, linking up with the Russians and bringing Turkey into the war on the Allied side. To stop Germany sending forces to resist this assault, there would be landings in both southern and northern France; and to get to southern France, the Allies would first take Sardinia and Corsica.

This wasn't, from the Allied perspective, a credible plan. British planners had insisted to the Americans that an invasion of France would be impossible that year, but here was a threat that involved landings in France and at both ends of the Mediterranean. Where were the troops and ships that would do all this?

Clarke proposed to conjure them from the air. Operation Cascade had been running for nearly a year now, trying to make the Allied forces in North Africa appear larger and stronger than they were.

Documents captured in the recent advances had shown the Axis assessment of the Allied order of battle in the Middle East. Almost all the fake units created by A Force appeared in it. Clarke had told the Americans it was risky to attempt to inflate numbers by more than 30 per cent, but when he looked at what the Axis believed, he found he'd actually achieved a 45 per cent inflation.

Now he was going to go further, with the creation of the 12th Army, an almost entirely fictional force supposedly being formed in Cairo. Its insignia, designed by Noel Wild, was a seal balancing a globe on its nose, designed to hint to an imaginative Axis intelligence officer that this was an amphibious outfit that would go anywhere.

Clarke's plan for implementing his deception was along the lines of his previous work: a mix of misleading orders, physical dummies, and false stories sent by double agents. His first act was to put out a call for troops who spoke Greek, Turkish, Bulgarian and Romanian.

As ever, he went deep into the detail, plotting out Barclay as though it were genuine: which units, real and notional, were to hit which targets when, which ships would carry them there, and where they would embark.

Barclay was the largest deception Clarke had run. The largest, up to that point, in history. It involved teams in Cairo, Algiers, Malta, London and Istanbul, putting over puzzle pieces in coordination, as well as hundreds more troops assisting in making it look real.

Naval officers in North Africa began asking for the names of local fishermen who were familiar with the waters off Corsica, Sardinia and southern France. In Algiers and Oran, American officers emptied the shops of guidebooks to the same places. The London Controlling Section dispatched fifty boxes marked as containing Greek bullion to Egypt. When it reached Suez, the cargo was transferred under heavy guard to a Cairo bank. The LCS also sent, rather more quietly, a small number of pound notes stamped 'France', 'Greece' and 'Bulgaria', which A Force proceeded to 'lose' in cities around the Mediterranean. Troops were handed specially printed guides to fighting in the Balkans and other 'target' areas. Greek and French troops were given special training in amphibious landing.

Clarke set his teams to work camouflaging the force massing in Eastern Tunisia and Malta, which could only plausibly be destined for Sicily. Ultra showed Axis photo-reconnaissance had worked out that dummy planes could be identified from the shadows on the ground of the struts that held up their wings. In the sort of double-bluff that explained why his staff regarded him as the master of his art, he ordered them to put wooden supports under the wings of real planes, so that they'd be identified as fakes.

At the other end of the Mediterranean, in the now-empty desert of Cyrenaica, the enemy was being asked to believe there was an army ready to invade Greece. It says a lot about A Force's reputation in early 1943 that no one seems to have questioned whether it would be possible to create an armoured division and an airborne division at a few weeks' notice. Dummy tanks were set up, and manoeuvred to look as though they were training. In the harbours dummy landing craft appeared. Seven airfields were made to appear operational, despite having a mere nine aircraft between them, busily taking off and landing whenever enemy planes were detected coming within sight.

There was a complex plan to create the fake radio traffic of the 12th Army, and a similar level of discipline to disguise the communications of the real forces. Planes flying across Africa were instructed to use their radios when they were going east, but not when they were going west, to give the impression that more were heading towards Egypt than were coming back. Uncle Sidney the magician would have recognised the technique of making attention-grabbing movements in one direction, and subtle ones in the other.

And some of the diversionary activity would have felt very real on the ground. Fighter planes intensified attacks on shipping off the Peloponnese. Teams of Commandos paid night-time visits to the supposed target beaches, leaving traces of their passing. The same beaches were the subject of intense photo-reconnaissance. He'd wanted heavy bombing of targets in Sardinia, but the RAF said it was too busy.

Then there were the newspapers. In Turkey, Wolfson got his special channel to work, planting another story in the Swiss press. But he and Clarke had plans to enlist journalists more directly. In London, the editor of the *Daily Mail* agreed to wire his correspondent Cedric Salter in Istanbul with instructions to position himself within easy reach of the Balkans at the end of June. Salter was in on the secret, under instructions to be judiciously indiscreet. 'I know my correspondents here well,' Wolfson wrote. 'They have been idle and too well fed for far too long and a warning to stand-by would set them off like a pistol shot. They would talk their heads off, however confidentially, and it would be bound to get to the enemy.' It was exactly the sort of rumour and speculation that Barclay needed.

Clarke had tried manipulating the press before, and found it fraught with unexpected complications. The previous year he'd approached Alexander Clifford, the *Mail*'s man in Cairo, and asked him to write a story about the difficulties Rommel might have launching an offensive in the heat of May, in the hope that enemy intelligence would draw the conclusion that the British were reluctant to attack at that time of year. The piece had appeared, 'most skilfully drafted', and A Force had briefly been delighted, until *The Times*'s correspondent, irritated at being scooped by a rival, had written a story rubbishing the *Mail*'s piece and insisting that the army was quite ready to attack.

In Algiers, he got around this problem by dealing with the press as a group. A select group of war correspondents was summoned and asked 'frankly' for their cooperation in spreading the false story. This was a tricky line to walk. The reporters who followed the Allied armies were in little doubt about whose side they were on, but were also clear that they were not supposed to be propagandists. In London there was a great fear of the consequences of planting misinformation. In early 1942, the government had blamed Shearer's optimistic briefing about Operation Crusader for some of its troubles, when his predictions hadn't come to pass.

But there was a middle path. 'It was never suggested that they should write untruths,' Clarke said. Instead, 'they were invited to stress certain aspects of current happenings so as to bring them into line with the general indications of Barclay.' Many of the 'current happenings' visible to a journalist were of course being stage managed by A Force, so they could be reported accurately and helpfully, if not entirely truthfully.

If Clarke had any anxiety that the assembled press would object to being asked to take part in deception, he needn't have. 'You cannot hope to bribe or twist, thank God! the British journalist,' the poet Humbert Wolfe had written a few years earlier. 'But, seeing what the man will do unbribed, there's no occasion to.' A Force's invitation was taken up with enthusiasm. One reporter in particular emphasised in his copy the focus on training troops in the dark of the moon, helping to mislead about the point in the month when any attack was likely.

There was a lot of focus in Barclay on misleading timing. It would be difficult for the soldiers defending Sicily to stay on high alert all the time, so Clarke repeated the trick that had worked in the desert, of seeming to build up to an attack, only to postpone at the last minute. He did this twice, hoping once again that 'our repeated cry of "wolf" would produce a sharp drop in vigilance just after the second notional D-Day had passed without incident.' Initially, all leave was to be refused after 20 June. On 15 June, that order was rescinded.

The chiefs of staff weighed in with their own ideas, too. To lend credibility to the idea that a Greek invasion was imminent, they ordered the guerrilla warriors of the Special Operations Executive to launch a campaign of sabotage against Axis communication lines in the country. Bevan was against this: like the rest of the British intelligence establishment, he viewed the SOE as insecure, its foreign networks liable to penetration by the enemy. But he was overruled, and on 21 June a key viaduct was blown up at the start of a wave of attacks.

All this deception certainly worked on the Allied side. A small group of Greek officers were attached to British units in the run-up to the attack. So certain was one of them that his homeland was going to be liberated that he contrived to stay with his unit even after he was supposed to have moved on. His reaction upon discovering that he was on a Sicilian beach, rather than a Greek one, wasn't recorded.

Elsewhere, the Allies were at pains to ensure that their deception efforts avoided more painful unforeseen consequences. Fearful that members of the French resistance might conclude liberation was imminent, and decide to rise up, they ordered propaganda broadcasts warning against 'premature action'.

Although Cheese was still a big part of his plans, Clarke now had more double agents he could call on. A French intelligence officer, who had maintained a covert network of double agents in unoccupied France, Spain and North Africa after his country's surrender, made his way to North Africa and put his agents at the disposal of A Force.

There were plenty of them, ranging from a smuggler-pimp who'd been given a wireless by Italian intelligence to a bar manager who wrote once a week to her German handler using invisible ink. In June, A Force reckoned it had seventeen wireless channels in North Africa, on top of Middle Eastern outlets like Cheese.

That didn't mean security was sewn up. Setting off for Tunis after it fell, an A Force officer was told that Bletchley Park was aware of eight Axis agents transmitting from the city. When he got there, he learned that only four had been identified.

But leakages weren't Clarke's biggest worry. He was counting on a few. What was the benefit of procuring large amounts of drachma, of issuing information to troops on Bulgaria and Romania, if none of this was going to make its way to Berlin?

No, his biggest issue, as he drew up his plan, was the sheer obviousness of the Allies' target. 'It seemed that the enemy could scarcely avoid the one conclusion that an attack on Sicily must be General Eisenhower's next move, no matter what his ultimate strategic intentions might be,' he wrote later. 'It was a painful realisation.'

Fortunately for Clarke, back in London two members of the Twenty Committee had come up with an idea to help with that. Even by wartime standards, it was a grisly one.

Chapter 39

Operation Mincemeat has been the subject of at least four non-fiction books, one novel, two films and a West End musical. It has a fair claim to be the best-known spy story of the Second World War. It is also the most misunderstood.

It had started back in September 1942, when a plane flying to Gibraltar crashed off Cadiz, killing all on board. This had caused a security panic back in London when they realised that one of the passengers had been carrying a letter from the US General Mark Clark containing details of the forthcoming Torch landings.

The courier's body had washed up on a Spanish beach, and had been returned to the British, the letter still in his pocket and apparently unopened. But the incident started cogs whirring in the mind of Charles Cholmondeley (pronounced 'Chumley', obviously), an RAF officer seconded to MI5 and serving as secretary of the Twenty Committee. He took an idea in: they should obtain a corpse, fill its lungs with water, dress it in uniform, slip some false documents in his pockets, and drop him from a plane somewhere he was likely to be washed ashore.

In essence, the idea was a haversack ruse, as considered by Clarke earlier in 1942 and implemented by Freddie de Guingand at Alam Halfa. Peter Fleming had tried one against the Japanese, leaving papers in an apparently crashed car in Burma, but there was little evidence the enemy had even noticed. The trick with haversack ruses was making them believable. Cholmondeley's hope was that the corpse would authenticate the document.

Because the plan involved dropping the body at sea, he was assigned to work on it with the Navy's representative on the committee, Ewen Montagu, the barrister who had sabotaged Oliver Stanley at the London Controlling Section. The idea would have seemed familiar to Montagu, because his boss, Admiral Godfrey, had proposed something similar in a memo listing possible deception ideas at the start of the war.

Cholmondeley's idea appealed to Montagu on a number of levels. First, it was clever, and Montagu was a clever man who liked clever things. It had about it all the qualities that are appealing about the secret world: it was theatrical, gruesome, a thing that others might not think of or dare to do. Finally, it would require an elaborate fraud, and Montagu found this sort of crime fascinating and even a little appealing.

He set about investigating the possibilities with alacrity, consulting a pathologist about how easy it was to determine a cause of death, and a coroner about the difficulties of procuring the right kind of corpse.

The plan was adjusted: dropping the body from a plane wasn't feasible, so they would need a submarine. The papers should be a letter between two generals, something candid that briefly made the Abwehr feel like they were right in the room. Authorities in Roman Catholic Spain might be squeamish about searching a body, so the papers would have to be in an attaché case attached to the corpse. That would mean they would need a reason for him having such a case. A side story was produced about asking Eisenhower to write the introduction to a book, so that the dead courier could be carrying a manuscript. The plan was given an appropriately gruesome codename. Even then, Montagu may have been preparing the tale he was going to tell his grandchildren – and the rest of the world.

Meanwhile the hunt went on for a corpse. It wasn't that people weren't dying in London. There was a war on, after all. But they weren't dying of the right things. Cholmondeley and Montagu needed a body that looked like it could have been the victim of a drowning. They found one at the end of January. Glyndwr Michael, a 34-year-old Welshman, homeless and with mental health problems, had been found in an abandoned London warehouse. He'd eaten rat poison, whether intentionally or not wasn't clear. The coroner told Montagu that this would be hard to distinguish from drowning, but warned that even kept cold, the body would need to be used within three months. A clock was now ticking.

By good fortune, from Montagu's perspective, Mincemeat was coming together just as there was a need for it. In the days before Michael had taken his poison, the Allies had agreed that Sicily was the next target. Unfortunately, as Churchill said, 'everyone but a bloody fool would know it'. But Montagu and Cholmondeley believed they had the perfect plan to put a different idea in Hitler's head, just at the moment it was needed.

Like a lot of brilliant individuals who believe they have an important idea, Montagu quickly became frustrated at the people he saw as obstructing him. When it came to naval deception, he was used to acting more or less as he saw fit. His main efforts thus far had been passing misleading information about the Navy's ships and their equipment: that warships still being built were operational, or that weapons were more effective than they really were. Although he'd welcomed the idea of Bevan coordinating deception work, he doesn't seem to have expected that this would include him.

But Bevan understood that deception needed one governing mind. At the London Controlling Section's October conference, he'd raised the issue of Naval Intelligence, who 'initiated their own deceptions in a small way', and Clarke replied that he 'considered this wrong in principle'. There could be no freelancers, and Naval Intelligence would have to start clearing their work with the LCS.

Bevan and Montagu had a fair amount in common: both came from wealthy backgrounds and enjoyed the sorts of countryside pursuits available to the English gentleman. Both were keen fly fishermen. And at first Montagu had been helpful to the new man. Part of his job was reading Ultra decrypts and parcelling them out within the Admiralty. Learning that MI6 was being slow to pass messages to the LCS, he had added Bevan to his distribution list on the sly.

But by the end of February 1943, he was furious with Bevan's approach. He had been circulating increasingly grumpy attacks on the LCS, accusing it of inexperience – which was fair enough, but also a reflection of the way he'd blocked its work for most of the previous year – and not understanding the Abwehr – again, the result of the struggle to get access to intelligence material such as Ultra. Now, when he, Montagu, had come up with a marvellous means of confounding the enemy, Bevan was getting in his way, insisting that Clarke, as the man running Operation Barclay, would have to sign Mincemeat off. Montagu was fully aware of the circumstances of Clarke's arrest in 1941, and may well have felt that such a ridiculous person had no right to a veto over his work.

As Bevan was preparing to head to Algiers to meet Clarke, Montagu was handed an Ultra decrypt that caused him to explode with frustration. It was an assessment from German Supreme Command. 'It is apparent that the enemy is practising deception on a large scale,' it began, although Montagu's view was that they weren't doing nearly enough. The message went on to say that the Mediterranean was likely to be the site of future action, with an attack on an island, 'the order of probability being Sicily first, Crete second, and Sardinia and Corsica third.'

Crete's presence in there, completely inaccurately, reflected a success for A Force, though Montagu is unlikely to have appreciated this. His anger was focused on the fact that Sicily was at the top of the list, and that Bevan seemed to be doing nothing about this.

Montagu drafted a furious five-page memo – followed up a few days later with a four-page appendix – denouncing Bevan. He was, he said, 'almost completely ignorant of the German Intelligence Service, how they work and what they are likely to believe'. More than that, he was 'completely inexperienced in any form of deception work'. He was charming, sure, but 'he has not a first grade brain'. He had exaggerated the success of his work on Torch, and was good at sucking up to superiors, but all he did was 'delay action'.

It was a rant that seems not to have left the Admiralty. Montagu's superiors wisely decided to do nothing about it, probably taking the view that their man was venting his frustration that people were blocking his great project.

Montagu might have been a little more circumspect had he known that he too was capable of making mistakes. In particular, he was unaware that his own brother Ivor, a convinced and very public communist, was also a Soviet agent, who had for the previous two years been supplying scientific intelligence gathered by a spy ring he'd built up. He may also have been going through the secret documents that Ewen liked to bring home from the office. (By coincidence, Ivor Montagu had been the co-director, with camouflage chief Geoffrey Barkas, of *Wings Over Everest*. Surely no other 22-minute Oscar-winning film has had more connections to secret intelligence.)

Clarke and Bevan meanwhile held their mini summit in the middle of March in a garage in Algiers, because there was no room for them at the nearest hotel. They drew up a draft of Barclay, and discussed Mincemeat's place in it.

In a way, Montagu was answering a question that Clarke had asked him and the rest of the Twenty Committee when he'd joined them back in 1941. Could they, he'd wanted to know, arrange to plant a document on the Germans? The reply had been that 'a document could be planted through more than one channel provided that the document was available in this country, and that he could provide a reasonable story to account for its presence in this country and its availability to the selected agent.' This was the difficulty of running double agents: you had to explain how they had access to the information they were passing over. There was no one on the Twenty Committee's roster who would plausibly have been told the details of Allied plans in the Mediterranean, but here was a chance to pass just such information over.

Clarke, though, had his doubts. He must have been torn. At one level Mincemeat's boldness and theatricality appealed to him. It's not difficult to imagine him being annoyed he hadn't thought of it first. But for all its appeal, this sort of flashy, complicated operation was a long way from his preferred approach.

The A Force deception method was to pass puzzle pieces to the enemy in a way that led them to assemble the wrong picture. Giving high-level documents felt more like simply passing them the picture all at once. On top of that, Clarke didn't like to draw the enemy's attention to the way he was giving them information. A stunt like this would by its nature be noticed, forcing the enemy to think about whether the letter was real, whether the corpse was genuine. It was always better not to have the target asking questions about their sources.

And if they realised they were being conned, it risked all the other work of Operation Barclay. 'It would be a mistake to play for high deception stakes,' he warned. He drafted a letter that the courier could carry which he deemed safe.

Montagu blew up – again – at this. What was the point of going to all this trouble to play for low stakes? Clarke's draft contained 'lowish grade innuendo' that could easily be put over by a double agent. Mincemeat, on the other hand, was a one-off chance to plausibly pass over false information of the highest level, and they should take it.

And now Bevan, in the face of all the things Montagu had said of him, agreed. 'We feel Mincemeat gives an unrivalled opportunity for

providing definite information and consequently we can go further,'
he cabled Clarke.

British intelligence was like any large organisation, riddled with
jealousies and internal factions periodically more enthusiastic
about attacking each other than the enemy. There would certainly
be tensions between the London Controlling Section and A Force
as the war went on, and the older organisation saw itself eclipsed
by its junior sibling. But Clarke, whatever his initial thoughts about
Mincemeat, yielded to Bevan. Perhaps he felt it was important to
support his colleague. Or perhaps he had decided that, on reflection,
he liked the idea of Mincemeat more than he worried about it.

If it succeeded, he wrote, 'the major part of the Barclay story
would have been carried in one bound right into the inmost circles
of the German war machine.' So the important thing was to make
it succeed.

Chapter 40

Montagu had grasped that the body on its own wouldn't be enough to sell the deception. They had to create a story around it, so he began writing one. It was a tragic wartime tale of a Royal Marine, 'Major Martin', who had met a girl and fallen in love, only to die just as they had become engaged. He would carry letters from 'Pam', his fiancée, written with a possible excess of pathos, as well as theatre tickets, a letter from his father, and a receipt for an engagement ring he couldn't afford. Cholmondeley was a similar build to the corpse, so he got himself fitted for a Royal Marines battledress, and dressed in it daily, to give it some wear.

It was thorough work, though open to the criticism that Montagu and Cholmondeley were trying a bit too hard, having a bit too much fun. The biggest danger with passing high-level deception documents to the enemy was that someone would suspect the information was too good. Such a suspicious mind might also wonder if the supporting evidence of Major Martin's life was too perfect.

The deception letters themselves were the subject of intense debate. The first was to be a letter from General Archie Nye, the vice-chief of the general staff, to General Alexander in Cairo. It went through multiple drafts by different hands, with Montagu typically furious and frustrated. As it was to be a personal note, he wanted to put in personal jokes at Montgomery's expense. His superiors, in the best traditions of anxious bureaucrats everywhere, forbade the mocking of Monty even in a false letter. In the end, they asked Nye, the general who was supposed to be writing the letter, to come up with a draft. Unsurprisingly, he did a better job, producing a letter to Alexander that had just the right level of behind-the-scenes gossip of the sort that someone might prefer to put into a private letter.

Crucially, it offered a few details of plans to invade Greece, and explained London had decided that Sicily wouldn't be a plausible cover target for such an operation, because 'there wasn't much hope of persuading the Boche that the extensive preparations in the Eastern Mediterranean were also directed at Sicily'. Instead, Nye went on, Sicily would be the cover for another unspecified invasion at the western end of the Mediterranean.

The clue about the 'real' target was in another letter, explaining Major Martin's supposed mission in North Africa, as an expert on landing craft. In its final line, requesting Martin return to London when the assault was over, was a suggestion that he 'might bring some sardines with him'. Was it too heavy-handed a hint that the target was Sardinia? Montagu thought it was just heavy enough for humourless Germans to notice it.

Churchill, another fan of the theatrical and the macabre, gave enthusiastic approval to Mincemeat, and the unfortunate Glyndwr Michael, who in the weeks after his death received more attention from the British state than he ever had in life, was floated off the coast of Spain by a submarine at the end of April.

There would be more excitement to follow. The British representative in the region where the body washed up, Francis Haselden, played the role of anxious diplomat trying to recover lost documents. This was finely judged: he had to try hard, but not so hard that he actually got the letters back before they'd been copied and passed to the Germans. At one point he had to stop a Spaniard from simply handing them to him.

It was here that the whole operation nearly fell apart. Montagu had been assured, and had assured himself, that Spanish pathologists weren't a patch on their British counterparts, and would never spot the issues with the dead body. But the man who carried out the work had seen a lot of drowning victims, and noticed some oddities about this corpse: there was no evidence that this body, which was supposed to have been in the water for several days, had been nibbled by fish, as would have been usual. Its hair and clothing didn't show the sort of effects he expected from that level of soaking, either.

That there weren't more questions was thanks in part to Haselden's quick-thinking. The diplomat wasn't in on the full Mincemeat story, but he knew the body needed to be accepted as drowned, and that the longer the autopsy went on, the more likely it was that a discrepancy would be spotted. The day was hot and the body stank. He told the pathologist that His Majesty's Government was quite prepared to accept the circumstances of this poor man's death, and given the state of the corpse, no further examination was needed. The pathologist, whatever his questions, was satisfied with the essential point: the man pulled dead from the water had drowned. That was, after all, the usual story with people pulled dead from water.

That evening, Haselden sent a telegram to the British embassy in Madrid. It was intended to be the message he would usually send in such circumstances. 'Body is identified as Major W Martin RM,' it said. 'Naval judge has taken possession of all papers. Death due to drowning probably 8 to 10 days at sea.'

As far as Haselden was concerned, he was signalling a success. The body had been accepted as a drowning, and the Spaniards had the paperwork. It was actually a message that revealed the greatest danger to Mincemeat.

The pathologist had judged that the body was so decomposed that it must have been in the water at least eight days. He'd actually only been in the water a few hours, of course, but he'd been in a fridge in a London morgue for several weeks and then a submarine, so it was hardly surprising he was a little ripe. This was a problem because Montagu's team had carefully loaded the body with a ticket stub putting Major Martin in London six days earlier. For anyone checking the story, it was an inconsistency that might lead to other questions.

If Mincemeat had been rumbled at this point, it could have backfired horribly. The Germans would have known they were the targets of a con, and have realised that the letters contained the opposite of the truth. Montagu spent a lot of time railing against the efforts of those he regarded as having lesser minds than his own – a category that seems to have included almost all of humanity – but he had, in his arrogance and his excitement, taken a terrible risk.

He got away with it partly because of what happened next. In the days that followed, there was a farce as German intelligence tried desperately to get hold of the contents of Martin's briefcase, and British intelligence tried to look like they wanted to stop them. In a further unforeseen problem, the letters were in the hands of the Spanish Navy, which was more pro-British than much of the government, and more resistant to the Abwehr. In London, Montagu went spare. In Madrid the naval attaché – last seen obtaining embarrassing pictures of Dudley Clarke for Churchill – played the straight spy, apparently doing his best to get the briefcase back, while making sure he didn't accidentally succeed until the enemy had taken a look inside. The result of this battle was that by the time the Abwehr finally got sight of the letters, they had fully convinced themselves of their importance and authenticity.

So much so, in fact, that even when they misread the ticket stub's date so that they believed Martin had been in London less than three days before he was found, the Abwehr persuaded themselves this was consistent with the state of the body, reasoning that 'the effect of the sun's rays on the floating corpse accelerated the rate of decomposition'.

Mincemeat was accepted all the way up the German intelligence chain, to Hitler himself. The Abwehr had no incentive to question what seemed to be a great coup, and those in military intelligence who might have raised doubts didn't. Only Joseph Goebbels seems to have had questions, but he didn't press them. So persuaded were senior officials of the tale of the 'English courier' that they became concerned the British would realise the letters had been opened and change their plans. The Abwehr gave assurances that the briefcase had been returned with no sign that the letters had been read.

The result would become known as one of the great intelligence triumphs of the war. There were proofs of success: at the start of March, the Axis had had eight divisions in the Balkans, one of them in Greece. Four months later there were eighteen, nine of them in Greece. In southern France the strength had been raised from two to three divisions, and two more had been sent to Sardinia and Corsica.

Mincemeat was indeed a great tale and a cunning operation, even if the risks associated with it hadn't been properly understood before it began. Bevan, showing a fair amount of grace in the circumstances, recommended Montagu and Cholmondeley for decorations.

Montagu was in no doubt that it was Mincemeat which made the difference. In his report of the operation, Sicily was the obvious target until 'Major Martin' floated off Huelva, at which point the Axis command changed their minds and started looking at Sardinia and Greece instead. He worked hard to ensure this became the accepted account within the military and government. Not that much work was needed: it was such a good tale.

But Montagu had fallen into the deception trap that Clarke had begun to identify two years earlier: the question isn't what you want your enemy to think – where Mincemeat was a huge triumph – but what you want him to do.

Even Montagu only claimed that one of the German divisions had moved as a result of Mincemeat. With the understandable focus on the body floating off the Spanish coast, the wider deception work gets lost: the reconnaissance of 'target' beaches, the bombing of Sardinia, the fake troop build-up in Libya, the double agents both in Britain and North Africa feeding a steady stream of misinformation back to Berlin, the intensifying SOE operations in Greece.

In suggesting they were going for the Balkans, the Allied deceivers were pushing at an open door. It was far easier to reinforce a mistaken belief than to lead someone to abandon a correct one, and Hitler was already worried about the Balkans.

Meanwhile there were many reasons Hitler didn't want to send too many soldiers to Sicily. He doubted – correctly, it would turn out – how committed the Italians really were to his war. Troops sent to an island off the southern tip of Italy were at serious risk of getting trapped there if things went wrong or his ally switched sides.

And the achievement of surprise on the night of the Sicily invasion itself owed more to A Force's work to build up the idea that any attack would come in the dark of the moon. The Italian army had never believed in Mincemeat. On the ground in Sicily, the soldiers knew they were the obvious target. It was, well, obvious. Where they were mistaken was on timing. Their commanders had believed the invasion was likeliest in the first ten days of the month, so the assault at the end of that period had come just as the defenders were relaxing.

Mincemeat's biggest flaw was the thing Montagu most liked about it: it was a great story. The body in the water carrying the secret letter drew everyone's attention. The moment it became clear to the Germans that Sicily had been the target all along, they were bound to question how they might have thought otherwise. In previous deceptions, A Force had given the enemy an 'out', allowing them to believe they'd simply drawn the wrong conclusion from their observations, or that plans had changed at the last minute.

As it happens, around this time in America, magicians had begun debating whether a trick could be 'too perfect'. If a missing card appeared on a part of the stage that the conjuror had never gone near, the danger was that the audience would conclude correctly that it wasn't the same card. According to this theory, the audience was bound to try to guess how a trick was done, and so it made sense to allow them several plausible options.

The vividness of Mincemeat meant any inquiry was bound to focus on the drowned courier, and the moment the Germans thought about that, the only possibility was that they had been the victims of an elaborate set-up. After the war, Clarke concluded that the invasion of Sicily had been the last time that the enemy weren't actively on the lookout for deception. From then on, the deceivers were working in an atmosphere of 'constant suspicion'.

The story of Mincemeat began to leak out even before the war had ended. Duff Cooper, a member of Churchill's Cabinet, fictionalised it in a 1950 novel, *Operation Heartbreak*. After a tip-off, the journalist Ian Colvin worked the story out, including finding Major Martin's grave. At this point Montagu persuaded the War Office that, as the tale was coming, they ought to release an approved version. He produced a manuscript which he claimed – implausibly – to have written over the weekend. Published in 1953, *The Man Who Never Was* became an instant hit. Security prevented any mention of wider deception operations, or the parts played by others in this one, meaning Montagu had to portray himself as a lone genius. He bore this burden, and the stardom that went with it, remarkably well.

Mincemeat was undoubtedly the biggest moment in Montagu's war, so it's understandable that he stressed its importance. It was a great stunt that continues to grab the imagination. Whereas much of the work that A Force did was painstaking, placing tiny clues here and there for months and years on end, the impact only comprehensible when the viewer stood back and saw the whole, here was an idea that was easy to understand, one so arresting that it would ultimately become impossible to keep secret.

But Mincemeat was only one trick in the performance that Clarke had been staging for Axis intelligence. It was undoubtedly the most memorable – indeed perhaps the best objection to it was that it was so vivid a clue that it risked revealing the entire story was false – but it sat within the much larger show that was Barclay.

No one was ever going to regale post-war dinner parties with hush-hush tales of the time that they renamed a series of units to create an imaginary infantry division, but the key to the success of the Mediterranean deception was Operation Cascade. However well-written the letters carried by Major Martin were, they would never have persuaded the Germans that the Allies were capable of launching assaults in three different parts of the Mediterranean in the space of a couple of months if the Abwehr's estimates of Allied strength in North Africa had not already been vastly inflated.

Mincemeat did help Clarke with his superiors. For most of the time he had been a deceiver, he'd been trying to explain the work to people at the top. But explanations about renaming units and creating fake divisions never really gripped an audience. Here at last was a deception that excited them. Even if they didn't understand quite how it had been done, both American and British commanders could see that the German army had been in the wrong place when Europe had been invaded.

And they were beginning to grasp that the idea Clarke had sketched out in 1941 might actually be plausible. In the run-up to El Alamein, A Force had helped to convince the enemy that the attack would come at a different time and in a different part of the line. In the run-up to Sicily, they persuaded Hitler that it would come in a different country.

Here, There or Where

July 1943–July 1946

The Magician pours rice into a vase, covers an orange with a tube and a bottle with a second tube. Then they lift the orange from the vase, reveal the bottle under the first tube, and lift the second tube to find rice gushing out of the bottom.

Chapter 41

The Allies attacked Sicily on 10 July 1943. The real landings on the southeast of the island were accompanied by deception efforts co-ordinated by Strangeways, to keep troops pinned down in the west. There were naval and aerial bombardments. Dummy parachutists, designed to explode on landing, were dropped, and Douglas Fairbanks' Beach Jumpers went into action for the first time, heading for the island playing the sound of an invading fleet. The defenders were convinced. When, the next day, they could find no one to fight, they announced they'd successfully seen off the invaders.

Back in Cairo, Cheese reported, probably accurately, that Greek troops were astonished to learn that Sicily had been invaded. His message was passed on: 'Reliable V-Man Roberto reports from Cairo,' an Abwehr message began. 'It is still believed that air attacks on Crete will result in a landing on Greece . . . The Twelfth Army, with its subordinate Greek units, is still here.' The Twelfth Army existed only in the files of A Force and the Abwehr, but it was holding very real German forces in place.

But for all the success of Operation Barclay, and despite all the claims made by Montagu for Operation Mincemeat, there were still Axis troops holding Sicily, and they still needed to be beaten. The mountainous terrain was ideal for defenders and the Germans made the most of it. It would take six weeks for the Allies to conquer the island. As they fought their way across, events moved fast in Rome. Mussolini was deposed, and the new Italian government began to negotiate a surrender. But even as it seemed Italy's war might be over, Hitler ordered German troops to occupy the country, while the Allies began moving up from the south.

This created jobs for both sides of A Force. Strangeways was deployed to help with tactical deception, and Simonds' MI9 team had to deal with a wave of Allied prisoners making a break for freedom from Italian prisoner-of-war camps.

Clarke suddenly found a new source of assistance. Back in England, the boffins at Bletchley Park had sensed for a while, reading German traffic, that someone must be doing something deceptive in Cairo. In November 1943 they finally learned of the existence of A Force and began formally working with them. It benefited both sides. Clarke was better able to understand the reliability of the intelligence he was receiving, and at Bletchley Park they realised a hidden significance in a lot of the messages that had previously passed them by: they showed the success, or not, of the efforts of Clarke's team. 'A Force,' a Bletchley Park note recorded, 'is one of the great successes of the war.'

The move into Italy also revealed the answer to a question that had been troubling SIME and A Force. Renato Levi, last seen leaving Istanbul more than two years earlier, wrote a letter to 'The Officer in Charge, British HQ, Intelligence Dept, CAIRO (Egypt)'. He had, somehow, survived, and was now free. SIME, delighted with this news and keen to hear his tale, brought him back to the fleshpots of Cairo for a lengthy debriefing and, doubtless, a little rest and relaxation. But if they were pleased with him, they still didn't trust him, and they had no intention of telling him how important his creation, 'Nicosoff', had become.

'He was a brave man,' Clarke concluded, 'full of resource and with an ever-ready wit. And if his moral character and past history are more colourful than respectable, at least he deserves well.'

After the invasion of Sicily, deception's place in Allied thinking was secure, but the strategic focus of the war began to shift away from the Mediterranean. The invasion of France was the next step, and that deception would be Johnny Bevan's show, run from London.

Clarke had known this day was coming and ceded the spotlight with good grace. He'd always been clear that 'one brain – and one alone – must be left unhampered to direct any one deception plan'. He explained why using his favourite analogy. 'It is after all little more than a drama played upon a vast stage, and the author and producer should be given as free a hand in the theatre of war as in any other theatre.'

Bevan was working, though, to Clarke's pattern. From double agents to dummy equipment to fake wireless signals, there was nothing that the London Controlling Section did in the run-up to D-Day that hadn't been pioneered by A Force. The very idea that the largest military operation ever mounted could be concealed and then passed off as something else was only plausible because of the work of the previous three years. That both Eisenhower and Montgomery were believers in deception by the start of 1944 was a tribute to Clarke's success over the previous three years. It was natural that two of Clarke's trusted team members, Strangeways and Wild, were sent to London to help. It would be a sequel to the desert war in another way, too: the German commander in charge of stopping the Allies entering France was Rommel.

The landings were to be at Normandy, under the codename Operation Overlord. Bevan's first draft of a deception plan, in summer 1943, was called Jael, after the Old Testament heroine who lured a Canaanite commander to her tent and then, while he was sleeping, drove a spike through his head. It was reworked after the 1943 Tehran conference between the leaders of Britain, the US and the Soviet Union. Bevan saw a minute of the meeting which had Churchill remarking to Stalin that 'truth deserved a bodyguard of lies'.* He rather liked the line, and called his grand deception Operation Bodyguard.

Things had seemed, frankly, pretty hopeless. 'Our first survey of the position showed a picture of almost unrelieved gloom,' Ronald Wingate, one of Bevan's staff, recalled. Politicians on both sides of the Atlantic had been talking publicly about opening up a second front in Europe, the only place they could do that from was Britain, and the closest bit of Europe to Britain was France. If that weren't all bad enough, the LCS deception policy for 1943 was to talk up the prospects of an attack in northern France – in one delightful piece of rumour-mongering, trusted officers were instructed to remark in their clubs that there was no point making plans for the usual August grouse shoots, because by then all leave would be cancelled. Now in 1944 they were supposed to talk it down. Those planning Overlord advised the LCS that they were 'beaten before they had begun'.

The deceivers could only reply, Wingate said, that it was 'worth trying'. 'Overlord' had to succeed. Anything that might increase its chances should be given a shot.

---

* Generally reported as: 'In wartime, truth is so precious that she should always be attended by a bodyguard of lies.' This version comes from an extract of the minutes in Clarke's files.

As it wasn't plausible to suggest that France wasn't a target at all, the story Bevan would tell was that it wasn't the main target. Instead, he said, the story would be that spring would see an attack in Norway, and a big Allied thrust in the Balkans. No cross-Channel efforts would be possible before late summer. Bevan's hope for the first part of the year was that he could keep as many German troops as he could as far away as possible from northern France.

Eyebrows continued to be raised. 'Do you suppose the Germans really are such suckers as to think we will attack through Norway?' Harry Butcher, one of Eisenhower's aides, wrote in his diary that April. 'They did during the North African invasion, and maybe it will happen again.'

There were good reasons for people to have their doubts about how much of this would work. The London Controlling Section were still finding their feet. In September 1943, they had sent a fake invasion fleet off to France with the goal of drawing the Luftwaffe out to fight so that the Allies could destroy them over the Channel. Fifty ships had set out and then turned back, but the enemy barely noticed.

The Germans though didn't have to think a Norway attack was a certainty, only that it was a serious possibility. Hitler had to defend his entire perimeter, and every soldier that he used to do it in Norway was one who wasn't going to be in Normandy.

In the same way, London tried to play on the uncertainty around neutral countries. With the war turning the Allies' way, might Sweden, or Spain, or Turkey be persuaded to join in on their side? The diplomats at the Foreign Office replied that this was extremely unlikely, but the deceivers replied that 'it was not what the neutral countries intended to do which mattered, but what the enemy might think that they intended to do'. A shift from any of the neutrals would suddenly alter the map of Europe as far as Hitler was concerned, so it was a natural worry.

Strangeways and Wild may have loathed each other, but one thing they agreed on was that they were the deception experts. That was, after all, why they were both in London at the start of 1944. While Wild irritated people with his manner, Strangeways did it by being cleverer than them.

He was there as Montgomery's deception man, in charge of implementing the cover plan for the invasion itself. At some point, the feeling was, it would become obvious to the Germans that a very large invasion force was building up in the south of England, and that neither Norway nor the Balkans had been attacked. At that stage, they were bound to conclude that northern France was the real target after all. The job of the cover plan was to conceal where and when this would be.

The draft handed to Strangeways at the start of the year was known as 'Appendix Y'. Its story was that the invasion was going to be in the Pas-de-Calais in the middle of July. It proposed putting this over by offering some dummy units in southeast England. The hope was that a landing in Normandy six weeks earlier would take them by surprise. After that, the story would be that a second set of landings were still planned for the Pas-de-Calais, in the hope of keeping some German forces there and away from Normandy.

Strangeways hated it. 'It was too complicated,' he recalled later. 'The people who made it had not ever done it before.' Apart from anything else, there was nothing in this story to stop the troops in the Calais region heading south in June to fight in Normandy, and then going back north in July. 'I rewrote it. Entirely.'

Strangeways approached the matter with Clarke's key question in mind: what did they want the Germans to DO? That was easy: to keep as many troops in Pas-de-Calais for as long as possible. What would induce them to do that? The thought that Normandy was not the main event. The cover story was changed: Normandy would now be presented as a feint, whose whole purpose was to draw troops away from the real target, the Pas-de-Calais.

But who was supposed to be making this second, main assault? This was Strangeways' other contribution. From Ultra, he knew that the Germans had detected the existence of a skeleton unit, the First United States Army Group (FUSAG). This, he proposed, should be offered as a real, vast force, sitting waiting to strike. Someone else suggested the final touch, that it should be commanded by General George S. Patton, who was in disgrace after slapping shell-shocked soldiers, and wasn't set to be involved in the early weeks of Overlord.

Here again was a story that relied on understanding the enemy's thinking. Hitler regarded Patton as one of the best generals that the Allies had, and the idea that he would be punished for being rough with his soldiers made little sense to the Nazi mind. It was easy for them to believe he was really going to be commanding the invasion.

His very name attached to FUSAG gave it credibility. And here too was a sign of how seriously deception was taken at the top of Allied command: one of their most senior generals assigned to play-acting in the run-up to the great invasion.

Strangeways' revised plan was received with resentment that matured into grudging admiration. 'Could we possibly get away with simulating an entirely fictitious army group?' asked one of those who read it. It showed how far ahead A Force was of London that Strangeways knew that had been done already, and could be again.

There were still Allied generals who struggled to grasp the entire concept, especially on the US side. One, informed of the plan to make the Germans concentrate on Pas-de-Calais, replied, baffled: 'But we're not going to land in the Pas-de-Calais.'

Clarke later described his order of battle deception as 'the basis of everything'. It had been, he said, 'undramatic and unnoticed', but also 'the instrument of success for Pas-de-Calais' and the Balkans. 'Even if no other deception is contemplated, I would recommend a commander to insist from the very start that a continuous and painstaking order of battle deception is put into operation. It cannot be done in a hurry, and one day he will be thankful for it. It will always repay the trouble it causes.'

It did. For first days, then weeks, then a month after the landings in Normandy, the Germans held troops back in readiness to fight off another invasion in Calais. Only later would Rommel realise this had been a decisive mistake. Forced to kill himself in the wake of the bomb plot against Hitler, he would never find out that the troops supposedly poised to attack Calais simply hadn't existed.

Bodyguard was put together using Clarke's methods, often by Clarke's people. His approach was everywhere. Even the idea of a feint that would at some point be revealed to have been so unexpectedly successful that it had become the real assault was a standard A Force routine. On the night of 5 June, as Overlord was beginning, the Twenty Committee's leading double agent, Pujol Garcia, codename Garbo, was allowed to send a warning transmission, just as Cheese had been two years earlier, on the eve of Montgomery's assault at El Alamein. And in an echo that no one could have planned but that was highly revealing of the state of the Abwehr, once again no one was listening at the other end.

A Force had its own role in Bodyguard, codenamed Operation Zeppelin, the 'longest and most elaborate operation it had yet undertaken'. There would be more bogus units, more dummy tanks and landing craft, this time assembled around Tobruk. Double agents, now operating the length of the Mediterranean, were put to work, providing puzzle pieces that pointed to a huge build-up of forces: Clarke calculated afterwards that Zeppelin had involved the transmission of 577 separate wireless reports. In a neat trick, a double agent in Britain told his handlers the codewords that the BBC would supposedly use in its Yugoslav service to give partisans a month's warning ahead of the invasion, as well as the words that would be used if the invasion had to be postponed. That enabled A Force to signal very precisely that there would be an invasion on 21 April, only to postpone it at a week's notice and set it for 21 May.

Clarke's problem was that Bodyguard described a series of wildly inconsistent stories in the Mediterranean. For the early part of the year, there was supposed to be an imminent invasion of the Balkans. Then in June, as troops were landing in northern France, A Force was asked to create an invasion threat in southern France, to try to keep German units pinned down there. Then in August, when there really was going to be an invasion of southern France, A Force was to say that there wasn't.

At another point in the war, Clarke might have objected to this, but he accepted that nothing was more important than the success of 'Overlord'. In May, he issued a 'special order of the day' to his team of double agent handlers: 'In the past, when nearing the climax of any plan, we have been at pains to conserve our machinery for another day. This time that policy will no longer hold.' If a successful deception destroyed a double agent's credibility, it was a price worth paying. 'Once we have entered the month of June, all considerations regarding the safety of our channels . . . are to be subordinated to the demands of the plans on which we are now working, and every risk accepted which can further the success of these plans.'

As Clarke and his team pondered how they might explain why the Allies would have called off an invasion of the Balkans at the last minute and decided to attack southern France instead, they got an unexpected helping hand. In April, Greek soldiers in Egypt mutinied, holding out for several weeks, until British forces fired on their camp, forcing them to surrender. It provided the ideal excuse for a change of plans: A Force put out the story that the Greeks were in no condition to liberate their homeland, and so France had become the target instead. The final twist came at the end of June when, having spent a month suggesting an invasion was imminent, they changed their story again, saying that it had been postponed because German forces hadn't left the French coast and gone north, as had been expected.

Zeppelin and its accompanying operations were judged a success. After the war, with access to German documents, Clarke calculated that in 1944 A Force's deception efforts had helped to pin 35 enemy divisions in the Mediterranean. Hitler needed troops in the Balkans to keep control and fight partisans, but not the 25 divisions that he kept there, ready to fight an invasion that he believed to be imminent but the Allies had neither intention nor capability to deliver. During June only one of the ten divisions on France's south coast moved north.

There was one more deception stunt in the days before D-Day that would become famous. It was Clarke's idea, and he was rather proud of it.

Chapter 42

At the start of January 1944, Clarke was just outside Naples, visiting Allied forces there. He was now largely based in Algiers, where he had a new secretary, Daphne Llewellyn, the 21-year-old sister of Hermione Ranfurly. She had discovered that order of battle deceptions had uses for manipulating allies as well as the enemy. The French administrators of Algiers frowned on frivolity while the mother country was under the fascist occupation, but had been persuaded to allow each army regiment to hold one dance a year. But Llewellyn, working for Clarke, knew that regiments only needed to be imagined to exist. She set about inventing fictional outfits to hold dances, soon known as 'Daphne's Dives'. Clarke was an enthusiastic supporter of such creativity.

Over in Italy, he'd worked in the morning, then headed away in the afternoon to do a spot of tourism, visiting the ruins of Pompeii. A nearby American unit was getting a screening of one of the previous year's hit films, *Five Graves to Cairo*, made by a talented new director, Billy Wilder. Clarke was never a man to miss a movie, especially one that promised to tell 'the startling inside story' of how Rommel had been defeated in the desert, so he went along.

It did not, whatever the trailer claimed, reveal the secrets of the victory at El Alamein, but it was an entertaining film for all that, telling the tale of a retreating British soldier who finds himself mistaken by Rommel for a top German agent. What caught Clarke's attention was one of the supporting actors, Miles Mander, who played an English colonel. Wearing a black beret, he bore a striking resemblance to General Montgomery. Something about his appearance in a film about mistaken identity set the cogs in Clarke's mind turning. Hollywood had been getting a lot of material from the war, and now Clarke was going to take an idea back.

There was no concealing the fact that there would be an Allied invasion that year. The question was where and when. There was value in misleading the enemy about timing, persuading them to relax a little at just the wrong moment.

Monty was now Britain's most famous commander, his movements the subject of intense enemy interest. Clarke had used that as part of Barclay, arranging a 'leave' in Palestine for the general in early July 1943 that was intended to show that no attack was imminent. Perhaps he could pull a similar trick again, and this time, with a bit more style.

It had just been announced that Montgomery was going to be commander-in-chief of the British group of invasion armies. 'Supposing,' Clarke mused, 'he were to be seen somewhere in the Mediterranean a day or two before the Normandy invasion, the Germans could take it as a certain indication that they had at least a week or more to wait before the landings came in North West Europe.'

Where could Monty reliably be seen? There was one place where Allied commanders came and went 'under the direct eyes of the enemy': Gibraltar. The airfield there was the northernmost part of the British territory, right next to the Spanish border. And just across the frontier, the Germans had set up an observation point where they could watch the comings and goings through binoculars.

Clarke presented a copy of his plan the following month. A Force's man on Gibraltar was an old friend of his, a one-eyed artilleryman named Harry Gummer, and he looked it over. Clarke's proposal was that the plane carrying 'Monty' simply stop to refuel, allowing the fake general to get out and be observed. But Gummer feared this was overestimating the competence of the German agent watching the airfield, who didn't usually report much more than aircraft or ship movements. It would be 'advantageous', he said, if 'Monty' could be met with a bit of ceremony, and leave the airport, a journey that would take him closer to the observation point. Gummer suggested a visit to the governor.

In April, plan 'Copperhead' was approved. In London Gilbert Lennox, an MI5 officer, was put in charge of finding an actor. His first thought was to get Miles Mander, as Clarke had suggested. Alas, Clarke recorded, 'discreet inquiries in Hollywood had shown that Mr Mander was unfortunately several inches taller than the general, and this was a physical handicap it was impossible to disguise.' Lennox found a substitute who immediately ruled himself out by breaking a leg in a road accident. Like a lot of clever schemes, this one was proving harder than it sounded.

And then, just as he was beginning to despair of finding a Montgomery impersonator, someone else did the job for him. 'Recognise the picture below?' began a brief article in the *News Chronicle* over a picture apparently of Montgomery. 'You're wrong. His name is James – Lieutenant Clifton James, producer and chief performer in the Royal Army Pay Corps Drama and Variety Group.'

Clifton James was, in the words of Noel Wild, 'a second-rate actor' who had so far spent the war making sure the rest of the army got paid. He didn't know why he'd been sent to the Pay Corps – he had no head for figures – but they let him put on shows for the troops in his spare time. Watching one of them, the *News Chronicle*'s photographer had noticed that James was the spitting image of Montgomery, and asked him to pose in the general's trademark beret. James, a nervous sort, feared he'd be disciplined for impersonating an officer. Instead he got a phone call the following month from David Niven.

The Hollywood star, still in touch with Clarke, was the perfect person to approach an actor. Niven asked James if he would mind popping down to London to discuss working on some military films. It was a plausible reason to take him away from his unit, but an unintentionally cruel one: James believed he was finally getting his big break. Instead, he was asked to sign the Official Secrets Act.

Wild had spoken to Montgomery about the operation. 'He is all out to support the plan,' he reported back, 'and has gone so far as to say he will lend us any clothing.' In the event, they approached his tailor instead. MI5's Guy Liddell was caustic about his motives: 'Monty is rather flattered by the whole plan, which of course is based on the theory that the Second Front cannot possibly start without him.'

Lennox set about preparing James for his role. Much of this work was mental. While James might have resembled Montgomery physically, psychologically he was as far from the general as it was possible to be. Unlike the man he would be impersonating, he was plagued by self-doubt. Watching newsreels of Montgomery, he worried he would struggle to match the 'tremendous air of assurance'. He was also weighed down by guilt at having to lie to his wife about what he was doing.

Over in Gibraltar, Gummer was having doubts, too. Having concluded that the German airport observer was not up to the job of spotting an intelligence scoop even when it got out of a plane in front of him, he was trying to construct a visit that would expose the fake Montgomery to as many Axis intelligence sources as possible. He'd arranged for a group of Spanish air force officers to run into him during a visit to Gibraltar, and for him to travel around in an open-top car. He wanted to prime locals as well, by getting a picture of Montgomery into the Gibraltar paper a couple of days before the visit. The care he was devoting to ensuring that enemy spies should recognise Britain's most famous general revealed a lot about the Allied assessment of enemy intelligence capabilities in 1944.

In London, James had got his uniform, and got the hang of Montgomery's salute. Dennis Wheatley was ordered to arrange for him to go up in a plane, to check he didn't suffer from airsickness – it would be no good if the Montgomery lookalike staggered onto the runway at Gibraltar and threw up. Finally, James was allowed to meet the general himself. The pair chatted about their childhoods in Australia, where James had been born, and Montgomery's father had been a bishop, and the actor tried to get a sense of the man he was going to impersonate.

Gummer meanwhile was encountering problem after problem. Wild had vetoed the newspaper article, presumably because it would have been laying things on a little too thick. The Spanish officers weren't going to be allowed to come. Instead one of the governor's aides, Miles Clifford, had been persuaded to invite the Spanish vice-consul to Government House, where he'd have a chance to accidentally see the bogus general. The vice-consul could be relied upon to report to the Spanish intelligence service, and they could be relied upon to pass the story to Berlin.

As the day approached, James felt increasing strain. The pressure of the role was unlike anything he was used to. Impersonating the abstemious Montgomery, he would be forbidden his usual nerve-steadying drinks and cigarettes. In a moment when it looked like the show might have to be called off, an MI5 officer suddenly noticed that James was missing the middle finger of his right hand, a wound from the previous war. A prosthetic was hastily crafted from sticking plaster and cotton wool.

On board the flight, things continued to go wrong. The journey was terrible, and the officer who was supposed to be playing one of Montgomery's aides was too airsick to get off the plane. The pilot feared the weather might be too bad to land at Gibraltar. On the ground, Gummer learned that the Spanish vice-consul had cancelled.

And then, just as with the best theatrical shows, everything came together. The pilot got the plane down. James, walking onto the stage, said his first line and realised that he might be able to pull it off. And best of all, Gummer learned that in the vice-consul's place the Spanish were sending Ignacio Molina.

This was a particularly happy moment. Though Molina was officially an employee of the Spanish government, MI5 knew him to be on the Abwehr payroll, and suspected him of having helped a team of Italian frogmen sent to plant mines on ships at Gibraltar. They had been trying to get him banned from the Rock for years. At one stage, they'd even considered kidnapping him and taking him to London. This would be better revenge.

Lieutenant Clifton James, Royal Army Pay Corps, saluted and waved to passers-by as he was driven to the governor's residence. The response was delight. Waiting there for him, with a guard of honour at attention, was the governor himself, an old friend of Montgomery's.

'Hello, Monty, glad to see you,' he said as his visitor got out of the car. 'Hello Rusty, how are you?' replied James, and the pair walked inside, chatting warmly. In private, at least according to James, the governor expressed his astonishment: 'You *are* Monty. I've known him for years.'

Next door, Miles Clifford, Colonial Secretary, was waiting to play his part. He hadn't been told that James was a fake, only that Montgomery was visiting, and that it was important he be identified by a Spaniard. At ten that morning, he received Molina, and the pair spent a few minutes discussing the official reason for the visit, before Clifford suggested they go and speak to one of the governor's staff. As they walked through the gate, they were greeted by the carefully timed sight of Sir Ralph putting 'Monty' back into the car.

Whatever Gummer's views of the rest of the Abwehr's agents, Molina didn't need any help identifying the visitor. He turned to Clifford who, 'with well-feigned embarrassment', confessed that this was indeed Montgomery, on his way to Algiers. It was all Molina could do to contain his excitement. The moment his meeting was over,

Gummer reported, 'he motored very fast' back across the border, and placed an 'urgent' long-distance telephone call. 'I imagine, therefore, that by now the good tidings are on their way to Berlin'.

The Monty's Double caper wasn't quite over. James would have to repeat his act three hours later in Algiers, where he was greeted by cheering crowds, before being driven, with American motorcycle outriders, to the Allied headquarters. There he was shown into a private room, where he changed into the uniform of a pay corps lieutenant, before sneaking out through the kitchens to an A Force villa, where Clarke was waiting to congratulate him on a part well-played.

The next day James flew to Cairo, badly in need of several drinks and under orders to lie low. Betty Crichton, who helped to look after him, was full of sympathy for a man who was finding coming off the stage as difficult as going onto it had been. According to A Force legend, her husband Michael invited James to join him for a whisky, and then excused himself and left the room, returning later to find James snoring and the bottle empty.

Copperhead was a terrific caper, but even Clarke was willing to concede there was no evidence it affected Germany's readiness for invasion. He had wanted 'Monty' to appear in Gibraltar close to D-Day, but the operation was pushed earlier, and the invasion was delayed, so that it would have been quite possible for the general to have got back to Britain in time.

Like Mincemeat, though, it was the kind of story people couldn't keep to themselves. While Clarke's team was busily restricting the number of people in the know around the Mediterranean, it was quickly the subject of gossip and jokes in Allied Headquarters in Britain. It reached the newspapers before the end of 1945, and Clifton James found he had a problem familiar to much more successful actors: he was typecast as Monty's Double, so famous in that role that nobody wanted to put him on stage in any other.

Years later, Strangeways recalled Copperhead. He was frustrated by the focus on the eye-catching ruses, and, speaking about this episode, more true to Clarke's vision than Clarke was himself. 'That wasn't the thing that did it,' he explained. 'It was some stuff dropped in Spain, something else somewhere else, something else somewhere else. And they all got together, all these little bits and pieces, to make the feed. And the icing on the cake was this chap. He did it very well, but it just was a bit extra.'

Chapter 43

In July 1946, three years after the Allied armies stormed the beaches of Sicily, two years after they landed at Normandy and one year after the German surrender, Brigadier Dudley Clarke walked into the lecture theatre of the Imperial Defence College, in Belgrave Square, London. He'd been promoted at the end of 1943. He might have hoped, at the start of the war, for faster and further advancement. When he'd joined up, thirty years earlier, he'd certainly hoped to lead men in combat. But aside from his duties in Palestine before the war and a night on a beach near Boulogne in 1940 with his Commandos, that hadn't happened.

He was leaving the army now, and looking for a new job. His curriculum vitae was detailed up to the end of 1940, and then vague. 'In recent years I have specialised in the subject of strategy,' he wrote. 'I was directly responsible for certain duties.'

It was to talk about some of those duties that he'd been invited to the college that Wednesday afternoon. His audience was the first post-war class in this school for high-flying officers and civil servants. On the front of his folder of notes were two words with which he was very familiar: 'TOP SECRET'. Deceivers, he began, are 'very shy people'. They had a duty to protect people who'd helped them, and they hoped that the work they'd done would be 'forgotten and generally discounted'.

That wasn't really true, at least as far as Clarke was concerned. He'd spent much of the previous year arguing that the deception story should be made public. It would be impossible, he'd argued, to write any proper history of the war without talking about deception, which had been 'inextricably interwoven into almost every strategic and major tactical plan since 1940'. What was more, all sorts of people were already writing histories, some of them clearly with a view to publication, and many of them unaware of the full picture. Clarke had proposed that someone who did know the full history – a list that really contained only his name – should write it, and it should be published. Official historians would need it, he said, before going on to what was really occupying his mind. 'There is also something to be said for revealing a colourful and often dramatic contribution to the conduct of the war which was wholly British in conception,' he wrote, in a line that gave a very clear idea of the sort of book he had in mind.

He wasn't the only person thinking along these lines. When he'd consulted colleagues about what secrets should be kept out of any public work, Naval Intelligence had replied that he shouldn't write about Mincemeat. It's not clear who told him this, but if, as seems likely, it was Ewen Montagu, it wasn't out of an excess of shyness on his part. Montagu had already begun discussions about selling the story, and he had no intention of letting Clarke scoop him.

Clarke's ambitions, meanwhile, went beyond literature. His younger brother Thomas had joined Ealing Studios during the war as a screenwriter, and Dudley, maker of home movies and de-vourer of Hollywood ones, saw a chance to get his own break. He had proposed that the government agree to what he described as a 'documentary film'. His description of the project suggested he had rather higher ambitions. A film, he said, 'can treat the subject to some extent on a fictional basis'. They would tell the stories of the El Alamein and Torch deceptions, and include Mincemeat as though it had been a part of those as well. Americans, he noted, might be more likely to watch a film than read a book.

This wasn't an offhand idea. Clarke had written a ten-page syn-opsis of his proposed movie, *Secret Weapon*, including what would be on the screen and the narration, and sent it to the Joint Intelli-gence Committee, seeking their permission to go ahead. 'This is the story of a Secret Weapon,' the voiceover would begin. 'Product of British brains . . . forged in the dark days of 1940 to the command of General Wavell . . . wielded to the greatest advantage in his skilled hands . . . tempered and finished by British experts.'

Like so many of Clarke's ideas, this was an ambitious one that was quite beyond the usual run of military thinking, and so it's not surprising that he was turned down. The Director of Military Intelligence was firm. All these releases of classified information, he had said, set 'a bad example'. Even if the content of the film were harmless, you couldn't have people getting the idea that Top Secret no longer meant anything once the war was over.

As he approached the end of his lecture, Clarke read out a quote from Alfred Jodl, chief of the German Army's operations staff. In March 1945, as the Allies closed in on victory, Jodl had issued a directive. 'Deception is a weapon which is still too little employed in the German method of warfare,' he began. 'Our enemies, especially the English, occupy themselves more with it and with more success.' It had been a little late to come to this realisation. Clarke had been ordered to cease deception operations in October 1944: the Germans were viewed as being so close to collapse that there was no point in trying to sell them any stories.

Germany had in fact enjoyed some notable deception successes, chiefly convincing Stalin in 1941 that there was no plan to invade Russia. But Jodl's memo showed that he still viewed the subject as mainly a matter of catching your enemy off guard.

With his disciples, Clarke had taken the weapon to another level. When Jodl signed the surrender in May 1945, he still had more than 300,000 men in Norway, three times what their commanders estimated was needed to secure the country.

These men were waiting for an attack that never came – the first Allied soldiers they met were the ones who came to take their guns – but more than that, they were waiting for an attack that had never been possible. The western Allies had simply not been capable of invading Norway and the Balkans as well as France and Italy. But the Germans had never realised this, accepting the imaginary soldiers of Cascade right to the end. One German general, in post-war interrogation, expressed his bafflement that the Allies had never deployed the 5th Airborne Division, unaware that it had never existed outside the files of A Force – and German intelligence.

Was Clarke right about the importance of his secret weapon? 'If I get to know how a trick is done, I lose my interest in it,' the Roman philosopher Seneca observed. Like any other illusion, deception can seem very ordinary once you know about the wires and the mirrors. Could all these elementary stunts – the tedious building up of imaginary forces, the slow passing over of misleading fragments of gossip, the fake wireless networks, the tanks that looked like trucks and the wood and canvas that looked like tanks – really have made that much difference?

The simple answer is to ask whether German commanders would have behaved differently if they'd had an accurate intelligence picture. Again and again in the second half of the war, their soldiers were in the wrong place, expecting the wrong thing. Hitler's weakness as a strategist was a large part of that, as was the poor quality of the Abwehr, but so, surely, was the deliberate and structured work of the Allies to deceive them, to put over what Clarke had imagined in 1941: 'a completely bogus plan for winning the war'.

And what was Clarke's contribution? Again, there's an easy counterfactual: how might events have panned out if things had gone differently after his Madrid arrest? Had German intelligence got their hands on him, it's certainly the case that the intelligence war would have followed a different course. At a minimum, MI5 would have had to assume that its entire Double-Cross network had been blown.

Imagine instead that Clarke had escaped Spain but failed to talk his way out of the trouble he was in with his superiors, and been shunted to some disgraced desk in the War Office. What would have happened to Allied deception? The likeliest outcome is that it would have ended up being run in the Middle East by Ralph Bagnold, a fine man but one who lacked Clarke's devious genius. There are hundreds of unknowables here. Would the El Alamein deception have worked as well without Clarke's suggestions about the timing? How would the battle have gone differently if Rommel had been on the scene when it started, with the instinct to order his reserve into the right place at once?

We can surely say that without Clarke, there would have been no Operation Cascade, steadily building up the size of Allied forces in the Abwehr's mind until it seemed plausible that 1943 might see simultaneous landings at both ends of the Mediterranean, and that there were enough soldiers in Britain in 1944 to invade Normandy, Calais and Norway, with sufficient left over in Egypt to attack the Balkans.

The scale of that work is breathtaking. The best estimate is that over the course of the war the Allies created 160 false units, ranging in size from Clarke's 1st Special Air Service Brigade, born at the start of 1941, to the First US Army Group, so important in 1944, and including bomber groups, fighter groups and even a US Navy fleet. In those years the Allies worked on more than 350 identifiable deception operations.

The triumph of Operation Bodyguard had many parents, but Johnny Bevan – his hair now grey after the strain of three years at the heart of war-planning – and his team in the London Controlling Section were always clear about the debt that they owed to A Force. Clarke's experience in North Africa had shown what was possible. He had selected and trained David Strangeways, whose rewriting was so critical to the cover plan for Normandy.

A lot of the arguments about deception get driven to extremes, with one side claiming that a single stunt won the war, and the other side furiously arguing that none of it made any difference at all. There is plenty of middle ground. Montgomery was clear that wars are won by killing, but he went to some effort to have surprise on his side at El Alamein. Likewise after D-Day, there are lots of reasons why the Germans didn't immediately move forces south from the Pas-de-Calais to meet the invaders. But Hitler's belief that this was where the real blow would fall – and the assessment of German intelligence that there was still an army group waiting in southern England – definitely helped.

In his 1946 lecture, Clarke listed his successes for his audience. At the end of the war a British analysis concluded that deception operations had tied down the equivalent of 50 German and Italian divisions in 1942 and 1943, and around 40 divisions in the build-up to D-Day in 1944.

The deception weapon had one very unusual quality. Did the deployment of 200,000 unnecessary German soldiers to Norway, rather than the banks of the Rhine, change the course of the war? It's unlikely: the Allies had superiority everywhere it mattered. Perhaps those troops could have delayed the inevitable for a few weeks.

But deception changed the course of the lives of those men, and the men on the Allied side who would have died while killing them. Deception was, Clarke said, a weapon 'designed to save lives rather than destroy'. And it achieved that, saving lives on both sides.

There are two persistent myths about deception. The first, relating to the Second World War, is that it relied on small bands of eccentrics, fighting rigid military bureaucracy. Cinematic versions feature moments when the brilliant deceivers have to go around unimaginative generals to the only man who will listen: Churchill himself. The great leader sees what the stuffed shirts can't: that the war will be won by brains and daring, as well as military might.

Nothing could be further from the truth. Deception in the Second World War was initiated by one of the most senior generals, Wavell, and willingly carried on by his successors. When Clarke presented his ideas to the chiefs of staff, they were immediately supportive. This is hardly a surprise. The British army spent the first half of the war losing. Commanders were eager to hear ideas that might help them win.

Eisenhower and Montgomery were both quickly persuaded of the benefits, with Eisenhower issuing orders that every genuine plan should come accompanied by a cover plan. It's not that the deceivers didn't face obstacles. There were fights over scarce resources, complaints from unimaginative staff officers, and issues with military bureaucracy, particularly when the freewheeling Brits of A Force encountered the rigidities of the US military staff. But even if few understood Clarke's weapon as he did, he always enjoyed the support of his commanders.

He could hardly have succeeded otherwise. While some of the deception capers were executed by small teams, many required a huge amount of organisation, equipment and manpower. There was the assembly of thousands of dummy tanks, planes and landing craft. The fake wireless networks needed radios and operators. The men doing all this work out in the desert needed food, water and shelter. Britain's deception and camouflage operations from 1942 involved over 4,000 soldiers – a tiny investment given the results they achieved, but still a long way from the idea of the lone genius.

This was why Wavell's appointment of Clarke had been inspired. He wasn't simply possessed of a rare imagination. He was an effective staff officer, a man who understood how to manage logistics. Much of this work wasn't glamorous or exciting, it was merely essential.

The second myth is that, although it worked in the past, it won't work again. This seems to be said after every war. It was to challenge that idea that Clarke was giving his lecture. Before the Second World War it had been suggested that aerial reconnaissance would make fooling the enemy impossible. In the event, Clarke and his team often relied on the Luftwaffe photographing their carefully displayed dummies to make their deceptions work.

After the Second World War it was assumed that developments such as satellite photography would finish deception. Russia's 2022 invasion of Ukraine showed different. Both sides used deception. Russia successfully persuaded the Ukrainians that their target wasn't Kyiv and kept defending forces away from the city. Unfortunately – for them – they had deceived their own soldiers as well, and their forces were unprepared to carry out the real plan.

The Ukrainians were more successful. After Russian strikes destroyed airfields, Ukraine photographed the damage, printed out the pictures onto large sheets, and used them to cover undamaged aircraft, successfully fooling the eyes in the sky. The Russian military began to wonder whether Ukrainian fighter jets were flying from underground shelters.

Likewise, twenty-first-century communications mean news is reported instantly from the front line. In theory this makes it much more difficult to put out false stories about what's happening. And yet the Ukrainians have proved adept at using the media to give a misleading impression of their plans, briefing the press that they're focusing in one place while attacking in another. As with stage magic, new technology just means new ways of delivering deception.

There was one mystery about deception that Clarke didn't address in his lecture: why did it keep working? Why did the Abwehr not realise that their sources were unreliable? Why was Rommel, fooled at El Alamein, fooled again at Normandy?

There were practical reasons. The deceivers were good at their jobs, and careful in their approach. The German intelligence organisations were badly led and riddled with corruption. The Nazi system made it dangerous to admit mistakes or tell Hitler things he didn't want to hear. The Allied codebreakers ensured the deceivers knew their enemy's fears and beliefs, and could reinforce them.

But there was another reason. A magician could tell you. 'Deception can never be effective either in love or in war,' the intelligence historian Michael Howard wrote, 'unless there is a certain willingness to be deceived.' For the Axis powers to admit they had been misled so comprehensively and repeatedly was too difficult. It was easier to believe the 'outs' that A Force kept offering. There is, the modern magician Teller says, no story as powerful as the one the audience tells itself. Clarke's audience, it turned out, preferred to be fooled.

And it was not just the enemy that was deceived. In late 1943, Churchill sent a grumpy note to his chiefs of staff, who had been complaining, as ever, about their lack of resources.

'To my certain knowledge there is the best part of an Army Corps in Cyprus,' he wrote. 'What is the total ration strength of the Middle East Command?'

The reply stayed just about on the correct side of politeness. 'The so-called Army Corps in Cyprus is for the purpose of deception,' it read. 'The only fighting troops available amount to one infantry brigade.'

Someone passed the exchange to Clarke, who placed it, with characteristic humour, at the start of a folder marked 'Results of the plan as shown by captured documents'.

Curtain

Exiting the Stage

David Strangeways stayed in the army after the war, eventually commanding a battalion in Malaya. He was asked to lead the force responsible for nuclear testing on Christmas Island in 1957, but he had moral problems with the atom bomb, so he resigned and became a Church of England vicar – switching sides, if you like, from deception to the service of truth.

Johnny Bevan also put his lies behind him and returned to gentlemanly stockbroking, his wartime work marked with an honour from the King. Once a year, he would host a dinner for wartime deceivers.

Michael Crichton too became a stockbroker on his return to England. His wife Betty, the nightclub hostess from Indiana, adjusted well to respectable life in the Home Counties, bringing with her a touch of the glamour that had bewitched the audience on the roof of the Continental in her days as Betty-to-You.

Carl Goldbranson, so sneered at by Clarke, stayed in the military after the war, working in deception for the rest of his career.

The Jewish political officer who in 1941 had helped Clarke spread stories about a desert glider crash as part of Abeam was called Reuven Shiloah. He spent much of the war recruiting Jews to fight in the British army, and trying to persuade the British to use them in operations to save Jews in occupied Europe. When the state of Israel was founded its first prime minister, David Ben-Gurion, asked Shiloah to set up and then head the Institute for Intelligence and Special Operations. It is better known as Mossad.

Vladimir Wolfson stayed involved with the Royal Naval Voluntary Reserve, playing a key role in persuading Ian Fleming to give up his own commission when he could no longer spare the time for the required annual fortnight's training. For all that, the Bond author had liked him. 'Made for the job,' he told a friend. He may have had him in mind when he created Darko Kerim, the fictional head of MI6's 'Station T' in Istanbul: 'Where had this exuberant shrewd pirate come from? And how had he come to work for the Service? He was the rare type of man that Bond loved.' Wolfson joined the British Overseas Airways Corporation, and was killed in 1954 when the de Havilland Comet he was flying in crashed off Italy. That meant this immigrant didn't live to see his son achieve what is surely the crowning glory of anyone who aspires to be an English gentleman: becoming the Conservative MP for Sevenoaks in 1979.

John Hutton, the artist whose airfield murals fooled friend and enemy alike, returned to England, where he was contacted by Basil Spence, an architect he'd got to know on the camouflage training course. Spence had been commissioned to design the new cathedral for bombed-out Coventry, and wanted Hutton to make a window for him. The Screen of Saints and Angels took him ten years. His ashes are buried at its foot.

Geoffrey Barkas returned home to his wife Natalie. He made a few more films, but nothing to match the great production he had put on at El Alamein. He wrote an account of that, admitting, with a little embarrassment, that he had rather enjoyed his war: 'One of the most interesting and absorbing assignments in a lifetime by no means lacking in variety.'

Evan John Simpson returned to writing, including a book, *Time in the East*, about his war years. Just after Christmas 1953 he was found shot dead in woods near his Oxfordshire home. He had taken his own life. A friend, writing to *The Times*, said he had been under strain since rushing to Greece earlier that year to help in the aftermath of an earthquake. 'He had a generous mind and great energy,' they wrote. 'He found no limits to the claims of friendship.'

R. J. Maunsell went on to set up Unilever's information division, keeping the relaxed management style that had served him so well at SIME. He wrote a brief memoir about his time in Cairo that is now in the Imperial War Museum. It is a frank and enjoyable read, and so scandalous that it can only be viewed under supervision.

Dominic Macadam-Sherwen, also known as Thomas Sherwen, but not, whatever his colleagues believed, known as Dominique, Vicomte de la Monte, is a mystery. Maunsell was fond of him: over the course of the war, he said, they 'became great personal friends. Indeed he still owes me £30.' He joined A Force on the MI9 side, and Simonds records that he volunteered to parachute into Yugoslavia, where his first message reported that the six bottles of whisky and four of gin that he'd carried in with him were destroyed in the drop.

What happened to him after the war? Maunsell said that a 'mysterious Colonel Emblanc' appeared in Cairo, recruiting Frenchmen to 'liberate' Indo-China. Macadam-Sherwen joined him and Maunsell never heard from him again. Clarke had an address for him on Martinique in his post-war files, but it is undated. Maunsell assumed he had been involved in France's disastrous attempt to hold onto its colony in what would become Vietnam. 'I have, for the last few years, presumed he was killed at Dien Bien Phu,' he wrote. 'He would never have been taken.' It is as good a story as any, and it might be true.

Ralph Bagnold, by then a brigadier, retired from the army in 1944, when it was clear there would be no more desert war. It would be unfair to remember him for his clash with Clarke: his military legacy was the foundation of the Long Range Desert Group, a pioneering unit in irregular warfare and one that contributed greatly to the success of others, including the SAS. After the war he continued his studies of sand, winning awards for his research, before living out his final years in Kent, an English county that is as unlike a desert as it is possible to be.

Laszlo Almasy (he may not have been a Count, as he claimed) received an Iron Cross for smuggling the Operation Condor spies into Egypt. If the operation yielded no useful intelligence for the Abwehr, it did at least deliver for popular culture. Embellished with fictional details – that the spies used a code based on Daphne du Maurier's *Rebecca*, that they were betrayed by the belly dancer – it would inspire a shelfful of books and a couple of films. Almasy himself found lasting fame as Michael Ondaatje's English Patient.

Anwar al-Sadat, the Egyptian officer arrested and interned for helping the two spies, found it did his prospects no harm in the long term. He went on to become president of Egypt.

Renato Levi's fate is unclear from his file. One report is that he returned to his family in Italy and then chartered a boat, filled it with Turkish carpets, and took them to Australia to sell. He is believed to have died in 1954. Though he never knew it, he was the genesis of the Allies' longest-running double agent operation. Between July 1941 and February 1945, the 'Cheese' channel, also known as Paul Nicosoff, also known as 'the Reliable V-Man Roberto', transmitted a total of 432 messages. It was also the first double agent channel to be used to put over a deception, ahead of Operation Crusader. Next to his final message, an A Force officer scrawled 'RIP'.

Jasper Maskelyne returned home to find London little interested in stage illusions. In an effort to cash in, he worked with a ghost writer to publish a memoir of his war years, *Magic – Top Secret*. There was no difficulty with the government agreeing to its publication because it was largely made up. His description of making the Suez Canal disappear, or moving the port of Alexandria, feature nowhere else in any of the records. It was, however, astonishingly enduring, with his claims regularly repeated seventy years later, most notably in David Fisher's *The War Magician*, which also credited him with coming up with the plan for the El Alamein deception. Despite having been a minor figure within A Force, Maskelyne became by some distance its most famous member. It is a little unfair to complain about a magician misleading their audience – that is, after all, the job – but most of the statements about Maskelyne's war years should be treated with the same scepticism we would reserve for his claim to be able to saw a woman in half. An audience, as both he and Clarke understood, generally prefers a good story to the truth.

Tony Simonds would have asked Maskelyne to stand as godfather to his daughter, but he was irritated by a prank the magician had played on him at his wedding, sewing up the arms and legs of all his clothes.

Instead he asked Clarke, who did the job reluctantly and without much idea what was expected of him. His gift of a snow globe of the Eiffel Tower would have been an ideal gift to a goddaughter, had she not been sixteen at the time, and distinctly unimpressed. Simonds himself stayed on the fringes of the secret world, writing for the *Intelligence Digest* from his house in Cyprus. He was, eventually, forced off the island after his house was destroyed in the Turkish invasion of Cyprus. He moved to Britain with little more than a duty-free bottle of Scotch. When, with his mind failing at the end of his life, his daughters found him a room in an old people's home, he became convinced he was in a prison camp. But the skills he'd learned in MI9 came back to him, and he escaped several times. It wasn't hard, he explained. You waited for the visitors to come, and then dressed up and slipped out with them. The guards, he said, were easily fooled.

Cedric Salter, the Turkish correspondent of the *Mail* whose willingness to deceive his fellow reporters was in the finest traditions of his trade, went on to join the *Express*. His war was a busy one, taking him from Poland through Romania, Bulgaria, Singapore, China, India, Tibet and Burma, where he was the last correspondent to leave Rangoon before it fell to the Japanese. It led to him being described as 'the most chased-about of British correspondents', which was probably a reference to the Gestapo, rather than his editors. He was in Turkey in 1945 when he received a Commander-in-Chief's Commendation in the King's Birthday Honours list for his help with deception. The citation remains classified to this day.

Dudley Clarke left the Army after the war and went to work for the Conservative Party, in its newly formed Opinion Research department. Its official role was to get to grips with the new tool of opinion polling, then in its infancy. This on its own was fascinating work, and he threw himself into the analysis of swings, floating voters and target seats, concepts that are routine now but were unexplored terrain in the 1940s. Churchill was still party leader, and six years after the war ended Clarke found himself, as his commanders had, explaining to the great man that he couldn't always have the numbers he wanted – in this case polling leads.

But as ever with Clarke, the official job title was, in part, a cover.

His team had 'a second – and secret – object', to gather information about their opponents. 'As in other battles,' he explained to a
colleague, 'successful planning can only result from plentiful and
accurate intelligence.'

Clarke ran the A Force veterans association, and wrote histories,
of the Eleventh Hussars, Noel Wild's cavalry unit, and of his own
life. *Seven Assignments*, a book covering his war up to the point he
joined Wavell's staff, was well-received.

Perhaps noting the success of Peter Fleming's younger brother
Ian, whose own visit to wartime Portugal had helped inspire the
best-selling *Casino Royale*, Clarke tried his hand at fiction. Published in 1955, *Golden Arrow*, his one novel (though very far from
his only attempt at story-telling) is an enjoyable adventure starring
a man who did something secret in the war and now works as a
high-end troubleshooter and mystery solver. This is clearly the man
Clarke would have loved to have become. His own passions and
experiences are visible in the tale: it centres on the luxury train route
from London to Paris; the villains are based on a houseboat – on
the Seine, not the Nile – and enlist the help of an exotic dancer.
The hero, it must be noted, is an unmarried man with an unusually
detailed knowledge of ladies' fashions.

But his request to write 'The Secret War', the story of A Force,
was refused by the government. As other histories began to drip out,
of Mincemeat, and of Double-Cross, his former comrades became
infuriated that others were – to their minds – taking credit for his
ideas. They took their own commitments to secrecy seriously: after
the first edition of this book was published, the grandson of one
of Clarke's men in Italy, Ron Harvie, got in touch to say that his
grandfather had never spoken about his work, to the extent that
for the rest of his life he feared he would talk about it in his sleep.
Like his team, Clarke wasn't going to to disobey an instruction
to stay silent. Instead he tended to appear, often unnamed, in
other people's war memoirs: a mysterious figure in a camel-hair
coat who seemed important but whose precise job no one quite
understood.

He almost vanished from the official memory. For most of the
time that I was working on this book, a mention of his name would
be greeted with a blank expression. And then, in the autumn of
2022, that changed, as the actor Dominic West pulled on a dress and

played Clarke, or at least a version of him, in the BBC's dramatisation of the desert war, *SAS: Rogue Heroes*.

The Clarke portrayed on screen was fictional, increasingly so as the drama went on: he may perhaps have tried cross-dressing in Cairo – though there's no evidence – but he certainly didn't wear Chanel gowns to the office. He was in North Africa, not London, ahead of the Sicily invasion. Although his drinking was probably heavy by modern standards, I've seen no suggestion that any of his contemporaries thought it noteworthy. Neither did he try to get David Stirling killed. But it's hard to know what Clarke himself would have made of it. He might, conceivably, have been prepared to overlook the transgressions in return for the recognition, of a sort, that was denied him in his lifetime. And perhaps he would have been pleased to know that a photograph from his 1941 arrest – the one with the dress, of course – now hangs in the officer's mess of 77 Brigade, the British Army's 'information operations' unit.

When he died in 1974, it was not big news. But his team knew what he'd done. A couple of weeks after *The Times* ran its brief obituary, the newspaper published an anonymous letter. It noted that, although there was no public record of his war work after 1940, it had received praise at the highest levels.

'The diminishing band of those who served in the dingy but exciting headquarters of A Force in Sharia Kasr-el-Nil,' it went on, 'cannot let his death pass without paying tribute to the energy (displayed at such unorthodox hours), the imagination (brightest as he pondered his plans in the loneliness of a crowded cinema), and the meticulous professionalism of his staff-work which made the most successfully secret of the "secret organizations" in Cairo exercise such a powerful influence.

'Whimsical, witty, far-sighted and always optimistic Clarke was a leader to admire then – and after 30 years.'

This was, as the letter-writer concluded, 'no ordinary man'.

Author's Note

One of the big challenges of historical research is that the memory plays tricks, and not simply at the distance of decades. It is only human to reinterpret our own actions in the light of subsequent events. Beyond this unconscious revisionism, memoirs are often written to settle scores and establish favourable narratives. Contemporaneous reports and even diaries are often written to justify decisions and seek credit.

It is no surprise that important events involving big personalities, such as the war in the desert, should be especially victim to this. The battles there chewed through plenty of reputations before they finally made Bernard Montgomery's.

But the deception campaign in North Africa and the Mediterranean has in the past been the subject not simply of partisan reinterpretation but of wholesale fabrication. Over the decades, several books have been written by those who were there, but the ones that deal most extensively with deception are, appropriately, the least reliable.

The charitable explanation for this is that the authors were making up tales to protect real secrets, mainly the identities of agents and the breaking of enemy codes. More harshly, it sometimes seems they – or their ghostwriters – felt free to spice up the dull bits of their war years. Of the most successful memoirs, one is more fiction than fact and another was written with government approval to put across a particular, and in parts deliberately false, version of events. Few of the others are much more reliable. Meanwhile those who best understood the truth were forbidden from telling their stories (though we should be clear that had Clarke been allowed to, he was planning to produce his own misleading memoir).

With the official files still classified, the next wave of historians often placed more weight on these 'first-hand' accounts than they could bear. Sometimes they added some inventions of their own.

The result is that what seem to be entirely fictional tales of, for instance, the *Rebecca* code and the 'Gauleiter of Mannheim' – who got the credit for Cheese's work for many years – endured longer than they should have. Jasper Maskelyne never made the Suez Canal disappear.

This is my attempt to get the facts straight, with access to archive material that those who went before me didn't have. There will be mistakes in here, too, and gentle corrections are always welcome. Every word that appears inside quotation marks is taken from sources I believe to be reliable, generally as close to contemporaneous as possible.

I've used Paul Findlay's translation of Rommel's papers, edited by Sir Basil Liddell Hart. For other translations, for instance of intercepted German transmissions, I've generally used the text produced by British intelligence at the time. The significant exception is the 'agent' Nicosoff, who communicated with his controllers in French. I've translated his messages myself, aiming to keep the sense of the transmissions as they were broadcast, supposedly by a cunning and resourceful spy in constant fear of his life.

Acknowledgements

I'm very grateful to all the people who have helped me as I've re-searched and written this book, especially the people I've forgotten to mention in the coming paragraphs. That error, and any others in the book, are my fault alone.

One of Britain's little secrets is that we have many well-organised archives where you can hold history in your hands, simply by asking. In particular, the staff of the National Archives at Kew and the Imperial War Museums in Kennington were a huge help with research, much of which took place during the constraints of lockdown. I'm also grateful to everyone at the Liddell Hart Centre for Military Archives, and to Catherine Smith at the Charterhouse Archive. Sheridan Westlake guided me towards the Conservative Party Archives at the Bodleian in Oxford. And Bloomsbury Publishing kindly facilitated access to the Churchill Archive at Cambridge University, where Andrew Riley was, as ever, a great help. The London Library offers everything a writer needs, and the staff are enthusiastic about tracking down obscure papers.

Various people patiently answered my questions, including Gustav Kuhn of the MAGIC-Lab, Dr David Abrutat at GCHQ, Lt-Col Dennis Vincent, Lt-Col John D Lock, Sheldon Rogers at the Tank Museum in Dorset, Bernadette Weber at the Neue Zürcher Zeitung AG and Dr Peter Quadflieg. Jane Pleydell-Bouverie's family shared her memories of her time in the London Controlling Section.

Richard Stokes has spent years digging away at the amazingly persistent fictions of Jasper Maskelyne. Every time I came across a fresh version of one, I could refer to his research for a reality check.

I'm indebted to everyone at the Magic Circle who talked to me about this project, in particular Terry Wright, who invited me to look at the non-secret shelves of the library (where I had two different versions of 'Any Card, Any Number' performed for me simultaneously) and Wayne Trice who gave me invaluable insights into magicians' jargon and their approach to their work. Shane Miller, who had already seen the parallels between stage magic and military deception, went to the trouble of designing and teaching me an illusion based on the El Alamein deception.

Clarke's great-nieces and -nephew, Fiona Buckland, Jenny Booth, Suzie Greenwood and Paul Greenwood, gave me insight into the legends of Great Uncle Dudley. Tony Simonds' daughter (and Clarke's goddaughter) Sally-Anne Olivier was generous with her time, as was the late Ann Weymss, Clarke's secretary at the Conservative Party's Opinion Research department.

At Weidenfeld & Nicolson, I'm grateful to Alan Samson who commissioned this book, Ed Lake who took it on and whose editing hugely improved it, Anne O'Brien for her copy-edit, Natalie Dawkins for finding the pictures and Frances Rooney and Clarissa Sutherland who got it into print. My agent Sally Holloway has steered me throughout the process with her usual firm hand and keen eye.

A few friends were willing to take on the burden of reading the first draft, offering the brutal criticism needed: Philip Cowley, Thomas Penny and Mark Mason, who also gave me an introduction to the principles of stage magic. Simon Clifford went through the manuscript from his hospital bed. I wish he could have seen the book published.

I am, finally, more thankful than I can say to my family – Sophie, Fraser and Cameron – for their love, support and patience in the writing of this book.

Further Reading

If you're interested in reading more on deception, magic or the intelligence war in the desert, here are some suggested starting points.

The Deceivers by Thaddeus Holt. This monumental history of Allied deception in the Second World War sets out to tell the entire story, listing every known operation and double agent in its 1,200 pages.

Churchill's Wizards by Nicholas Rankin. I first came across Clarke when the file on his Madrid arrest was released. But like other journalists writing it up, I didn't really have any idea who he was. It wasn't until I read this years later that I grasped the importance of his deception work. Rankin's wider history of British deception goes back to the First World War.

Speed, Aggression, Surprise by Tom Petch. The early history of the SAS, with a focus on the influence that Clarke's thinking had on the unit.

Operation Mincemeat and *Double Cross* by Ben Macintyre. Accounts of later Second World War deceptions. I'm sceptical of the impacts of Mincemeat, but this is the most enjoyable telling of the tale.

The Phantom Army of Alamein by Rick Stroud. The story of the artists and filmmakers who turned their hands to camouflage.

'A' *Force* and *Diversion and Deception* by Whitney T. Bendeck. Scholarly but affectionate accounts of Clarke's work.

Practise to Deceive by Barton Whaley. A series of short studies of military deception by the man who turned it into a proper academic subject.

War of Shadows by Gershom Gorenberg. A history of the intelligence war in the Middle East, with a great account of the British hunt for Rommel's 'Good Source'.

Hiding The Elephant by Jim Steinmeyer. A wonderful history of the Golden Age of stage magic.

Notes

1   'All warfare is based on deception . . .' Lionel Giles, trans. *The Art of War* by Sun Tzu.

4   'It was all that the younger man could do . . .' Papers of Lieutenant Colonel A. C. Simonds OBE. 2023. Imperial War Museums.

5   'all we could do was wait to grow old . . .' Dudley Wrangel Clarke, 'A Quarter of My Century'. Unpublished.

6   'roughly the right physique . . .' Clarke, 'A Quarter of My Century'.

7   'He merely smiled sweetly . . .' Private Papers of D. W. A. Mure. Imperial War Museums.

7   'I recognised an original . . .' Dudley Wrangel Clarke, *Seven Assignments* (Cape, 1948).

8   'Here was a professional soldier . . .' Clarke, *Seven Assignments*.

9   'I feel more and more convinced . . .' Private Papers of Brigadier D. W. Clarke CBE CB (Imperial War Museums). The author Tom Petch argues the word in Clarke's handwritten diary is 'subliminal'. The point is debatable – I think it looks more like 'subterranean', and this fits with Clarke's use of 'underground work' to describe his ideas a couple of weeks later. It doesn't make a huge difference.

11   'by the ankles . . .' Clarke, Private Papers.

12   'a war of continual mosquito tactics . . .' Clarke, Private Papers.

12   'intelligence, self-reliance and an independent frame of mind . . .' Clarke, Private Papers.

19   'I meant: when did you join . . .' Clarke, Private Papers.

19   'cat burglar, gunman, poacher . . .' A. P. Wavell, *The Good Soldier* (London: Macmillan, 1948).

19   'war is not only a grim . . .' A. P. Wavell, *Other Men's Flowers: An Anthology of Poetry* (Jonathan Cape, 1944).

19   'I soon learned to respect these silences . . .' Clarke, Private Papers.

20   'In his usual silent way . . .' Clarke, Private Papers.

20   'Wish to form special section . . .' WO 169/24866. The National Archives, Kew.

20   'they sold daisy-chains . . .' Dudley Wrangel Clarke, *Golden Arrow* (London: Hodder & Stoughton, 1955).

328 THE ILLUSIONIST

21 'as if he knew trouble well . . .' Hermione, Countess of Ranfurly, *To War with Whitaker: the wartime diaries of the Countess of Ranfurly 1939–1945* (London: Bello, 2014).

21 'slow, quiet manner . . .' Clarke, *Seven Assignments.*

22 'I have always believed in doing everything possible . . .' Clarke, *Seven Assignments.*

23 'The men of Ai looked back . . .' Joshua 8: 20–21, New International Version.

24 'Strong men fight their enemies . . .' Quintus of Smryna, *The War at Troy: what Homer didn't tell* (New York: Barnes & Noble, 1996).

25 'As a nation we are bred up . . .' Garnet Joseph Wolseley, *The Soldier's Pocket-Book for Field Service* (Minneapolis: Franklin Classics, 1869).

26 'for the ordinary general . . .' T. E. Lawrence, *Seven Pillars of Wisdom, A Triumph* (Jonathan Cape: 1935).

26 'all the business of war . . .' Duke of Wellington. Oxford Reference.

27 'the greatest show ever seen in Olympia . . .' Clarke, 'A Quarter of My Century'.

28 'Purely a matter of statistics, my boy . . .' Thomas Ernest Bennett Clarke, *This Is Where I Came In* (London: Joseph, 1974).

28 'Gave conjuring show in my bedroom . . .' Edwin A. Dawes, *The Barrister in the Circle* (London: The Magic Circle, 1983).

33 'The following is a picture of my plans . . .' WO 169/24903. The National Archives, Kew.

35 'helped considerably to oil the wheels . . .' Private Papers of Brigadier R. J. Maunsell CBE. Imperial War Museums.

35 'A secure Egypt behind my back . . .' Maunsell, Private Papers.

36 'with the professional help of the Port Said Police . . .' Maunsell, Private Papers.

36 'had the air of a man . . .' Clarke, *Golden Arrow.*

37 'the not inappropriately named Mr Ohno . . .' Maunsell, Private Papers.

41 '3 July. Late in the night, the group is informed . . .' WO 169/24904. The National Archives, Kew.

43 'Colonel Clarke . . . HQ Airborne Division 20 . . .' ibid.

43 'Ready to descend on Italy!' ibid.

44 'From tomorrow onwards . . .' ibid.

45 'We answered a lot of questions', ibid.

46 'Nobody could poke into what he was doing . . .' Martin Young and Robbie Stamp, *Trojan Horses: Extraordinary Stories of Deception Operations in the Second World War* (London: The Bodley Head, 1989).

46 'Nearly every conception of guerrilla warfare . . .' Clarke, Private Papers.

48 'an adventurous sound, with historic associations . . .' Clarke, Private Papers.

49 'If it had not been for your activities, the Green Beret . . .' Clarke, Private Papers.

53 'undefined secret activities . . .' WO 169/24847. The National Archives, Kew.

55 'No casualties on our side . . .' Sir Basil Henry Liddell Hart, ed., *The Rommel Papers* (London: Collins, 1953).

57 'Enemy probably knows we have a sea-borne expedition . . .' WO 169/24905. The National Archives, Kew.

58 'Mind your own tongue . . .' Young and Stamp, *Trojan Horses*.

60 'intended to avoid, in any circumstances, fighting a decisive action . . .' Liddell Hart, ed., *The Rommel Papers*.

61 'assume, incorrectly, that he would follow orders . . .' Ralph Bennett, *Ultra and Mediterranean Strategy: 1941–1945* (London: Hamish Hamilton, 1989).

66 'living a double life in a state of near terror . . .' Clarke, 'A Quarter of My Century'.

67 'unobtrusive rendezvous . . .' WO 169/24847. The National Archives, Kew.

67 'more English than any Englishman . . .' Robert Harling, *Ian Fleming: A Personal Memoir* (London: Biteback Publishing, 2022).

67 'left in peace to get on with spying on the Middle East . . .' Barry M. Rubin, *Istanbul Intrigues* (Istanbul: Boğaziçi University Press, 2002).

68 'We worked closely together . . .' Clarke, 'A Quarter of My Century'.

68 'He has been in London a good deal and is pro-British . . .' WO 169/24889. The National Archives, Kew.

69 'He is essentially a news hound . . .' ibid.

69 'He has contacts in Axis circles . . .' ibid.

69 'strong British sentiments . . .' ibid.

69 'He is very talkative and inquisitive . . .' ibid.

69 'There is a little man belonging to the Iraq consulate . . .' ibid.

70 'well-prepared trap . . .' WO 169/24905. The National Archives, Kew.

76 'he still disseminated a faint atmosphere of barns and hayfields . . .' Evan John, *Time in the East: An Entertainment* (London: William Heinemann, 1946).

76 'I didn't give a damn how they wore their uniforms', Maunsell, Private Papers.

76 'Since he was vouched for, he was treated in a friendly fashion . . .' Clarke, Private Papers.

76   'a natural liar, capable of inventing any story . . .' KV 2/1133. The National Archives, Kew.

77   'It was quite obvious that his main concern in life was women . . .' account from Kenyon Jones in Clarke, Private Papers.

77   'an intelligent, easy-going, lazy fellow . . .' ibid.

77   'Renato amused himself with his lady friends . . .' ibid.

78   'He seemed to have no idea that he might be risking his life . . .' ibid.

81   'Men of military age were in particular danger of being interned . . .' BBC, 'WW2 People's War – Our journey from Turkey in 1941'.

82   'It was impossible to sift the false from the true . . .' WO 169/24847. The National Archives, Kew.

82   'The road followed the coast the whole way . . .' WO 169/24847. The National Archives, Kew.

83   'does not come by any conceivable stretch within the scope . . .' John Buchan, Greenmantle (London: Hodder & Stoughton, 1916).

88   'remain silent against ordinary raids . . .' WO 169/24925. The National Archives, Kew.

90   'how can we undertake offensive operations on two fronts . . .' Alex Danchev and Dan Todman, eds, War Diaries 1939–1945, Field Marshal Lord Alanbrooke (London: Weidenfeld & Nicolson, 2015).

90   'capital of England . . .' Hans-Otto Behrendt, Rommel's Intelligence in the Desert Campaign, 1941–1943 (London: William Kimber, 1985).

91   'as they do not consider they deceive any German . . .' WO 169/24925. The National Archives, Kew.

92   'who was known to be in touch with Japanese intelligence. . .' WO 169/24847. The National Archives, Kew.

92   'Don't ask for less than one hundred Egyptian pounds . . .' WO 169/24925. The National Archives, Kew.

93   'Driver George Nathaniel Glover . . .' Geoffrey Barkas in collaboration with Natalie Barkas, The Camouflage Story: From Aintree to Alamein (London: Cassell & Co., 1952).

93   'Whatever Nature (or man) has placed upon the surface of the earth . . .' Barkas, The Camouflage Story.

96   'After the long strain you have borne . . .' Jonathan Dimbleby, Destiny in the Desert: The road to El Alamein – the Battle that Turned the Tide (London: Profile Books, 2013).

97   'I saw suddenly how sincere he was . . .' Alan Moorehead, The Desert War: The Classic Trilogy on the North African Campaign 1940–43 (London: Aurum Press, 2009).

98   'He needed just four months of steady preparation . . .' WO 169/24847. The National Archives, Kew.

103 'It's probably pure gossip . . .' Liddell Hart, *The Rommel Papers.*

103 'I work all day, and he works all night . . .' Clarke, 'A Quarter of My Century'.

104 'valuable centre for the collection of information . . .' WO 169/24847. The National Archives, Kew.

104 'no new experience or pleasure . . .' Clarke, *Golden Arrow.*

105 'for Jack from Mayhew . . .' WO 169/24889. The National Archives, Kew.

106 'This was not without some profit . . .' Clarke, 'A Quarter of My Century'.

107 'The aftermath will still be Communism . . .' Clarke, *Seven Assignments.*

107 'chief had contacts with Abwehr . . .' David Mure, *Master of Deception: Tangled webs in London and the Middle East* (London: Kimber, 1980).

112 'I said that if we had a really good liaison . . .' KV 4/188. The National Archives, Kew.

114 'must be prepared to go to endless inconvenience . . .' WO 169/24871. The National Archives, Kew.

115 'Never give the Boche the thing on a plate . . .' letter from Oliver Thynne in Mure, Private Papers.

118 'must possess considerable ingenuity . . .' WO 169/24871. The National Archives, Kew.

118 'who alone was conducting active operations . . .' Clarke, Private Papers.

119 'the news of "no desert offensive before Christmas" . . .' WO 169/24847. The National Archives, Kew.

119 'Abwehr employed between seventy and a hundred people . . .' Walter Schellenberg, *Walter Schellenberg: The Memoirs of Hitler's Spymaster* (London: Andre Deutsch, 2011).

120 'arrested in a main street dressed, down to a brassiere, as a woman . . .' FO 1093/252. The National Archives, Kew.

122 'It could not have been a worse affair . . .' Keith Jeffery, *MI6: The History of the Secret Intelligence Service 1909–1949* (London: Bloomsbury, 2011).

122 'particularly struck by his intimate knowledge of military secrets . . .' FO 1093/252. The National Archives, Kew.

125 'Everything was always funny . . .' Mure, *Master of Deception.*

125 'Wrangal Craker, the Madrid correspondent . . .' Jeffery, *MI6: The History of the Secret Intelligence Service.*

125 'I am afraid that after his stay in Lisbon . . .' KV 4/188. The National Archives, Kew.

126 'confirmed homosexuals whose rehabilitation is unlikely . . .' John Costello, *Love, Sex and War: Changing values 1939–45* (London: Pan, 1986).

127 'They all behaved in a perfectly civilised way . . .' Maunsell, Private Papers.

130 'nothing (repeat nothing) whatever compromised . . .' Jeffery, *MI6*.

137 'Auchinleck under pressure from Churchill . . .' WO 169/24847. The National Archives, Kew.

137 'It is difficult to know what is going on by way of deception in the Middle East . . .' KV 4/188. The National Archives, Kew.

140 'our friend Rommel is becoming a kind of magician . . .' Dimbleby, *Destiny in the Desert*.

144 'still in touch but I doubt future utility . . .' WO 169/24847. The National Archives, Kew.

144 'Reliable reports indicate that the reason for this replacement . . .' WO 169/24905. The National Archives, Kew.

153 'with people like Rommel, if you suggested you were going to attack . . .' WO 169/24874. The National Archives, Kew.

156 'dismissed the genuine papers as an obvious plant . . .' M. R. D. Foot, *The Oxford Companion to World War II* (Oxford: Oxford University Press, 2003).

157 'as though the tentage had been accidentally torn . . .' WO 169/24848. The National Archives, Kew.

160 'It is a source of real worry . . .' WO 169/24872. The National Archives, Kew.

163 'Clarke was running a racket . . .' Mure, *Master of Deception*.

163 'Knowing Dudley I accepted with alacrity . . .' letter from Oliver Thynne in Mure, Private Papers.

165 'One of our favourite people . . .' Hermione, Countess of Ranfurly, *To War with Whitaker*.

165 'quiet and authoritative', Joan Bright Astley, *The Inner Circle: A View of War at the Top* (Hutchinson, 1971).

165 'If you made a mistake . . .' Clarke, Private Papers.

166 'one straightforward, perfectly simple object . . .' WO 169/24871. The National Archives, Kew.

166 'the only purpose of any deception . . .' WO 169/24848. The National Archives, Kew.

166 'The story must be complete enough to have a clear picture . . .' WO 169/24871. The National Archives, Kew.

167 'a deception plan must never rely upon implementation by one method alone . . .' WO 169/24848. The National Archives, Kew.

167 'This is a very cheap form of deception . . .' WO 169/24874. The National Archives, Kew.

169 'The total strength of the Middle East forces . . .' WO 169/24926. The National Archives, Kew.

169 'one of the biggest strategic problems facing the British was a shortage of troops . . .' John Ellis, *The World War II Databook. The Essential Facts and Figures for All the Combatants* (London: Aurum, 1993).

169 'no deceptive threat to any chink in the enemy's armour . . .' WO 169/24848. The National Archives, Kew.

172 'He had the most all-containing brain . . .' letter from Oliver Thynne in Mure, Private Papers.

173 'create from the written pages of a manuscript a living play . . .' WO 169/24848. The National Archives, Kew.

175 'of no outstanding physique . . .' *The Times Archive.*

175 'unusual channels', Evan John, *Time in the East.*

175 'one of the most fascinating paper-games in the world . . .' ibid.

176 'is likewise very striking . . .' KV 2/1133. The National Archives, Kew.

178 'unimportant tit-bits of information . . .' WO 169/24891. The National Archives, Kew.

181 'Ranfurly captured. Last seen in good health . . .' Hermione, Countess of Ranfurly, *To War with Whitaker.*

182 'He was the ideal spy, touring battlefields . . .' David Kahn, *The Codebreakers: The story of secret writing* (London: Weidenfeld & Nicolson, 1966).

182 'stupefying in its openness . . .' Behrendt, *Rommel's Intelligence in the Desert Campaign.*

182 'How did they know that we had told the Army in Egypt . . .' C. J. Jenner, 'Turning the Hinge of Fate: Good Source and the U.K.–U.S. Intelligence Alliance, 1940–1942', *Diplomatic History* Vol. 32, April 2008, pp. 165–205. Oxford University Press.

183 'Another long report to German Army in Africa from "Good Source" . . .' C. J. Jenner, op. cit.

184 'Training inferior according to American ideas . . .' Gershom Gorenberg, *War of Shadows: codebreakers, spies, and the secret struggle to drive the Nazis from the Middle East* (New York: PublicAffairs, 2021).

184 'I am satisfied that the American ciphers in Cairo are compromised . . .' Jenner, op. cit.

185 'Further information from Good Source reveals our future plans . . .' Gorenberg, *War of Shadows.*

187 'The battle has been won . . .' Liddell Hart, *The Rommel Papers*.

190 'The Arabs seemed to view the struggle with the Axis . . .' Maunsell, Private Papers.

190 'Today, I drive you to Groppi's . . .' Thaddeus Holt, *The Deceivers: Allied military deception in the Second World War* (London: Weidenfeld & Nicolson, 2004).

192 'Look at this lady!' Thaddeus Holt, *The Deceivers*.

195 'US-made Grant tanks turned out to be far more effective . . .' John Ferris, review of 'Turning the Hinge of Fate', *H-Diplo* 199, 4 November 2008.

195 'suddenly forced to grope around in the pitch dark . . .' Behrendt, *Rommel's Intelligence in the Desert Campaign*.

197 'Be very active these days . . .' WO 169/24848. The National Archives, Kew.

198 'He chose worthless officers . . .' CAB 154/105. The National Archives, Kew.

199 'The whole organisation was permeated with "pins in the map syndrome" . . .' Maunsell, Private Papers.

199 'corrupt enough to see the necessity of preventing it . . .' Undated. CAB 154/105. The National Archives, Kew.

200 'burning through their cash without anything to show for it . . .' KV 2/1467. The National Archives, Kew.

205 'Though the submarine quickly sank again, all 48 members of the crew were rescued . . .' www.hmstetcott.co.uk/u-372.php.

205 'It will be her role not willingly to reveal information . . .' WO 169/24893. The National Archives, Kew.

206 'Nicosoff's a Russian name . . .' Mure, *Master of Deception*.

208 'This was balm to the soul . . .' Barkas, *The Camouflage Story*.

209 'carefully photographed by the watchful Boche . . .' WO 169/24848. The National Archives, Kew.

215 'Ground that had been "firm and fast" was now labelled "generally impassable" . . .' WO 201/2852. The National Archives, Kew.

216 'It looks as if it probably helped . . .' Sir Francis De Guingand, *Operation Victory* (London: Hodder and Stoughton, 1947).

219 'our own troops cannot be taken by surprise provided they keep their eyes open . . .' Behrendt, *Rommel's Intelligence in the Desert Campaign*.

220 'Nothing to report . . .' Charles Richardson, *Flashback: a soldier's story* (London: Kimber, 1985).

220 'Enemy situation unchanged . . .' Behrendt, *Rommel's Intelligence in the Desert Campaign*.

220 'silly little blabbing phrases, repeated over and over again . . .'

Alexander Clifford, *Three Against Rommel* (London: George G. Harrap & Co., 1943).

225 'Under Monty's teaching the whole thing suddenly became plain and simple . . .' Clarke, 'A Quarter of My Century'.

225 'It will be a killing match . . .' WO 201/444. The National Archives, Kew.

226 'horribly obvious . . .' Richardson, *Flashback*.

228 'Believe English are worried about Caucasus . . .' WO 169/24894. The National Archives, Kew.

229 'You must conceal 150,000 men . . .' Anthony Cave Brown, *Bodyguard of Lies* 4th edn (London: Comet, 1986).

231 'There is no better test of a conjurer's skill . . .' Sidney W. Clarke and Todd Karr, *The Annals of Conjuring*, ed. Edwin A. Dawes (Los Angeles: Miracle Factory, 2001).

239 'I thought it best to stress only the "defensive positions" part of your telegram . . .' WO 169/24906. The National Archives, Kew.

240 'When, how and where?' WO 169/24894. The National Archives, Kew.

242 'WAIT FIVE MINUTES. WAIT FIVE MINUTES . . .' ibid.

243 'he is very angry, discouraged and a trifle windy . . .' ibid.

244 'now the finished product . . .' WO 169/24848. The National Archives, Kew.

245 'His work has created the nervousness you speak of . . .' CHAR 20/80. Churchill Archive.

250 'I have always had considerable belief in deceiving . . .' CAB 120/769. The National Archives, Kew.

250 'rather frail-looking man of medium build . . .' Dennis Wheatley, *The Deception Planners: My secret war* (London: Hutchinson, 1980).

250 'When things were looking pretty bad for his side at cricket . . .' ibid.

251 'any matter calculated to mystify or mislead the enemy . . .' CAB 154/100. The National Archives, Kew.

252 'greatest amphibious operation since the Spanish Armada . . .' Wheatley, *The Deception Planners*.

252 'Deception is merely a side-line . . .' KV 4/190. The National Archives, Kew.

254 'ambiguity-decreasing deception . . .' Mike Martin, *How to Fight a War* (London: C. Hurst & Co., 2023).

254 'a complete surprise . . .' WO 169/24848. The National Archives, Kew.

255 'it would be invaluable', WO 169/24872. The National Archives, Kew.

256 'Too far-fetched even for Hitler . . .' CAB 120/468. The National Archives, Kew.

256 'we were most intrigued to see the "great deceiver" in the flesh . . .' Wheatley, *The Deception Planners*.

256 'To God and history . . .' Holt, *The Deceivers*.

259 'a great song and dance over the whole thing with masses of orders . . .' Young and Stamp, *Trojan Horses*.

259 'eggs and bacon with marmalade . . .' Mure, *Masters of Deception*.

260 'You always had this strange contradiction within you . . .' Young and Stamp, *Trojan Horses*.

261 'claimed he shot his way in – and blowing open the safe . . .' Obituary: Canon David Strangeways, *The Independent*, 23 October 2011.

261 'He said I was very naughty . . .' Young and Stamp, *Trojan Horses*.

261 'resourcefulness, determination and coolness in difficult situations . . .' WO 373/2/50. The National Archives, Kew.

265 'the rather vague hope that someone on the operations . . .' HW 3/125. The National Archives, Kew.

266 'received a flood of reports from their agents . . .' CAB 154/96. The National Archives, Kew.

266 'All cover plans should be based on what the enemy . . .' David Mure, *Practise to Deceive* (London: Kimber, 1977).

267 'a 45 per cent inflation . . .' WO 169/24926. The National Archives, Kew.

268 'I know my correspondents here well . . .' WO 169/24912. The National Archives, Kew.

270 'our repeated cry of "wolf" . . .' WO 169/24849. The National Archives, Kew.

270 'propaganda broadcasts warning against "premature action" . . .' WO 169/24849. The National Archives, Kew.

271 'It seemed that the enemy could scarcely avoid the one conclusion . . .' ibid.

275 'everyone but a bloody fool would know it . . .' Ewen Montagu, *Beyond Top Secret Ultra* (New York: Coward, McCann & Geoghegan, 1978).

275 'considered this wrong in principle . . .' WO 169/24872. The National Archives, Kew.

276 'the order of probability being Sicily first . . .' ADM 223/794. The National Archives, Kew.

276 'almost completely ignorant of the German Intelligence Service . . .' ibid.

277 'a document could be planted through more than one channel . . .' KV 4/64. The National Archives, Kew.

277 'It would be a mistake to play for high deception stakes . . .' CAB 154/67. The National Archives, Kew.

277 'We feel Mincemeat gives an unrivalled opportunity . . .' ibid.

278 'the major part of the Barclay story . . .' WO 169/24849. The National Archives, Kew.

280 'there wasn't much hope of persuading the Boche . . .' CAB 154/67. The National Archives, Kew.

280 'noticed some oddities about this corpse . . .' Ben Macintyre, *Operation Mincemeat: the true spy story that changed the course of World War II* (London: Bloomsbury, 2010).

284 'an atmosphere of "constant suspicion" . . .' WO 169/24849. The National Archives, Kew.

290 'one of the great successes of the war . . .' HW 3/125. The National Archives, Kew.

290 'It is after all little more than a drama . . .' WO 169/24874. The National Archives, Kew.

291 'truth deserved a bodyguard of lies . . .' WO 169/24876. The National Archives, Kew.

291 'Our first survey of the position . . .' CAB 154/101. The National Archives, Kew.

291 'beaten before they had begun . . .' CAB 154/101. The National Archives, Kew.

292 'They did during the North African invasion . . .' Harry C. Butcher, *My Three Years With Eisenhower: The Personal Diary of Captain Harry C. Butcher 1942–1945* (New York: Simon and Schuster, 1946).

292 'it was not what the neutral countries intended to do . . .' CAB 154/101. The National Archives, Kew.

293 'I rewrote it. Entirely . . .' David Inderwick Strangeways (Oral history). Imperial War Museums.

294 'Could we possibly get away with simulating an entirely fictitious army group . . .' Joshua Levine, *Operation Fortitude: The story of the spies and the spy operation that saved D-Day* (London: Collins, 2011).

294 'But we're not going to land in the Pas-de-Calais . . .' Holt, *The Deceivers*.

295 'longest and most elaborate operation it had yet undertaken . . .' WO 169/24850. The National Archives, Kew.

295 'every risk accepted which can further the success of these plans . . .' WO 169/24850. The National Archives, Kew.

298 'a week or more to wait before the landings came in North West Europe . . .' WO 169/24850. The National Archives, Kew.

298 'Gummer suggested a visit to the governor . . .' WO 169/24923. The National Archives, Kew.

299 'a second-rate actor . . .' WO 169/24923. The National Archives, Kew.

299 'Monty is rather flattered by the whole plan . . .' KV 4/194. The National Archives, Kew.

299 'tremendous air of assurance . . .' M. E. Clifton James, *I Was Monty's Double* (London: Rider, 1954).

301 'Hello, Monty, glad to see you . . .' WO 169/24850. The National Archives, Kew.

301 'You *are* Monty. I've known him for years . . .' James, *I Was Monty's Double*.

301 'with well-feigned embarrassment . . .' WO 169/24850. The National Archives, Kew.

302 'good tidings are on their way to Berlin . . .' WO 169/24923. The National Archives, Kew.

302 'James snoring and the bottle empty . . .' Mure, *Master of Deception*.

302 'It was some stuff dropped in Spain . . .' Strangeways (Oral history). Imperial War Museums.

303 'inextricably interwoven into almost every strategic and major tactical plan . . .' WO 169/24875. The National Archives, Kew.

305 'bafflement that the Allies had never deployed the 5th Airborne Division . . .' Holt, *The Deceivers*.

307 'designed to save lives rather than destroy . . .' WO 169/24875. The National Archives, Kew.

309 'their forces were unprepared to carry out the real plan . . .' Mykhaylo Zabrodskyi, 'Preliminary Lessons in Conventional Warfighting from Russia's Invasion of Ukraine: February–July 2022' (London: Royal United Services Institute for Defence Studies, 2022).

309 'Deception can never be effective either in love or in war . . .' Michael Howard, *British Intelligence in the Second World War: Volume 5, Strategic Deception* (London: HMSO, 1990).

310 'Results of the plan as shown by captured documents . . .' WO 169/24925. The National Archives, Kew.

314 'Made for the job . . .' Robert Harling, *Ian Fleming: A Personal Memoir*.

314 'Where had this exuberant shrewd pirate come from? . . .' Ian Fleming, *From Russia, with Love* (London: Random House, 2012).

316 'He is believed to have died in 1954 . . .' Nigel West, *Double Cross in Cairo: The true story of the spy who turned the tide of war in the Middle East* (London: Biteback, 2015).

317 'a second – and secret – object . . .' CCO 180/1/1, Conservative Party Archive, Bodleian Libraries, Oxford.

317 'as in other battles . . .' CCO 180/1/2, Conservative Party Archive, Bodleian Libraries, Oxford.

Bibliography

Alanbrooke, Lord, *Alanbrooke War Diaries 1939–1945: Field Marshall Lord Alanbrooke*, ed. by Alex Danchev and Dan Todman, Later Edition (London: Weidenfeld & Nicolson, 2002)

Barkas, Geoffrey, with Barkas, Natalie, *The Camouflage Story. From Aintree to Alamein* (London: Cassell & Co., 1952)

Barr, Niall, *Pendulum of War: The Three Battles of El Alamein* (Pimlico, 2004)

Behrendt, Hans-Otto, *Rommel's Intelligence in the Desert Campaign, 1941–1943* (London: William Kimber, 1985)

Bell, J. Bowyer, *Cheating and Deception* (New Brunswick, N.J.: Transaction, 1991)

Bendeck, Whitney T., *'A' Force: The Origins of British Deception During the Second World War* (Annapolis, Maryland: Naval Institute Press, 2013)

———, *Diversion and Deception: Dudley Clarke's 'A' Force and Allied operations in World War II* (University of Oklahoma Press, 2021)

Bennett, Ralph, *Ultra And Mediterranean Strategy: 1941–1945* (London; New York, N.Y., USA: Hamish Hamilton, 1989)

Bijl, Nicholas van der, *Sharing the Secret: The History of the Intelligence Corps 1940–2010* (Pen and Sword, 2013)

Bright Astley, Joan, *The Inner Circle: A View of War at the Top* (Hutchinson, 1971)

Brown, Anthony Cave, *Bodyguard of Lies*, New edition (Comet, 1986)

Buchan, John, *Greenmantle* (London: Hodder & Stoughton, 1916)

Butcher, Harry C., *My Three Years With Eisenhower 1942–1945* (William Heinemann, 1946)

Caddick-Adams, Peter, *Monty and Rommel: Parallel Lives* (Preface, 2011)

Clarke, Dudley Wrangel, *A Quarter of My Century* (Unpublished), Imperial War Museum

———, *Golden Arrow* (London: Hodder & Stoughton, 1955)

———, *Seven Assignments* (Alden Press, 1948)

———, *The Eleventh at War* (Michael Joseph, 1952)

Clarke, Sidney W., *Annals of Conjuring*, ed. by Edwin A. Dawes and Todd Karr (The Miracle Factory, 2001)

Clarke, Thomas Ernest Bennett, *This Is Where I Came In* (London: Joseph, 1974)

Clifford, Alexander, *Three Against Rommel* (George G. Harrap & Co., 1943)

Colvin, Ian Goodhope, *The Unknown Courier: With a Note on the Situation Confronting the Axis in the Mediterranean in the Spring of 1943* (London: William Kimber, 1953)

Cooper, Artemis, *Cairo in the War* (Hamish Hamilton, 1989)

Costello, John, *Love, Sex and War: Changing Values 1939–45* (London: Pan in association with Collins, 1986)

Cowles, Virginia, *The Phantom Major: The Story of David Stirling and His Desert Command* (New York: Ballantine Books, 1966)

Crowdy, Terry, *Deceiving Hitler* (Osprey, 2008)

Cruikshank, Charles, *Deception in World War II* (Oxford University Press, 1979)

Dawes, Edwin A., *The Barrister In The Circle* (The Magic Circle, 1983)

De Guingand, Sir Francis, *Operation Victory* (London: Hodder & Stoughton, 1947)

Dear, I. C. B. and Foot, M. R. D., eds, *The Oxford Companion to World War II* (Oxford University Press, 1995)

Deletant, Dennis, *British Clandestine Activities in Romania during the Second World War* (Springer, 2016)

Dimbleby, Jonathan, *Destiny in the Desert: The Road to El Alamein – the Battle That Turned the Tide* (Profile Books, 2013)

Downing, Taylor, *1942: Britain at the Brink* (Little, Brown, 2022)

Dykes, Vivian, *Establishing the Anglo-American Alliance: The Second World War Diaries of Brigadier Vivian Dykes*, ed. by Alex Danchev (Oxford: Brassey's Defence, 1990)

Ellis, John, *The World War II Databook. The Essential Facts and Figures for All the Combatants* (BCA, 2005)

Fairbanks, Douglas Jr, *A Hell of a War* (Robson Books, 1995)

Ferris, John, *Behind the Enigma: The Authorised History of GCHQ, Britain's Secret Cyber-Intelligence Agency* (Bloomsbury, 2021)

Fleming, Ian, *From Russia, with Love* (Jonathan Cape, 1957)

Gershom Gorenberg, *War of Shadows: Codebreakers, Spies, and the Secret Struggle to Drive the Nazis from the Middle East* (New York: PublicAffairs, 2021)

Handel, Michael, ed., *Strategic and Operational Deception in the Second World War* (Frank Cass & Co., 1987)

Hart, B. H. Liddell, *The Rommel Papers* (Collins, 1953)

Hocus Pocus Junior, *The Anatomy of Legerdemain; or The Art of Juggling Set Forth in His Proper Colours* (T. H, 1635)

Holt, Thaddeus, *The Deceivers: Allied Military Deception in the Second World War* (London: Weidenfeld & Nicolson, 2004)

Hoffman, 'Professor' Louis, *Modern Magic* (George Routledge & Sons, 1893)

Hopkins, Albert A., *Magic: Stage Illusions, Special Effects and Trick Photography* (Dover, 1976)

Howard, Michael, *British Intelligence in the Second World War, Vol. 5, Strategic Deception,* History of the Second World War (London: H.M.S.O., 1990)

James, M. E. Clifton, *I Was Monty's Double* (Rider And Company, 1954)

Jeffery, Keith, *MI6: The History of the Secret Intelligence Service 1909–1949* (London, Berlin: Bloomsbury Paperbacks, 2011)

John, Evan, *Time in the East: An Entertainment* (William Heinemann, 1946)

Johnson, David Alan, *Righteous Deception* (Praeger, 2001)

Kahn, David, *The Codebreakers: The Story of Secret Writing* (Weidenfeld & Nicolson, 1966)

Kwong, David, *Spellbound* (Harper Business, 2017)

Kuhn, Gustav, *Experiencing the Impossible: The Science of Magic* (Massachusetts Institute of Technology, 2019)

Lamont, Peter and Wiseman, Richard, *Magic in Theory* (University of Hertfordshire Press, 1999)

Latimer, Jon, *Deception in War* (Lume Books, 2020)

Lawrence, T. E., *Seven Pillars of Wisdom* (Jonathan Cape, 1926)

Levine, Joshua, *Operation Fortitude: The True Story of the Key Spy Operation of WWII That Saved D-Day* (Collins, 2011)

Lintott, Brett, *The Mediterranean Double-cross System, 1941–1945* (Routledge Studies in Modern European History, 2018)

Lochery, Neill, *Lisbon: War in the Shadows of the City of Light, 1939–45* (PublicAffairs, 2011)

Macintyre, Ben, *Operation Mincemeat: The True Spy Story That Changed the Course of World War II* (London: Bloomsbury, 2010)

———, *Double Cross: The True Story of the D-Day Spies* (London: Bloomsbury, 2012)

Martin, Mike, *How to Fight a War* (C. Hurst & Co., 2023)

Masterman, J. C., *The Double Cross System* (Pimlico, 1995)

Meneses, Filipe de, *Salazar: A Political Biography* (Enigma Books, 2010)

Montagu, Ewen, *Beyond Top Secret Ultra* (New York: Coward, McCann & Geoghegan, 1978)

———, The Man Who Never Was (Evans, 1953)

Montgomery, Bernard Law, *The Memoirs of Field-Marshal the Viscount Montgomery of Alamein, K.G.* (London: Collins, 1960)

Moorehead, Alan, *The Desert War: The Classic Trilogy on the North African Campaign 1940–43*, UK edition (London: Aurum Press Ltd, 2009)

Mortimer, Gavin, *The Long Range Desert Group in World War II* (Bloomsbury, 2017)

Mure, David, *Master of Deception* (London: Kimber, 1980)

———, *Practise to Deceive* (London: Kimber, 1977)

Petch, Tom, *Speed, Aggression, Surprise: the Untold Secret Origins of the SAS* (W. H. Allen, 2022)

Ranfurly, Hermione, *To War with Whitaker: The Wartime Diaries of the Countess of Ranfurly 1939–1945* (London: Bello, 2014)

Rankin, Nicholas, *Churchill's Wizards: the British Genius for Deception 1914–1945* (Faber & Faber, 2009)

Richardson, Charles, *Flashback: A Soldier's Story* (London: Kimber, 1985)

Robert-Houdin, Jean Eugene, *The Secrets of Conjuring and Magic* (Public Domain, first published 1868)

———, *The Secrets of Stage Conjuring* (Milton Keynes: Wildside Press, 2008)

Rubin, Barry, *Istanbul Intrigues* (McGraw Hill, 1989)

Sansom, Major A. W., *I Spied Spies* (George G. Harrap & Co., 1965)

Sawyer, Ralph D., *Lever of Power: Military Deception in China and the West* (CreateSpace, 2017)

Schellenberg, Walter, *Walter Schellenberg: The Memoirs of Hitler's Spymaster* (Andre Deutsch, 2011)

Scot, Reginald, *The Discouverie of Witchcraft, Being a Reprint of the First Edition Published in 1584* (Elliot Stock, 1886)

Smart, Nicholas, *Biographical Dictionary of British Generals of the Second World War*, Illustrated edition (Pen & Sword Military, 2005)

Smyth, Denis, *Deathly Deception: The Real Story of Operation Mincemeat* (Oxford; New York; Oxford University Press, 2010)

Steinmeyer, Jim, *Hiding The Elephant: How Magicians Invented the Impossible* (London: Arrow, 2005)

Stroud, Rick, *The Phantom Army of Alamein* (Bloomsbury, 2012)

Sykes, Steven, *Deceivers Ever* (Spellmount, 1990)

Tamkin, N., *Britain, Turkey and the Soviet Union, 1940–45: Strategy, Diplomacy and Intelligence in the Eastern Mediterranean* (Springer, 2009)

Urban, Mark, *Generals* (Faber & Faber, 2005)

Wavell, A. P., *The Good Soldier* (Macmillan, 1948)

————, *Other Men's Flowers: An Anthology of Poetry* (Jonathan Cape, 1944)

Weber, Ronald, *The Lisbon Route: Entry and Escape in Nazi Europe* (Government Institutes, 2011)

West, Nigel, *Double Cross in Cairo: The True Story of the Spy Who Turned the Tide of War in the Middle East* (London: Biteback, 2015)

————, *Hitler's Nest of Vipers: The Rise of the Abwehr* (Frontline, 2022)

Whaley, Barton, *Practise to Deceive* (Naval Institute Press, 2016)

Wheatley, Dennis, *The Deception Planners: My Secret War* (London: Hutchinson, 1980)

Wilson, John Howard, *Evelyn Waugh: 1924–1966* (Fairleigh Dickinson University Press, 1996)

Wirtz, James, ed., *Strategic Denial and Deception: The Twenty-First Century Challenge* (Routledge, 2017)

Young, Martin, and Stamp, Robbie, *Trojan Horses: Extraordinary Stories of Deception Operations in the Second World War* (London: The Bodley Head Ltd, 1989)

Index